# WAR TO THE KNIFE

*Also by the author:*

**Black Flag**
**Bloody Dawn**
**Scalp Dance**

# WAR TO THE KNIFE

Bleeding Kansas, 1854–1861

Thomas Goodrich

STACKPOLE
BOOKS

Published by
STACKPOLE BOOKS
5067 Ritter Road
Mechanicsburg, PA 17055

Printed in the United States of America

10 9 8 7 6 5 4 3 2 1

FIRST EDITION

**Library of Congress Cataloging-in-Publication Data**

Goodrich, Th.
    War to the knife : bleeding Kansas, 1854–1861 / Thomas Goodrich
      p.      cm.
    Includes bibliographical references (p.     ) and index.
    ISBN 0-8117-1921-9
    1. Kansas—Politics and government—1854–1861.   2. Kansas—History, Military.
    3. United States—History—Civil War, 1861–1865—Causes.  I. Title.
    F685.G66     1998
    978.1'02—dc21                              98-9293
                                                    CIP

# TABLE OF CONTENTS

# List of Illustrations

*To Maurine*

*I know of no transaction in human history which has been covered up with such abundant lying. . . .*

—Abolitionist Theodore Parker, 1856

HE WAS OLD FOR HIS DAY. HIS LONG WHITE BEARD AND DEEPLY FURROWED FACE readily revealed a life far beyond its prime. A man his age looked strangely out of place here in the field among so much youth and vitality. A man his age should have been rocking away this winter's morn by a warm fireplace, enjoying his last days with a grandson on one knee and a granddaughter on the other. Instead, the old man was being hauled in the back of an open freight wagon through a stubble field in Virginia. The seat beneath him was a rude wooden coffin.

All was silent now. The buzzing and laughter of the soldiers, the shouting and commands of the officers that had filled the air this morning, had suddenly ceased. Among the waiting hundreds, anxious eyes were now focused on the wagon and the gaunt figure in black as they approached. With quiet surprise, the man in the rumbling wagon looked up and scanned the scene surrounding him.

"I was very near the old man," a reporter for the *New York Tribune* wrote, "and scrutinized him closely."

> He seemed to take in the whole scene at a glance, and he straightened himself up proudly, as if to set to the soldiers an example of a soldier's courage. The only motion he made, beyond a swaying to and fro of his body, was . . . [a] patting of his knees with his hands. . . . As he came upon an eminence . . . he cast his eyes over the beautiful landscape and followed the windings of the Blue Ridge Mountains in the distance. He looked up earnestly at the sun and sky, and all about, and then remarked, "This is a beautiful country."[1]

The old man's eyes returned to earth. Looming just ahead, the great, grim monster stood ready to receive him. The old man's million-mile wander of fifty-nine years was now but a footfall and a heartbeat from journey's end. A rogue's death on the gallows awaited. Most men, old or young, might have trembled at the sight; most men might have bowed down in terror at the fate awaiting them. The old man was not like most men, however, and far from being afraid, he would not have traded places with anyone in the world. As he well knew, he was bound for God—and Glory. His final battle in the Army of the Lord was being waged, and victory was within reach. He would not disappoint either himself or his Maker.

At last the wagon drew up beside the scaffold and halted. Two men quickly moved forward to help the old man down. Gazing up the steps at the platform momentarily, the victim did not hesitate, but led the way in his bright red slippers "as calmly and quietly as if he had been going to his dinner," noted a young soldier nearby.[2]

"There is no faltering in his step," another witness added when the old man reached the top, "but firmly and erect he stands amid the almost breathless lines of soldiery that surround him. With a graceful motion of his piniored right arm he takes the slouched hat from his head and carelessly casts it upon the platform by his side."[3]

Recorded another spectator to the drama:

He stood upon the scaffold but a short time . . . when . . . the white cap [was] drawn over his face, the noose adjusted and attached to the hook above, and he was moved, blindfolded, a few steps forward. It was curious to note how the instincts of nature operated to make him careful in putting out his feet, as if afraid he would walk off the scaffold. The man who stood unblenched on the brink of eternity was afraid of falling a few feet to the ground!

Everything was now in readiness. The sheriff asked the prisoner if he should give him a private signal before the fatal moment. He replied, in a voice that sounded to me unnaturally natural . . . that it did not matter to him, if only they would not keep him too long waiting. . . . I was close to him, and watched him narrowly to see if I could detect any signs of shrinking or trembling in his person, but there was none. Once I thought I saw his knees tremble, but it was only the wind blowing his loose trousers.[4]

At length, all departed the platform except the old man and the sheriff. While the military companies marched and countermarched into final positions, others stared in awe as the victim stood quietly on the trapdoor with a hood over his head and a noose around his neck. Among those who watched was another old man, one with long white hair, who was destined to fire the first cannon shot of the coming conflagration a year and a half hence. Also on the field this day was a handsome young actor whose pistol report at Ford's theater would prove the last and most tragic bullet fired of the war. These two men and scores of others around them, who had cut slivers from the gallows as souvenirs, knew that they were now a part of history in the making—that something mighty was about to occur over which they would have no more control than would a reed against the wind.

When all was in place, a signal was given, and the sheriff descended the steps. Reaching for a sharp hatchet nearby, the officer glanced up at the old man one last time. As before, the prisoner stood patiently waiting, not a trace of fear visible even though he was for the first time in his long life completely alone. Gripping the hatchet firmly, the sheriff eyed the rope that held the trapdoor. Then, with one swift motion, the blade flashed forward. With a loud screech, the trapdoor opened, and the old man in black came down with a sickening thud. The rough rope dug viciously into his neck—his face quickly distorted into a horrible purple grimace and the eyes bulged hideously from their sockets.

"There was but one spasmodic effort of the hands to clutch at the neck," a horrified eyewitness said, "but for nearly five minutes the limbs jerked and quivered. He seemed to retain an extraordinary hold upon life. One who has seen numbers of men hung before, told me he had never seen so hard a struggle."[5]

"He did not die easily," remarked another onlooker. "The animal heat remained in his body . . . long."[6]

*The execution of John Brown.* KANSAS STATE HISTORICAL SOCIETY, TOPEKA.

The minutes passed. The drama in the field continued as the stunned spectators stared in silence at the struggle between life and death. Eventually, the spasms and shudders grew less violent, then ceased altogether, and the body was at last at peace. "Not a sound was heard," a spellbound viewer remembered, "except the creaking of the timbers of the scaffold and the whipping sound of the wind, as it played with the naked branches of the trees."[7]

And so it was. The old man was no more. His end was also the final chapter in another story, a story which he had a large hand in writing. Like his life and death, the story is a violent one to relate—a story about blood and fire and war and how Americans learned to hate and kill each other. The old man was dead now, and nothing could start his feverish pulse pounding again. Of that, most on the field this day were heartily relieved, and some felt that for his terrible sins, he should and indeed would burn in hell forever and ever. Others though, beyond Virginia, beyond even America, believed that the old man's spirit had taken wings when his body had fallen, and his soul was now soaring upward to a greater and grander glory.

> [T]he man of strong and bloody hand, of fierce passions, of iron will, of wonderful vicissitudes . . . the man execrated and lauded, damned and prayed for, the man who in his motives, his means, his plans, and his successes, must ever be a wonder, a puzzle and a mystery. John Brown was hanging between heaven and earth.[8]

# CHAPTER ONE

# *ISLANDS IN THE NIGHT*

TOMORROW, I BELIEVE, THERE IS TO BE AN ECLIPSE OF THE SUN, AND I think that the sun in the heavens and the glory of this republic should both go into obscurity and darkness together. Let the bill then pass. It is a proper occasion for so dark and damning a deed.[1]

Thus thundered Benjamin Wade of Michigan from the floor of the United States Senate. Even as the senator's apocalyptic forecast was echoing through the upper chamber, a cloud of black betrayal was blanketing the North. For more than thirty years the dam known as the Missouri Compromise had held back the dark and dangerous waters of American slavery. Now, with repeal of that seemingly sacrosanct law, the dike had burst, and the vast unsettled domain west of the great rivers lay threatened with immediate inundation. The debate in Congress had been long and heated. The arguments against abrogation had seemed clear, concise, and convincing. As Wade and other antislavery senators were soon made to discover, however, the might of the South and its grip on Washington was virtually unbreakable. On May 30, 1854, with a stroke of the pen, the Kansas-Nebraska Bill was signed into life, and the Missouri Compromise was declared null and void. Henceforth, the law of the land would lay with the settlers themselves—should a majority in a new territory vote for slavery, then, upon admission to the Union, a slave state would join the ranks of the South. If free-soil was their choice, then the North would gain. The first test of this theory in "popular sovereignty" would come on the virgin plains of Kansas and Nebraska. And Benjamin Wade was stunned.

From the very birth of the nation, Americans had been painfully aware that human bondage was an anachronism in a republican form of government. The Declaration of Independence, the Constitution, the Rights of Man, liberty, freedom, justice—all seemed a mockery as long as one American remained enslaved. As the years passed there was hope that, in an increasingly industrialized world, slavery would die on the vine for want of sustenance. But suddenly, and paradoxically, a product of the mechanical age—the cotton gin—pumped new life into the system by making the cultivation of cotton vastly more profitable. Far from fading, slavery grew fourfold because of the invention, and by the 1840s the system was more firmly rooted than ever. Hopes in the antislavery North were raised by the Missouri Compromise and other measures aimed at halting the spread of the "peculiar institution." If slavery could not be ended any time soon, they felt, perhaps it might be confined to a relatively small area and dealt with diplomatically in the not-too-distant future. But then came the thunderclap of repeal, and while Benjamin Wade and the North reeled in disbelief, many others, particularly in the South, rejoiced.

Since the signing of the Missouri Compromise in 1820, opinion had changed dramatically in the southern states. Equitable and fair though it may have seemed a generation earlier, the compromise and its restrictions were by 1854 viewed among many as unequal, unjust, and ultimately fatal to slavery. Barred on the north by the compromise line of 36° 30', locked out from the Pacific Coast by Free-States, only the bleak and barren sands of New Mexico Territory seemed a safe, if dubious, haven for slavery. To maintain the delicate political balance in an increasingly hostile Congress, new lands, new men, and new votes had to be won for the South. Some cast longing, warlike eyes to Mexico, Cuba, Nicaragua, and other tropic lands, but more were determined to meet the foe head-on and claim their fair share of the North American continent. Many Southerners had earlier commiserated with all Americans over the dilemma they faced regarding slavery, but by the middle of the nineteenth century human bondage had become such a fundamental part of their life that to talk of destroying the one was to talk of destroying the other.

As a siege mentality settled into southern minds with the passage of years, a suspicion and distrust for the rest of the nation correspondingly grew. It was a relatively small, strident group of emancipationists, however, for which slave owners held the deepest fear and loathing, and it was their actions more than any others that solidified southern sentiment against all Northerners. Centered in New England, many of these men and women saw war or disunion as the only salvation of the nation. Not content with containment, a few "brain-sick abolitionists," through the pen and the lectern, even urged servile revolt. Others encouraged slaves to flee their masters and established "underground railroads" to aid the runaways in their flight to Canada, beyond the grasp of the Fugitive Slave Law.

As the assaults on slavery became increasingly strong and shrill, southern efforts to defend the system in turn became stronger and even more shrill. "Let us declare," announced the *Columbia* (S. C.) *Courier*, "that the very moment any private individual attempts to lecture us upon its evils and morality . . . in the same moment his tongue shall be cut out and cast upon the dunghill."[2]

"[T]he gallows and the stake await . . . the abolitionist who should dare to appear in person among us," added a Charleston paper from the same state.[3]

As the circle closed tighter around the South, and as the menacing attacks of abolitionists continued apace, including all-out assaults by northern writers like Harriet Beecher Stowe, with her devastating antislavery novel, *Uncle Tom's Cabin*, more and more Southerners saw secession as the only means of preserving their way of life. Then, with repeal of the Missouri Compromise, many in the Slave States thought that they saw for the first time in a generation a glimmer of hope and a peaceful way out of a spiraling situation.

As the impassioned words of Ben Wade had made dramatically clear, however, the scrapping of the sacred treaty was viewed in the North as more than a political maneuver; it was a breach of faith. With it came the sudden realization that the hunger of the "slavocracy" was insatiable. Too, there was a genuine fear that even the heretofore secure northern states might ultimately be strapped with slavery. Stunned disbelief soon gave way to flaming outrage. Wrote William Cullen Bryant of the *New York Evening Post*:

> If this paper was three times its present size, and if it were issued three times its present size, and if it were issued three times a day instead of once, we could not then have space enough to record the action of patriotic meetings throughout the Northern States protesting against the repeal of the Missouri Compromise by the passage of the Kansas-Nebraska Bill.[4]

In spite of the mass demonstrations, a general feeling of helplessness crushed many. Archabolitionist and editor William Lloyd Garrison paused momentarily to express the mood of the North, as well as his own deep despair.

> The deed is done—the Slave Power is again victorious. . . . And so, against the strongest popular remonstrances—against an unprecedented demonstration of religious sentiment—against the laws of God and the rights of universal man—in subversion of plighted faith, in utter disregard of the scorn of the world, and for purposes as diabolical as can be conceived of or consummated here on earth—the deed is accomplished. A thousand times accursed be the Union which has made this possible![5]

Though few and far between, some were not yet ready to surrender on Nebraska or even Kansas. Senator William H. Seward of New York was one. "Come on then, gentlemen of the slave states!" Seward growled defiantly from the floor of the Senate. "Since there is no escaping your challenge, I accept it, in behalf of freedom. We will engage in a competition for the virgin soil of Kansas and God give the victory to the side that is stronger in numbers, as it is in right!"[6]

Eli Thayer was another. Even as Seward was delivering his dramatic, defiant, though hopelessly hollow, challenge, Thayer was quietly at work, preparing to meet the peril head-on—not with ringing words or resolutions, but with men, money, and, above all, with action. While many in the North saw only doom and despair following passage of the Kansas-Nebraska Bill, Thayer saw only opportunity. Unlike the armchair abolitionists and pessimists around him, who waged war on slavery with treatises, tracts, and high-sounding though impotent declarations, the Massachusetts businessman was a philanthropist who believed in deeds over words. From his Worcester office, Thayer devised a plan to deliver a devastating and perhaps lethal blow at slavery; he would drive an "entering wedge" into the new territories—a wedge of freedom. In words clear and unmistakable, Thayer charted his course.

> [S]lavery was a great national curse. . . . [I]t practically ruined one-half of the nation and greatly impeded the progress of the other half. . . . [I]t was a curse to the negro, but a much greater curse to the white man. It made the slaveholders petty tyrants. . . . It made the poor whites of the South more abject and degraded than the slaves themselves. That it was an insurmountable obstacle in the way of the nation's progress and prosperity. That it must be overcome and extirpated. That the way to do this was to go to the prairies . . . and show the superiority of free-labor civilization; to go with all our free-labor trophies; churches and schools, printing presses, steam-engines, and mills; and in a peaceful contest convince every poor man from the South of the superiority of free labor. That it was much better to go and do something for free labor than to stay at home and talk of manacles and auction-blocks and bloodhounds. . . . That our work was not to make women and children cry in anti-slavery conventions, by sentimental appeals, BUT TO GO AND PUT AN END TO SLAVERY.[7]

Anticipating the worst, Thayer had set to work even before repeal of the Missouri Compromise. As stated, the promoter's plan was to literally transplant as much of New England to the plains as possible by forming a company of wealthy stockholders who would, for a profit, equip, pay passage, and establish colonies in the new territories. The focus of the New England Emigrant Aid Society would be Kansas. With the Free State of Iowa abutting Nebraska, there seemed small cause for concern in that quarter. Kansas was another matter. Straddled by the rough and raw Slave State of Missouri to the east, the full blast of the South would undoubtedly be aimed at Kansas. Here, then, Thayer rightly guessed, was to be the battleground, and here it was that antislavery colonies were to be situated. If such outposts could hang on and weather the initial southern storm, they could then serve as bulwarks for other free-soilers who came later from Illinois, Indiana, and Ohio. Should the plan succeed and should Kansas be admitted to the Union as a Free-State, not only would another territory be saved for freedom, but the political setback to the South might cause the entire structure of slavery to come crashing down.

Although a bold, exciting plan, it was one that some cautioned could not succeed. "Many looked upon Eli Thayer as mad, and his project as madness," wrote a man who did believe, Dr. Charles Robinson. "Who could be found to go to Kansas with the certainty of meeting a hostile greeting of revolvers, bowie-knives, and all the desperadoes of the border?"[8]

Surprisingly, when Thayer made his plan public, a host of eager supporters rushed forth. Not only did subscriptions from wealthy patrons pour in, but hundreds of idealistic pioneers signed on. Many Northerners, Horace Greeley of the *New York Tribune* included, were thrilled by the simplicity of the scheme.

> The plan is no less than one to found free cities and extemporize free States. . . . The contest already takes the form of the People against Tyranny and Slavery. The whole crowd of slave-drivers and traitors, backed by a party organization, a corrupt majority in Congress, a soul-less partisan press, an administration with its law officers armed with revolvers, and sustained by the bayonets of a mercenary soldiery, will altogether prove totally insufficient to cope with an aroused people.[9]

"I know people," added poet and philosopher Ralph Waldo Emerson, "who are making haste to reduce their expenses and pay their debts, not with a view to new accumulations, but in preparation to save and earn for the benefit of Kansas emigrants."[10]

"The enthusiasm increased," reminisced Thayer's treasurer, Amos A. Lawrence, and parties were formed all over the Northern States. The Emigrant Aid Company undertook to give character and direction to the whole."[11]

"At length," Charles Robinson continued, "after great labor, a party of twenty-nine men, who were willing to take their lives in their hands . . . [prepared to leave]. These men were regarded with as much interest as would be a like number of gladiators about to enter into deadly conflict with wild beasts. . . ."[12]

*Charles Robinson.* KANSAS COLLECTION,
UNIVERSITY OF KANSAS LIBRARIES.

Recalls a proud, if equally apprehensive, Eli Thayer:

> This pioneer colony left Boston on the 17th of July, 1854. Immense
> crowds had gathered at the station to give them the parting godspeed and
> the pledge of their future cordial care. They moved out of the station
> amid the cheering crowds who lined the track for several blocks. The fact
> of this intense public interest impelled others to prepare to join the
> colony, intending to go one month later. . . . The emigrants remained in
> Worcester the first night and received a suitable ovation. . . . The next day I
> took charge of the party, and we were met in the evening at Albany by a
> good number of the citizens, who welcomed us with great cordiality.
> The next day we were cheered at all the principal stations as we passed
> on our westward journey. . . .[13]

Although Thayer soon turned back to organize future efforts, the advance
group continued on its mission to select town sites and smooth the way for those
to come. Leading them west was the director's trusted agent, Charles Robinson.
"A wiser and more sagacious man for this work could not have been found within
the borders of the nation," praised Thayer of his lieutenant.[14]

Meanwhile, on the untamed plains of Kansas, proslavery Missourians were already rushing in. While much of the best bottom and timberland was owned by the Shawnee, Delaware, Kaw, Pottawatomie, and other reservation Indian tribes, white land seekers staked claims to most of the choice sites that remained. As was often the case, after laying down a token foundation of logs or rocks, the Missourians tacked notes of ownership to trees and promptly returned home, satisfied that their claims were secure.

"If I find any damned rascal tearing this foundation down," ran a typical threat, "I'll cut his liver out."[15]

Understandably, many Missourians considered Kansas their birthright. "Missouri wagons had left deep scars upon the plains to witness possession by the right of conquest," one observer explained, referring to the Santa Fe trade. "Rightly the Missouri farmer . . . [viewed Kansas as] his particular domain; it belonged to him as new lands had traditionally belonged to settlers nearest their borders."[16] And what belonged to Missouri belonged to the South. Slavery was already an established fact in the territory, with many Indians as well as missionaries owning chattel.[17] In spite of the flaming eastern rhetoric, some Southerners felt a backroom deal had been cut in Washington whereby Kansas was secure for slavery and Nebraska safe for free-soil. It was only because of this understood if unspoken "compromise," so the reasoning ran, that the balance of power in Congress could be maintained and the horrors of disunion and civil war avoided. Thus, when the first rumors reached the western border hinting that Eli Thayer was shipping Yankee "mercenaries" west to vote in the territorial elections, many Missourians initially laughed.

To the typical Missouri frontiersman, who considered himself "half horse, half alligator" and whose boast was that he could "scream louder, jump higher, shoot closer, get drunker at night . . . than any man this side of the Rocky Mountains," the thought that clerks, peddlers, and "white-livered Abolitionists" from New England would dare tread the semisavage border to contest Kansas seemed a good jest, indeed. "Humans were divided into three classes," sneered one Southerner. "Yankees, niggers, and white people."[18] As the tales of westering abolitionists became increasingly ominous, however, the proslavery laughter soon turned to concern . . . then anger . . . then threats.

"Citizens of the West, of the South, and Illinois!" growled the *Weston Platte County Argus,* "stake out your claim, and woe be to the abolitionist . . . who shall intrude upon it, or come within reach of your long and true rifles, or within point-blank shot of your revolvers."[19] In the same county, another murderous Missourian vowed that he would meet the Yankees on the border the moment they arrived "and with my own hand help hang every one of them on the first tree."

Even as threats of doom were being uttered on the western border, over a thousand miles to the east, a second wave of the New England Emigrant Aid Society prepared to embark. As the sixty-seven men, women, and children boarded the train in Boston, they were urged onward with speeches, shouts, and a ringing rhetoric to match that of Missouri.

> Down with the slavery extentionists and dough-faces. . . . No union with slave-holders. . . . Let us pour such an antislavery element into [Kansas] that whatever political success slavery may obtain there, the very atmosphere shall be pestilential to it; yea, that it shall feel . . . a fire burning in its very vitals, and destined speedily to consume it.

With John Greenleaf Whittier's words wedded to "Auld Lang Syne" wafting sweetly in their ears, the antislavery emigrants turned hard, grim faces westward and made ready to war with slavery.

> We cross the prairies as of old,
> our fathers crossed the sea.
> To make the West as they the East,
> the homestead of the free.

As the bitter opponents moved closer to collision that summer of 1854, another movement, much quieter but much larger, was taking place. Indeed, in a mass migration reminiscent of the Gold Rush days, from Ohio, Indiana, Illinois, and other states of the old northwest, thousands of small farmers, merchants, and mechanics were unceremoniously packing family and furniture, setting their sights on Kansas. For most of these immigrants the opening of the territory was viewed not as an opportunity to either end or extend slavery, but as a chance to better themselves. As their mothers and fathers before them, the trek west was the defining event of their lives. The magic of rolling wheels, the thrill of new sights and sounds during the first days of travel, were experiences few "pilgrims" ever forgot.

"Have passed beautiful green fields of wheat, and fine tall trees all in leaf," wrote a wonder-filled Miriam Colt from a westbound train in Ohio.

> [H]ave seen gardens being made, and wild flowers blooming. Here is an apple tree close by the window, almost in full blossom—surely we are moving southward! southward! How quick the transition from winter to spring. . . . [H]ave travelled from snow banks and ice-bound streams, to green fields, leafy woods, smiling flowers, and the merry notes of birds.[20]

And, as their parents before them had discovered, the emigrants' first heady days of excitement and adventure rapidly gave ground to bone-jarring monotony and sleepless nights on impossible seats. Miriam Colts' "smiling

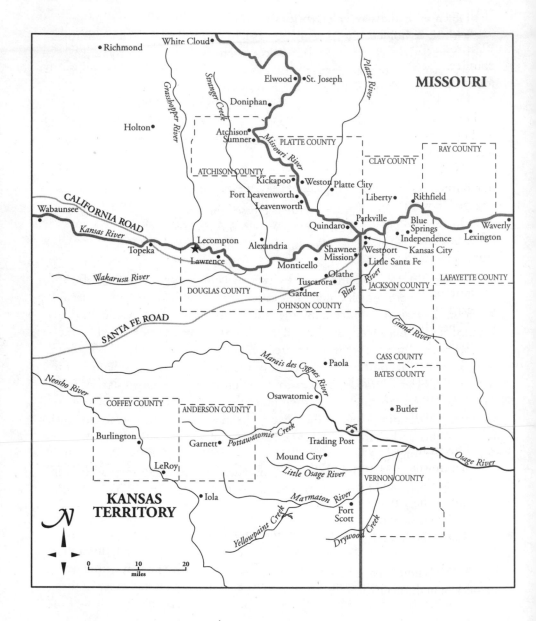

flowers and merry notes of birds" quickly succumbed to "miserable fare and miserable, dirty beds."

Likewise, the rolling world of John J. Ingalls was soon colored gray and grim. "[A]ll the railroad depots west of Cleveland are meaner than the one in Haverhill, if such a thing were possible," the young man groaned in a note to his father. "The route of the railroad lies through a desolate, forlorn, unproductive-looking country, sparsely populated, poorly cultivated, interspersed with unhealthy forests and stagnant expanses of marshy waters."[21]

Unbeknownst to Ingalls, Colt, and thousands more traveling to Kansas, rough and rattling railroads were the easiest leg of the trip. Once the pioneers reached St. Louis, many opted to catch a Missouri River packet for the final pull to the territory. This, for most, was where the true trial began.

"When we started from St. Louis, we began to think we were near the end of our journey," ran a typical emigrant's letter, "but the most tedious business that I ever engaged in was that . . . passage up the Missouri."[22]

On new, swift craft, at high stage, a voyage up the "Big Muddy" to Kansas City could be accomplished in under a week. More commonly, however, a slow, aging "tub," crammed with passengers, set sail on a shallow stream "too dry for navigation and too wet for agriculture." Because of snags and sandbars, it was not uncommon for a trip west to take ten days, and a voyage of two weeks was not unheard of.

"The Missouri is a strange river, at least it seems so to us Eastern people," scribbled Thomas Wells to those back home. "Every few minutes we run against a snag which one would think would knock a hole through the bottom of the boat, and every day, and sometimes several times a day we are delayed from half an hour to three or four hours on a sand bar."[23]

Wells went on:

This steamboating up the Missouri, when the water is as low as it is now, in a crowded boat is just the meanest way of getting along that ever I tried. By far the greater portion of us have to sleep on mattresses on the floor, and I believe that we should be more comfortable and less liable to catch cold if we slept out of doors. As it is I do not believe there are a dozen on board who have not taken a severe cold and I have not escaped.[24]

As Wells noted, passengers without berths managed as best they could, either on deck or in the main dining cabin. Richard Cordley recalls his first night on board.

At bedtime they put down about one hundred and fifty . . . cots, covering the cabin from end to end. They were about as big as door-mats and a trifle thicker. Over them they spread what they called quilts, each quilt about three feet wide and five feet long. . . . They also gave each a pillow which we could easily have carried off in our pockets. . . .

The early part of the night was quite warm and the lack of bedding was not felt. But a little after midnight we were awakened by one of the wildest storms I ever knew, a regular northwester, a blizzard of the bitterest kind. . . . The boat was still lashed to the shore, but she creaked and tossed about as if she would be thrown from the water. The intense cold pierced the thin sides of the cabin, and our little quilts seemed to shrivel up like cabbage leaves. . . . We endured it as long as we could, then one by one we rose . . . and went to the stove. In an hour after the storm began, the whole one hundred and fifty were trying to crowd around that little stove in the fore part of the cabin.[25]

Those individuals who secured private cabins fared little better, as John J. Ingalls soon discovered.

My stateroom was directly over the engines and close by the escape pipe; the thin partitions were painful with heat. . . . There was a perfect pandemonium of sound. The dull thunder of the paddles, the rattling of the tiller chains, which ran directly over my head; the trembling of the boat, the panting roar of the escaping steam . . . and the dull "thud" which brought everything up standing as we occasionally ran aground. I was almost parboiled during the night.[26]

Whether roasting or freezing, the miserable emigrants found small solace with the dawn. Ingalls continued:

At 6:30 the first breakfast gong sounds, the beds are taken from the floor and the tables elongated and spread. The frowsy, dirty passengers emerge from their berths and rush to the washroom to perform their ablutions in water dirtier than any I ever saw thrown away before. At seven the gong again sounds, and the hungry wretches devour greasy meats and chicory coffee for about five minutes, and then smoke, gamble and read novels till dinner at one; and then smoke, gamble and read novels till supper at six; and then smoke, gamble and read novels till bedtime.[27]

"It was the most unpleasant . . . days I ever journeyed," admitted John Everett to his wife in New York. "I do not remember hearing a man speak . . . who did not swear."[28]

Given the conditions, nerves understandably were frayed, particularly among the New Englanders. Although the anticipated confrontation with slaveholders at St. Louis had failed to materialize, anger was redirected toward the New England Emigrant Aid Society, which, despite promises, had been remiss in providing for its immigrants. "Our Yankees . . . expected to meet with some hardships in Kanzas [*sic*] and have prepared for it," one Rhode Islander wrote, "but such hard times in the cars and on the boat is something that they had no reason to expect."[29]

The general misery had a way of infecting everything associated with the trip. Said sour, misnamed Julia Lovejoy:

> We saw some places of interest, on the river, but "few and far between," and not one that looked home-like, or that would compare in tastefulness of Architecture with a New England cottage. Even Jefferson, the Capitol [*sic*] of the State, had nothing peculiarly attracting. . . . The Capitol was a spacious building on a beautiful eminence overlooking the river, but we thought it would look very contemptible along-side of the one in the Green Mountain State.[30]

While little actual violence occurred onboard, crowded conditions made certain that anti- and proslavery passengers would occasionally pass words. Tired, dirty, wretched, both sides were quick to resent perceived insults. "We have . . . some Southern folks who think they are_____," spit Edward Fitch to friends in Massachusetts. "[They] have tried to insult me and my family in every possible way. They will set down and stop up one passage in the aft Deck and have told some of our folks that the *second class* did not belong on that side."[31]

Though their view was limited, the New Englanders also got a first glimpse of slavery on their trip up the Missouri. Near the same capitol that she found so loathsome, Julia Lovejoy and others in her party saw a sight on shore that elicited their "disapprobation and disgust."

> A cart drawn by mules, was being relieved from it "contents" of manure, by a hoe in the hands of a colored woman, whilst her overseer stood by with an air of content, giving directions that it should be properly done, whilst he moved not a finger to assist the poor creature in her masculine task! O slavery, thou unsexing demon, how art thou cursed of God and humanity.[32]

"We have six slaves with their masters going to work hemp in Lexington, Missouri . . . ," added a physician from another boat. "The master of one said he paid $1,400 for him. One poor fellow has left a wife and five children in Kentucky, but his master was compelled to sell him to save himself from ruin. We had many slaveowners on board, some of whom talked loud about tar and feathers on our arrival."[33]

To the relief of this doctor and other Yankees, no mob was waiting when the seemingly interminable voyage ended. "We hail Kansas City in the distance," Hannah Ropes sighed, "looking really more pleasant than one could anticipate; and glad we all are to anticipate a release from the river, or at any rate a change."[34]

"Change" it was; "pleasant" it was not. What may have beckoned from several miles downstream fled like a mirage once the boat docked. Newspaper correspondent Albert Richardson sketches the scene:

> In front of the town the broad bouldered landing sloping down to the water's edge presented a confused picture of immense piles of freight, horse, ox, and mule teams receiving merchandise from the steamers, scores of immigrant wagons, and a busy crowd of whites, Indians, half-breeds, negroes and Mexicans. There were solid brick houses and low frame shanties along the levee, and scattered unfinished buildings on the hill above, where "the Grade" was being cut fifteen or twenty feet deep, through abrupt bluffs. Carts and horses wallowed in the mud of these deep excavations; and the houses stood trembling on the verge as if in fear of tumbling over. Drinking saloons abounded, and everything wore the accidental, transition look of new settlements.[35]

"There are any quantity of pigs in this place," Charles Loomer of Massachusetts noted; "they run wild all over the fields and in the streets. You can 'smell pork' anywhere."[36]

Understandably, many emigrants who had either shipped their wagons by boat or arrived in them overland struck off almost immediately for the territory or nearby Westport. Some, however, were compelled to linger days, even weeks in Kansas City, until the necessary equipment was purchased or repaired. While the men of the aid society and other "greenhorns" ran the daily gauntlet of gamblers, pickpockets and "jackals" of all description, sights witnessed by the ladies seemed perfectly designed to offend eastern sensibilities. Agonized Julia Lovejoy:

> Our first impressions of this city were extremely unfavorable; and boarding in this hotel as we have for weeks past, confirms us in the belief, that . . . the inhabitants and the morals, are of an indescribably repulsive and undesirable character. . . . There is but one Church edifice in the city, and this unpainted, uncarpeted, and as filthy as any incorrigible tobacco chewer would wish to have it; stove, benches, and other "fixtures" bearing unmistakable evidence that the delicious weed, had been thoroughly masticated.[37]

In addition to the filth and "infamous" odors in the streets, there were other reasons to escape the town. Julia continues:

> During our stay . . . hundreds were almost constantly thronging the house, bringing various diseases with them, and seldom a boat load without more or less sick, until the very air in the different rooms seemed impregnated with disease and death. Within a few feet of our own room, lay at one time four men, sick with lung fever. A little further on, in the passage that led to our room, within a short time lay two dead bodies. In another room lay our beloved Bro. D . . . sick with fever for weeks; and many from different boarding places found a grave in Kansas City.[38]

Not surprisingly, when the pioneers at last set out for the final leg into the territory, it was with a great sense of relief that Kansas City was left behind. While many settlers continued up the Missouri to take claims in northern Kansas, more struck overland on the Santa Fe–California Road. For those who had spent weary days and weeks in the closed and confined river valleys, the transition between Missouri and Kansas could hardly have been sharper.

"The road out from the river is on the state line," Joseph Trego observed, "and . . . it is fenced all up on one side with old and well improved farms as far east as we could see, while to the right—in the territory . . . it is open, wild prairie."[39]

East of the line the land was indeed cleanly defined by fields and forests that ran south for miles; to the west, the earth spread out into an awe-inspiring spectacle that left many speechless. "The feelings that come over a person, as he first views this immense ocean of land, are indescribable," one stunned New Englander said. "As far as the eye can reach, he sees nothing but a beautiful green carpet, save here and there perhaps a cluster of trees; he hears nothing but the feathered songsters of the air, and feels nothing but a solemn awe in view of this infinite display."[40]

"The land around . . . is beautiful. I never saw a place I liked so well," echoed an equally excited Bay Stater. "What I have seen of Kansas is all it is cracked up to be."[41]

For many a worn-out emigrant, though, the euphoria was short-lived. "Our ardor exhausted itself . . . ," remembered Hannah Ropes, who, like other women, only longed for the interminable journey to end. "Our way now ran along the dull prose of a country road, settling us back into the full consciousness of the cart—its sail-cloth covering knocking against our bonnets at every jolt; its plank seats without backs; its cramped, uncomfortable crowdedness of people, of children, of baskets, of carpet-bags, of cloaks and shawls; its sickening odor of crumbled gingerbread, of bread and butter, of cheese and dried beef."[42]

Though generally friendly, resident Indians sometimes set a brake to the emigrant's runaway rapture, as the diary of Chestina Allen makes clear.

> While journeying to day met perhaps fifty Kaw Indians. They were the most savage men & women I ever saw; begged of us but got little. . . . The Indians surrounded Cary and frightened him by their savage gestures, got his wallet and took three half dollars all he had, as Bisbee came up he gave them ten cts. They began to follow him. He shook a stick at them, and the cowards retreated. Poor Cary was wofully scared. We continued to meet squads of them for some time . . . [and the] men loaded their guns, but our driver expressed much bravado.[43]

And for more than a few, the short trip into the territory was filled with heart-rending grief. Four days short of her sixth birthday, Julia Lovejoy's little daughter was taken violently ill.

> [She] was borne in the arms of an agonizing father from the baggage wagon, into a cabin by the wayside . . . and in a few hours of unconsciousness to her, her spirit went to God. . . . [W]e laid the precious casket . . . away in a cold damp grave, in a lone spot. . . . [I]n a few hours from the time we saw the cold clods heaped upon our darling, we were obliged by force of circumstances, to tear ourselves from the grave of our loved one, and continue our journey of nearly 90 miles, scattering our tears along the road, as we turned our eyes across the prairies that stretched away toward her grave.[44]

While Julia's grieving family continued up the Kansas, or Kaw, River to its union with the Blue, many more from the aid society stopped short on a beautiful plain in the shadow of a towering bluff. Here, two days out of Missouri, where the valleys of the Kansas and Wakarusa Rivers joined, the main colony of the antislavery East was to be sited. Reasoned Eli Thayer:

> It seemed wise to plant the first town at such a distance from the Missouri line that it could not be easily assailed by hostile forces from that State without ample notice to our people and some chance for preparations for defence. I therefore decided that our town should be about fifty miles from Missouri. I chose the valley of the Kaw as being in the central portion of the Territory. . . . I chose the south bank of the Kaw, so that [much of] Missouri and the new town would have two wide rivers between them.[45]

On August 1, 1854, the first aid society contingent pitched their tents above the river on a high, windswept bluff soon to be named Mount Oread. "[T]he sun was pouring down its beams with terrific fierceness, and all nature shrank under the infliction," one company member recounted. "A high wind swept over the prairies, but it resembled the blast of a furnace."

> [A]lthough the weather continued intensely warm, parties went out to secure claims in the neighborhood, and within three days each individual had contented himself with his prescribed 160 acres. . . . Little difficulty was found in selecting on the open prairie, but a great deal of the water frontage, comprising the wood land, had been already staked into claims. Where our new city was to be we found the log habitations of some four or five settlers of from four to six months standing. They were of that class which exists in the west, who are pioneers by profession, and who seek to be always in the advance guard of the army which invades the wilderness.[46]

A short time later the second New England party, led by agent Charles Robinson, arrived on the scene, only to find the initial group still encamped on the bluff. When it was learned that the "professional pioneers" below were only willing to sell for outrageous fees, Robinson acted swiftly. Moving down the hill, the doctor and his followers pitched a tent by the riverside and quietly surveyed their town site. The response was equally swift.

> Dr. Robinson:—Yourself and friends are hereby notified that you will have one-half hour to move the tent which you have on my undisputed claim, and from this date desist from surveying on said claim. If the tent is not moved within one-half hour, we shall take the trouble to move the same.
>
> John Baldwin and Friends[47]

A leader in the California land riots of several years before, Robinson was not a man easily cowed.

> To John Baldwin and Friends:
>
> If you molest our property, you do it at your peril.
>
> C. Robinson and Friends[48]

As the deadline approached, additional threats were hurled by both parties, with Robinson's men marching and countermarching in a menacing military display. According to one of the Yankee claim jumpers, Erastus Ladd, the heavily outnumbered land owners vowed to

> proceed at all hazards to remove the tent, and if they fell in the attempt, our fate would be sealed, our extermination certain, for three thousand, and if necessary thirty thousand, men would immediately be raised in Missouri to sweep us and our enterprise from the face of the earth. . . . But there were strong arms and determined wills there. Had a man laid a finger on that tent, he would have been sacrificed instantly, and had another single offensive movement been made by one of them, there would not have been a man left to tell the tale. . . . Well, the half-hour passed, and another quarter, the enemy in full view in consultation, occasionally making a movement as if about to form in order for the execution of their threat, then seating themselves upon the ground for further consultation. . . . While thus waiting, John Hutchinson asked Dr. Robinson what he would do if they should attempt to remove the tent? would he fire to hit them, or would he fire over them? Dr. Robinson replied that he "would be ashamed to fire at a man and not hit him." Immediately after this reply, a man who had been with the Free-State men, and till then supposed to be one of them, went over to the other party, which soon after dispersed. It was supposed at the time that the report of this spy brought the "war" to an end.[49]

As the beaten squatters cleared their claim, the Yankees moved in and soon named the town site Lawrence, in honor of aid society treasurer Amos Lawrence. Although the veteran Robinson viewed the affair as little more than a trifling land squabble—"[T]he claimants . . . , cared nothing for the slavery question, but simply wanted to be bought off," he laughed—many of his awed admirers considered the victory their first over slavery since all of the dispossessed were Missourians.[50] Indeed, despite earlier fears, most in Lawrence were amazed by the ease with which not only their colony but those at Topeka, Manhattan, Wabaunsee, and Osawatomie, were established. Far from a Missouri mob waiting to lynch them on the line, as threatened, the traders and merchants of Kansas City, Weston, St. Joseph, Parkville, and other towns along the border had been civil, even friendly, and sold all that was wanted.

"I was much mistaken in the character of the Missourians," a relieved Sam Wood remarked. "A few fanatics, who were resolved to extend slavery at all hazards, seem for the time being to give tone to the whole people; but a better acquaintance convinces me that a great majority of the people condemn the violent resolutions. . . ."[51]

"I think there is more danger of being frightened than hurt by them," added another free-soiler.[52] Nevertheless, there were several ominous incidents that occurred that autumn of 1854, which augured ill in the days to come.

Despite the obvious hazards, one bold free-stater was among the first squatters to enter the territory when it opened to settlement. Staking his claim in the heavily proslave Salt Creek Valley near Leavenworth, the Iowan mowed hay for the federal government at the nearby fort. "Father was a plain spoken man, and . . . he *would* talk," recalled the pioneer's daughter, Julia. "My father had been Talking very freely about Kansas being like Iowa was, not to have any slaves or to hold Negroes in Kansas."[53] On September 18, the man was returning home from the fort with his ten-year-old son when he noticed a crowd milling outside a store. As Julia revealed:

They stopped him and wanted him to give them a speech. He tried to beg off, offering every excuse. . . . [H]e got off of his Horse, and they grabbed him, and put him up on a big Dry goods box, and he seen no way out of it when they called out, Speech, Speech. He began by saying that he hoped they could all live in this territory without having any trouble about any question. One of the men called out, You are the man that wants Kansas Territory to be a Free state, don't you? He went on talking on verrious questions and some one called out again, Say . . . you want to make Kansas a Free state[?] He sayed yes.[54]

Sitting in his saddle, frightened and trembling, the man's little boy, Willie, continued:

Men began crowding around him, cursing and shaking their fists. One of them . . . worked his way through the crowd, and jumped up on a box directly behind father. I saw the gleam of a knife. The next instant, without a groan, father fell forward stabbed in the back. Somehow I got off my pony and ran to his assistance, catching him as he fell. . . . With the help of a friend I got father into a wagon when the crowd had gone. I held his head in my lap during the ride home. . . . He had been stabbed down through the kidneys, leaving an ugly wound.[55]

*William F. Cody.* KANSAS STATE HISTORICAL SOCIETY, TOPEKA.

Dangerously, though not mortally, wounded, Isaac Cody made a slow and painful recovery. "Willie would cry,"

Julia said, recalling a baby brother who would one day be known worldwide as Buffalo Bill, "and then he would say, Oh, I wish I was a man. I would just love to kill all of those Bad men that want to kill my father, and I will when I get big. . . ."[56]

Later, an argument along the Kaw Valley escalated to guns and knives, leaving one man dead. While the dispute was seemingly nonpolitical, it was nevertheless a fact that the victim was proslave while his murderer was free-state.[57]

Though traumatic to those involved, isolated and largely unreported incidents such as the above did little to dent the surprisingly placid political climate. While welcomed by those intent on building homes and clearing land, the blessed calm was not enough to mollify many New Englanders. Topping the list of grievances was a simmering resentment with Eli Thayer's aid society. Complained one pioneer to the eastern press:

> We were told . . . that wherever we stopped on our journey, suitable accommodations would be prepared at half the usual price. Also, that our meals on the road need not average 20 cents per meal; that when we arrived in Kansas City we could immediately enter a hotel, conducted by their agents, and remain for half price. . . . How did we find these things . . . ? After [Albany] no arrangements whatever were made, that I could learn. At Chicago we were cooly informed . . . that no hotel in the place could keep us. Consequently, two car loads remained in the cars all night. The rest wandered about the streets, some going to hotels and paying $2 for a breakfast and lodging. Coming up the Missouri, we were stowed into a miserable old boat . . . and about 75 of us slept on the floor, and many of us found our own blankets. . . . Arriving at Kansas City, we were ushered into a house capable of holding about 150 persons. This, too, was half full. Some 75 or 100 slept on the floor, and 20 of us went to the stable and turned in on the hay. For these *accommodations* we were obliged to pay in advance. Such have been the arrangements which we have met throughout at the hands of this company. We . . . were told we should have first class passage, instead of which we barely got third-rate.[58]

Disenchantment with the aid society did not diminish once the Yankees reached the territory. Some shepherding agents seemed more intent on making money than fighting slavery, and Sara Everett of Osawatomie regarded one official there as little more than a "moral pest."

"Not a person who knows him speaks well of him," Sara snapped. "Himself and family are all thoroughly detested."[59]

Ferocious heat, blinding dust, and unwonted toil were other factors that quickly sapped the spirit of new arrivals. Not surprisingly, beset by one trial after another, the humanitarian pulse of many eastern immigrants soon stopped beating and large numbers left for home weeks, even days, after arrival. In a typical article, the *Boston Daily Evening Traveller* reported the experiences of one young clerk.

> He declares that of the party of one hundred and sixty who left with him, at least ninety are on their way back to the Eastward, well satisfied that they are not fitted to settle a new and unbroken country, and quite disposed to pronounce the whole Kanzas [*sic*] scheme a grand humbug."[60]

"Some seemed to think they should find farms all fenced, and houses built ready for their reception . . . in short all the luxuries of the . . . [East]," grumbled Samuel Grey of Topeka, after witnessing the hasty exit of his comrades.[61]

For every two who left, however, there was always one who, like Samuel Grey, was determined to stay. Indeed, despite the prophets of doom, the first stage of Eli Thayer's plan had become a reality—antislavery colonies had been successfully planted in the heart of the proslavery West. The job now, as Thayer and his Kansas representative, Charles Robinson, saw it, was simply to hang on and ride out the storm, for, as one observer sagely noted, the eyes of the civilized world were turning westward toward the looming battle in Kansas.

> Like islands that have been formed in the night by volcanic action, or mountains suddenly lifted out of the plains of South America, Kansas has been upheaved from the political ocean, by the internal fires of party, and has become at once one of the most prominent objects on our continent. With thousands, who a few months ago had never even heard of Kansas, it is now the chief subject of thought and inquiry.[62]

## CHAPTER TWO

# IN AWFUL
# EARNEST

THE SWIFTNESS OF EASTERN IMMIGRATION TO KANSAS WAS AN EVENT THAT CAUGHT many Missourians by surprise. Shocked not only by their boldness but by their aggressiveness, few Westerners could believe that this handful of intrepid Yankees were the same "white-livered" cowards so vividly portrayed in the proslavery press. To meet the coming crisis, U.S. Senator David Atchison and other prominent Missourians swung into action. "We will before six months rolls round, have the Devil to play in Kansas and in this State," the nervous former vice president warned.[1]

In a letter to the senator from the territory itself, William Walker, a well-educated Wyandotte, agreed. Wrote the wealthy, slave-holding Indian:

> I greatly fear we are destined to be visited by a curse equalling . . . the plagues of Egypt, in being made the unwilling recepticle of the filth, scum and off scourings of the East and Europe—to polute our fair land, to dictate to us a government, to preach Abolitionism and dig underground Rail Roads. A heavenly time we will have of it if they gain the ascendency here! I tremble when I contemplate the threatening prospect. . . . The Abolitionists will compass Sea and land[,] heaven & hell to prevent the establishment of slavery in this Territory.[2]

"If [Kansas] is to become 'free-nigger' territory," echoed Claiborne Jackson ominously from Missouri, "[we] must become so too. . . ."[3]

While vowing he would sooner see Kansas "sunk in the bottom of Hell than come in a free state," Atchison—known fondly as "Old Bourbon" for his love of liquor—and other Missourians began stumping the state to rally support.[4] Blue

Lodges, Social Bands, Self-Defensives, and other semisecret organizations mush-roomed in Missouri to meet the free-soil peril head-on. "Sound on the goose," "Alright on the hemp," and other coded greetings were devised to reveal the politics of a stranger. Whereas much of western Missouri had been strangely silent on the subject of slavery prior to the advent of free-soilers in Kansas, a great many now found themselves directly threatened.

"We have no sympathy for Abolitionism," seethed the editor of the *Kickapoo Kansas Pioneer*, "and the sooner they are made to believe that the squatters of Kansas Territory have no sympathy for their black, nefarious, contemptible dogmas the better. We want no negro-sympathizing thieves among us; they will be run-ning off our slaves whenever a chance offers. Their hearts are as black as the darkest deeds of hell. Away with them; send them back where they belong."[5]

With winter and the approach of the first territorial election—set to select a delegate to the U.S. House of Representatives—Atchison and other anxious Missouri leaders were determined to seize the initiative. Although many rightly guessed the actual proslavery settlers in the territory handily outnumbered free-staters, disquieting rumors hinted that the New England Emigrant Aid Society was shipping hordes of "hired paupers" to vote in the contest. Consequently, and in part because of nebulous residency requirements, Missourians were urged to invade the precincts on polling day, November 29, and help their friends in Kansas.

"For days before the election they crowded by hundreds the roads leading to the various districts," one shocked Northerner noted, "always carrying with them a liberal supply of bad whiskey. Maddened by its influence, they were ready for any dishonorable or violent course."[6]

Continued a witness from Douglas, a hamlet seven miles west of Lawrence:

On the morning of the election they gathered around the house where the election was to be held. Two of the judges . . . did not appear, and other judges were selected by the crowd; all then voted. In order to make a pretense of right to vote, some persons of the company kept a pretended register of squatter claims, on which any one could enter his name, and then assert he had a claim in the Territory. A citizen of the District, who was himself a candidate for Delegate to Congress, was told by one of the strangers, that he would be abused, and probably killed if he challenged a vote. He was seized by the collar, called a damned Abolitionist, and was compelled to seek protection in the room of the judges. About the time the polls were closed, the strangers mounted their horses and got into their wagons and cried out, "All aboard for Westport and Kansas City. . . ." Like frauds, only varying in particulars and persons were reported in seven other districts, the most shameless of which was the precinct designated as "110," where 584 bogus votes were thrown in a total vote of 604.[7]

*David Atchison.* KANSAS STATE HISTORICAL SOCIETY, TOPEKA.

When the ballots were tallied, the proslavery candidate, John Whitfield, had defeated his closest rival by a count of 2,258 to 305. Moreover, while it soon became clear that Whitfield would have handily won the contest even without Missouri support, David Atchison felt entirely justified, especially when newspapers such as the *Washington Star* reported on similar fraud committed by free-staters. "[I]t is a fact beyond controversy," argued the senator in a Kansas City paper, "that many, very many Northern men came from New England, New York and, other remote points *to vote*, and for no other purpose; for not less than one hundred and fifty of them left for the East together with their candidate, on the day after the election."[8]

If the Missouri march on Kansas was demoralizing to some free-soilers and proved the last straw in their decision to quit the territory, others, like Charles Robinson, saw the invasion as a serious strategic mistake. This "inexcusable blunder," Robinson wrote,

> served to expose the game the pro-slavery men proposed to play, and increased the agitation and determination in the North. . . . [T]he anti-slavery sentiment of the country, had received a serious shock in the repeal of the Missouri Compromise, and was in no mood for foul play in the game set by the slave interest. . . . [T]his invasion [also] showed conclusively that . . . the Free-State men, were rated as inferiors and to be despised, trodden upon and crushed without ceremony.[9]

Another who sniffed the advantage was Eli Thayer. Well tuned to the caliber of men and women he had helped west, the shrewd Yankee knew his emigrants would exploit every opening. Indeed, the last Missouri "Border Ruffian" had scarcely cleared Kansas before the free-staters went to work. Said Thayer:

> [N]early all these colonists were liberally educated. No sooner had they constructed their rude cabins than their letters began to be forwarded to the East. . . . If one letter was sent to a town, copies of it were made and every citizen had a chance to read it. Young and spirited men volunteered to go and share with their brave comrades the duties and the dangers of this new way of fighting slavery. For three or four months my own voice had been the only one urging this action. Now at least two hundred pens, all in awful earnest, reinforced my arguments. . . . [O]ne incident [will] show how these letters united all parties in the North in the cause of free Kansas. In . . . a little town in New Hampshire . . . the post-office was in the village store. Letters were displayed in the window so that the addresses could be read in the street. I observed there a letter postmarked with a pen, "Lawrence, K.T." The people going by soon discovered it and gave a boy a few cents to go and bring the man to whom it was addressed. Meanwhile the waiting number was increasing. Soon came the owner of the letter and opened it. The clamor was, "Read it aloud." This he did; but when he had finished, others had come who had not heard the first

part of it. It was read in this way the second, third, and fourth time. Then one of the young men requested and obtained a copy for the county paper. The result was that the letter of my helper in Lawrence was probably read by almost every one in that county. Who can ever tell the influence of that single letter?"[10]

When missives such as the above reported the rape of the ballot box in Kansas, a wave of outrage rolled over the North. Many, who had formerly considered abolitionists dangerous fanatics and disunionists, now began to heed their words on slavery. Others began to actively identify with them.

"I am an Anti-Slavery man, and could now take by the hand an 'Abolitionist' of any kind," one angered Kansan avowed in the *New York Tribune*.[11]

In an effort to annul the "bogus" election, a small group of free-soilers petitioned Andrew Reeder, the territorial governor. Although increasingly sympathetic to anti-slavery views, Reeder—an appointment of the pro-southern administration of President Franklin Pierce—dared do little more than admonish the Missourians.

> We shall always be glad to see our neighbors across the river as friends and visitors among us, and will endeavor to treat them with kindness and hospitality. We shall be still more pleased if they will abandon their present homes and dot our beautiful country with their residences to contribute to our wealth and progress; but until they do the latter, we must respectfully, but determinedly, decline to allow them any participation in regulating our affairs.[12]

While Reeder made his ineffectual plea, Missouri slaveholders and their allies in the territory celebrated. "There is not a single doubt that Kansas will be a slave State . . .," rang the *Kansas Herald* from the proslavery boomtown of Leavenworth. "And notwithstanding the Aid Societies [that] have poured in hordes of her paupers for the purpose of abolitionizing Kansas, they either become initiated in our institutions, or leave as fast as they arrive. Now, if the South does her duty, and especially Missouri, the Northern hope of abolitionizing Kansas will be a *phantom hope*."[13]

During the winter of 1854–55, emigrants continued to trickle into the territory. To the dismay of the *Kansas Herald* and other proslavery paladins, however, most newcomers were free-soil. Hence, with the approach of the next election, set for March to select the all-important territorial legislature, David Atchison and his lieutenants began marshaling their forces once more. In January and February, slavers throughout western Missouri held "incessant" meetings, enlisting recruits and plotting spring strategy. As the date for the polling drew nigh, southern news-men on both sides of the line intensified their attack. Fearful that apathy had set in following the easy victory in October, editors were quick to remind readers of the dire consequences of remaining passive.

"[T]his triumph was a mere skirmish, calculated to lull the energies of the South into a peaceful slumber," the *Westport Frontier News* warned. "The real battle, the decisive conflict, has yet to be fought."[14]

"Like the rude hordes from the North," added a St. Joseph journalist, "that invaded Rome in olden times and on being repulsed returned in ten-fold numbers, so will our Northern invaders return with new recruits to carry out their schemes. . . .The reality is before us. It stands out in the acts of the 'Emigrant Aid Society,' who ship paupers west as if they were so many cattle."[15]

When word reached the border in mid-March that a new "herd of barbarians" was indeed headed west to vote in the election, Dr. John Stringfellow of the *Atchison (Kan.) Squatter Sovereign* rang the tocsin.

> We are credibly informed that quite a large number, probably several hun-dred, of these purchased voters are now on their way up the Missouri River, consigned to . . . different points for distribution in lots to suit. . . . A still larger number are said to be in St. Louis, ready for shipment on the first boat. . . . A cargo of rotten oranges once introduced death by thousands in Philadelphia (in the shape of yellow fever). A more horrible disease, and one followed by many deaths, we fear, may be the conse-quence if this mass of corruption, and worse than leprous loathsomeness, is permitted to land and traverse our beautiful country.[16]

Speaking to an angry audience in Platte County, David Atchison roused Missourians to "fight the devil with fire."

> [I]f a set of fanatics and demagogues a thousand miles off [can] advance their money and exert every nerve to abolitionize the Territory . . . , what is your duty? When you reside within one day's journey of the Territory, and when your peace, your quiet, and your property depend upon your action, you can without an exertion send five hundred of your young men who will vote in favor of your institutions. Should each county in the State of Missouri only do its duty, the question will be decided quietly and peaceably at the ballot-box. . . . [I am] for meeting these philanthropic knaves . . . and out-voting them.[17]

"To those who have qualms of conscience as to violating laws, state or national," justified John Stringfellow's equally fiery, equally diminutive, brother, Benjamin, "the crisis has arrived when such impositions must be disregarded, as your rights and property are in danger, and I advise one and all to . . . vote at the point of the bowie-knife and the revolver. . . . I tell you to mark every scoundrel among you that is in the least tainted with free-soilism or abolitionism and exterminate him."[18]

"Missourians," the *Leavenworth Herald* cried, "remember the 30th day of March, A. D. 1855, as Texans once remembered the Alamo."[19]

By the last week of March, thousands of men, many with identifying ribbons or bits of rope hemp in their buttonholes, kept the ferries over the Missouri in constant motion.[20] To the south, hundreds more streamed across the open border. Wrote Thomas Wells of Rhode Island, who had himself come west to vote:

*Sara Robinson.* KANSAS STATE HISTORICAL SOCIETY, TOPEKA.

> We traveled nearly all day among a large party of Missourians . . . and a pretty rough looking set they were, some on horseback, some in covered wagons, and others on foot, all hardy, sunburnt, frontier men, and all well armed with guns, revolvers and bowie knives. We were often asked what county (in Missouri) we came from, and when they learned that we were from the East we had the pleasure of being called "damned Yankees," etc., but they did not succeed in frightening us. . . . The thing which I was most afraid of was a barrel of whiskey which we discovered in one of their wagons.[21]

"The whole week they were encamped all up and down the roads, like filthy plague spots, on the face of these beautiful prairies," seethed another eastern voter. "Drunk and loathsome, [they were] a sight to make the heart sick."[22] By election eve, hundreds of campfires flickered in the woods surrounding territorial polling places.

"Upon the morning of the 30th of March, a clear sunshiny day," James Christian recalled, "the voters of Lawrence District began assembling about the door of the polls, which was held in a small log shanty . . . situated upon the outskirts of the city."[23] And then, said Sara Robinson, wife of the aid society agent,

> about one thousand men, under the command of Col. Samuel Young, of Boone county [Missouri], and Claiborne F. Jackson, came into Lawrence. They came in about one hundred and ten wagons, and upon horseback, with music, and banners flying. . . . They brought two cannon loaded with musket balls. . . . When this band of men were coming to Lawrence, they met Mr. N[apoleon] B. Blanton . . . who had been appointed one of the judges of election by Gov. Reeder. Upon his saying that he should feel bound, in executing the duties of his office, to demand the oath as to residence in the territory, they attempted, by bribes first, and then with threats of hanging, to induce him to receive their votes without the oath. Mr. Blanton not appearing . . . , a new judge, by name Robert A. Cummins, who claimed that a man had a right to vote if he had been in the territory but an hour, was appointed in his place. The Missourians . . . said, that "if the judges appointed by the governor did not allow them to vote, they would appoint judges who would."[24]

"At 9 A.M., the hour appointed for the opening of the polls," continued James Christian, "the Missourians, well armed, walked down to the one-horse shanty, before alluded to. . . . To avoid the rush, and prevent unnecessary crowding, the Missourians then formed a line some hundred yards in length, on either side of the shanty window, in which the voters were to deposit their ballots."[25]

Returning to Sara Robinson:

> The crowd was often so great around the log cabin, that many of the
> voters, having voted, were hoisted on to the roof of the building, thus
> making room for others. . . . [W]hen the citizens began to vote, a passage-
> way was made through the crowd. Between a double file of armed men . . .,
> with threats of shooting, or hanging, our citizens passed to the polls.
> Several citizens of Lawrence were driven from the ground during the
> day, with threats of fatal violence.[26]

One of those who did vote was a well-armed George Washington Brown,
editor of the *Lawrence Herald of Freedom.* "It was the first time we ever appeared
at the ballot box with an instrument of defense," noted the newsman, who was
escorted by several friends.[27]

One of those who did not vote, Brown added, was Edwin Bond.

> [He] was forcibly ejected from the ground, and pursued by an angry
> crowd to the bank of the river with curses and threatenings of destruction,
> and compelled to jump down the declivity, when a revolver was discharged
> at him, and a ball narrowly escaped his head. He ran along the beach,
> and finally escaped unscathed.[28]

When a reporter for the *New York Tribune* was spied taking notes, then refused
to desist as ordered, he was saved from the howling mob only when big Sam
Young picked him up bodily and toted him to safety.[29] Meanwhile, similar events
were transpiring throughout the territory. As soon as it became evident that the
proslavery party had more than enough to carry any given precinct, the surplus
was pointed to other polls. Ten miles up the Wakarusa from Lawrence, a swarm
of voters converged on Bloomington. Said Sara Robinson:

> Samuel J. Jones, of Westport, Claiborne F. Jackson, with his volunteers from
> the camp at Lawrence, and a Mr. Steely, of Independence, were the leaders
> of this motley gang. . . . Scarcely were the polls open, before Jones marched
> up to the window, at the head of the crowd, and demanded that they be
> allowed to vote without being sworn as to their residence. Little bands of
> fifteen or twenty men were formed by Jackson. He gave to them the guns
> from the wagons, which some of them loaded. Jackson had previously
> declared, amid repeated cheers, that "they came there to vote . . . [and]
> that they would not go home without voting." Upon the refusal of the
> judges to resign, the mob broke in the windows, glass, and sash, and,
> presenting pistols and guns, threatened to shoot them. A voice from the

outside cried, "Do not shoot them; there are pro-slavery men in the house!" A pry was then put under the corner of the log cabin, letting it rise and fall. . . . The two judges still remaining firm in their refusal to allow them to vote, Jones led on a party with bowie-knives drawn, and pistols cocked. With watch in hand, he declared to the judges, "he would give them five minutes in which to resign, or die." The five minutes passed by. Jones said he "would give another minute, but no more." The pro-slavery judge snatched up the ballot-boxes, and, crying out "Hurrah for Missouri!" ran into the crowd. The other judges, persuaded by their friends, who thought them in imminent peril . . . passed out [and left].[30]

After routing the opposition, the southerners got down to business. "Not satisfied with once voting," continued Sara, "many of them, by changing hats and coats repeatedly voted. . . ."[31]

Someone seemingly undeterred by the situation was J. N. Mace, a Bay Stater who had come west to cast a ballot.

I hastened to get near the box, when I heard them say: no Yankee should vote there to-day, and the first man who took the oath required by the law, should lose his life. . . . It now came my turn. I moved forward. There were two of these desperate fellows at the window; one at each side as I came up with my vote folded. One of them took me by the coat, and said, "Open that vote, and let us look at it." I said I came here under the protection of the United States to vote; it guarantees to me the right to vote by ballot, which is to vote secretly, and I will show no man my vote. . . . An old man then came up, and they asked me if I would give way for him to vote. I at once did so. Meanwhile, I was asked from what State I came. I told the questioner that it was from Massachusetts. . . . After the old man had voted, I reached my hand inside of the window, with the ballot in it, and gave my name to the judges.—Immediately on this, at a word from one of the inquisitors, I was seized and dragged through the crowd, amidst cries of "Kill the nigger thief!" "Cut his throat!" Around me, on all sides, were flourished bowie-knives, pistols, clubs, and guns. I struggled, and gained my feet. . . . There was one bowie-knife within two inches of my heart, one revolver at my ear, and how many more drawn about me, I cannot say. One man struck at me with a club, but the blow was warded off by one of my friends, catching his arm as he struck. At this moment, something caught the attention of the crowd, and drew them in another direction.[32]

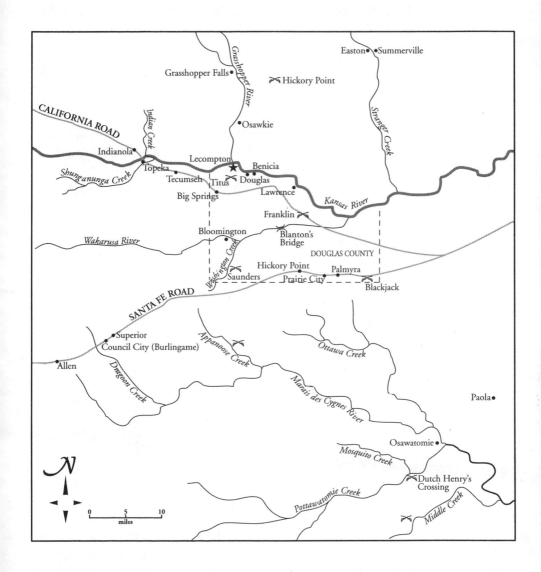

Although Mace made a miraculous escape, free-soilers at Tecumseh, Leavenworth, and other polling places had even closer calls. "We've come to vote, and will vote, or kill every God Damned abolitionist in the territory," David Atchison shouted to a mob in northern Kansas.[33] By the time the polls closed later that day, only a handful of free-staters had cast ballots. The frustration of Cyrus K. Holliday of Topeka, himself a candidate for office, was the experience of most.

"When we went to the polls," complained the future founder of the Santa Fe Railroad to his wife in Pennsylvania, "the Missourians had charge of the grounds—had driven off the Judges of the election and taken the matter into their own hands. We therefore did not vote at all. . . . "[34]

"All Hail!" crowed the Missouri headlines, even before the ballots were counted. "Pro-slavery Party Victorious!! The Smoke of the Battle is Over."[35] When word of the "clean sweep" became official, spontaneous demonstrations erupted across western Missouri with marching bands, speeches, and parades.[36] "The fanatical propagandists of the North have only received a lesson in the Southern political alphabet," the *Independence Messenger* laughed. "What comes now of the Northern boast that they were going to abolitionize Kansas, and make it a free State?"[37]

There were additional reasons to celebrate. Revealed the *Leavenworth Herald*:

It is well known that the seeming uncertainty of Kansas becoming a slave State, and the stupendous efforts of the so-called Emigrant Aid societies to abolitionize our Territory by the importation of hordes of paupers, hirelings, and convicts have served in a great measure to discourage and impede emigration from the South. . . . This obstruction is now obliterated, for the infernal machinations of the Emigrant Aid societies have been defeated.[38]

A Richfield, Missouri, editor agreed.

Come on, Southern men; bring your slaves and fill up the Territory. Kansas is saved . . . ! [T]he pro-slavery party have carried their tickets in every district by a vote so decisive that the free-soil party will return to their masters, Thayer and Company. . . . Our opponents are chopfallen; they look most dolefully, they talk most hopelessly, and feel, no doubt, awfully bad.[39]

As the journalist suggested, free-soilers in the territory did indeed feel "awfully bad." They, as well as others throughout the North, also felt highly enraged. Of the 6,000 votes cast, nearly 5,000 were deemed fraudulent. As word of the Missouri invasion swept east, a tidal wave of anger rolled with it.

"The last election in Kansas was more outrageously conducted than the first," one stunned Connecticut editor said.[40]

"[I]t . . . seems scarcely possible," added an equally incredulous Massachusetts newsman, ". . . that men bearing the names of 'American freemen' could be guilty of such cowardly assaults . . . such dastardly attacks . . . and such unprovoked, unjustifiable assaults . . . as have been committed by Atchison and Stringfellow, and the scoundrels with whom they have twice carried war into Kansas."[41]

Raged Horace Greeley's *New York Tribune*:

[A] more stupendous fraud was never perpetrated since the invention of the ballot-box. The crew who will assemble under the title of the Kansas Territorial Legislature, by virtue of this outrage, will be a body of men to whose acts no more respect will be due . . . than a Legislature chosen by a tribe of wandering Arabs. . . .[42]

Overlooked almost entirely in the flaming northern rhetoric was the free-soil attempt to foist a similar fraud on Kansas with its itinerant voters, a plan foiled only by the overwhelming might of its foe. The hypocrisy was not overlooked, however, by the *Charleston (S.C.) Mercury*.

Never, since the world began . . . has there been heard such a howl as is now set up all over the North, by the dogs of fanaticism, upon the recent drubbing in Kansas. The abolition journals pour out daily diatribes against the hardy Missourians who drove away from their doors the horde of negro-stealers who threatened to overwhelm them. . . . The abolitionists find themselves beaten, routed at their own game. . . .[43]

One item not overlooked by either party, however, was the performance of the lead actor in the late election. While the northern press pilloried David Atchison as a "boozy backwoods speaker," "a man little better than a roving bandit . . . marching at the head of an infuriated mob," proslavery journals praised "Old Davy" as a hero who had saved the day for Missouri and the South. Frontier politician that he was, Atchison understood the nature of the struggle perhaps better than any, and despite the storm of abuse, to defeat the "infernal machinations" of his abolition adversaries the Missourian was fully committed to a no-holds-barred fight to the finish.

"We are playing for a mighty stake," the hard-drinking firebrand confided to a friend, "[and] the game must be played boldly."[44]

As Atchison well knew, although the first round of the "game" had been won, the contest was not over. Even as Southerners noisily celebrated the victory, one free-soiler was quietly girding for round two.

# CHAPTER THREE

# TO A BLOODY ISSUE

THE EASE WITH WHICH THE PROSLAVERY PARTY CARRIED THE POLLS IN KANSAS caused general demoralization among Northerners, both within the territory and beyond. Hundreds of fearful free-soilers fled Kansas in dismay, while among many eastern abolitionists, the first crack brought their wall of words tumbling down.[1]

"The moment you throw the struggle with slavery into the half-barbarous West, where things are decided by the revolver and bowie-knife, slavery triumphs," wrote one hand-wringing emancipationist.[2]

"Beyond a doubt the fate of Kansas is sealed," echoed William Lloyd Garrison in his paper, *The Liberator*. "Will Kansas be a free State? We answer no, not while the existing Union stands. Its fate is settled."[3] Others felt as Garrison. With slavery seemingly safe and secure in Kansas, some, like the *New Haven (Conn.) Palladium*, adopted a policy of rule or ruin.

"We would have the admission of that State to this Union resisted," the editor threatened, "though it costs rivers of blood and a hundred millions of treasure."[4]

One of the few free-soilers in America not despondent over the recent reverses—and certainly not accepting defeat in Kansas—was Eli Thayer of the New England Emigrant Aid Society. Another was his agent in the territory, Charles Robinson. As he had proven during the land dispute in Lawrence, as he had also demonstrated during the California squatter riots in which he not only slew a man but was himself dangerously wounded, Dr. Robinson was not a faint heart who frightened easily. Although the fire of battle burned within, Robinson was also a man who could act with surprising patience and pragmatism. When the odds were heavily stacked against him, as was the case in Kansas, the doctor was capable of moving with cold and deadly deliberation.

Like his opposite in Missouri, David Atchison, Robinson understood frontier politics and the direction the struggle for Kansas had to ultimately assume. In a holy crusade to smite slavery, the end, as Robinson saw it, justified the means. If truth, honor, and fair play could not win the prize, then the free-soil physician, like the proslavery politician, was ready to use any and all means at his disposal.

While many, North and South, viewed the Missouri invasion as a great victory for slavery, Robinson once again recognized it for the strategic blunder that it was. As the bespectacled doctor, his friend Amos Lawrence, and others admitted in private—and occasionally in print—there had indeed been numerous instances of free-state vote fraud. Not only had hundreds of Easterners arrived on election day simply to vote, but in the northern precincts of the territory free-soilers from Nebraska and Iowa had also invaded the polls. Additionally, there were gross irregularities among the actual residents themselves, with some Yankees voting three, four, even five times.[5] Nevertheless, the mistake Southerners had made, as Robinson saw it, was in the sheer enormity of the fraud. Much like shooting gnats with shotguns, whereas hundreds of voters would have sufficed to carry the election, a massive army of thousands had swamped the territory. In the battle for the hearts and minds of the politically indifferent settlers of Kansas, who formed the vast majority, few could fail to see that slavery was willing to use brute force to crush all who resisted. It was the doctor's hope, as well as Eli Thayer's, that the average squatter would soon come to view the struggle between freedom and slavery as "them against us," of the bona fide settlers of Kansas versus the foreign invaders from Missouri.

"What steps were to be taken?" Robinson later asked rhetorically. "The first," he answered himself, "was to be repudiation of the fraud."[6]

Along with others, Robinson petitioned Governor Reeder to toss out the results of the recent election. Although he owed his present position to the proslavery Pierce administration in Washington, Andrew Reeder had shown an increasing tendency to sail independently in Kansas. The governor agreed that flagrant fraud had indeed occurred. Instead of upending the entire election, however, Reeder declared the results in only several precincts invalid. The gesture satisfied no one. Already incensed by the governor's decision to delay the election until March, ostensibly so that eastern "hirelings" might arrive in time to vote, this latest act, to southern minds at least, illustrated a growing trend on Reeder's part to side with free-soilers.[7]

Failing in his first attempt, Robinson adopted a more radical plan: "Immediately after the decision of Governor Reeder . . . [I] came to the conclusion that there was but one hope for a free State, and that was to repudiate not only the election, but Governor Reeder's action in giving certificates to the invaders."[8]

While Robinson and a growing number of adherents simply ignored the proslavery "bogus" legislature, the doctor began building behind the scenes a free-state government. Although the action was patently illegal and revolutionary, if free-soilers were firm and refrained from violence, only some overt act on the part of the proslavery party could disrupt their plan. In that event, both Missouri and the South would once again be tarred as the aggressors in the northern press. That Missourians would obligingly fall into Robinson's cunning trap became all too obvious all too soon.

Despite reassurances that Kansas was secure for slavery following the March election, most Missourians realized that so long as even one abolitionist remained in the region, the war would not be won. But rooting out "revolutionists" in the territory would take time; dealing with renegades in their own backyard was another matter.

Originally from Illinois, George Park had become by the 1850s one of the largest landholders in Platte County, Missouri.[9] Not only did he own the biggest and best hotel in town, but the town itself, Parkville, was named for him. George Park was also proprietor of the *Parkville Luminary*. In another time, the *Luminary's* moderate tone and mild reproach of slavery might have been watched but tolerated. By the spring of 1855, however, western Missouri was in no mood to split hairs or argue fine points. When the unwitting journalist made the mistake of gently chiding his neighbors for invading Kansas on March 30, it was the last straw.[10] Though Park was fortunately absent April 14, his colleague at the *Luminary*, William Patterson, was not. According to a witness:

> [A]bout 10 o'clock this morning, we were surprised to see about ten or fifteen of our most respectable country acquaintances ride into town and go to the printing office and put Patterson under guard. . . . At 12 o'clock about two hundred men had arrived. The Press was very quietly taken down and paraded into the street. The crowd was called to order, and Patterson was brought forth to receive his sentence. . . . One speaker stated that they all were aware that they came there with the firm determination to black, tar and feather, and ride on a rail . . . Park and . . . Patterson, but that, as Park had escaped, and left this scapegoat to suffer for both, he wished the meeting to decide what should now be done with the prisoner. Another speaker declared his voice was for mercy, not that he had any excuses to offer for Patterson, for he despised him as strongly as any man could but that Patterson's wife throughout the morning, had hung to him like a leech; that she now held on to him, and that we could not inflict the punishment without gross violence to her feelings, and perhaps rudeness to her person. . . . [H]e was therefore set at large. . . . The Press was then shouldered with

a white cap drawn over its head and labelled "Boston Aid," the crowd following in regular order, it was marched up through town nearly to the upper landing and there with three hearty cheers, it was deposited in . . . the Missouri River.[11]

Not everyone condoned the action. Tom Thorpe, for one, was outraged. "Boys, this is breakin' down the rights of American citizens . . . ," the farmer protested. "[Y]ou might as well put my hoss or my old woman's bureau into the river, as that 'ere press. That's personal property."[12]

When a drunken physician told an equally drunken Thorpe to "shut up," the two squared off. "Well . . . [t]he fact is," Thorpe recalled, "I spoke pretty sharp, an' he spoke back sharper, an' I hit him, an' he pitched into me, an' then we had at it. . . . [T]he boys was busy pitchin' in them type, an' breakin' up the wooden dishes, and when the doctor an' I got to fightin', they screeched an' hollered an' went to bettin' on it; an' then some o' them separated us."[13]

Before the mob dispersed, a series of resolutions were passed, one of which stated: "That we meet here again on this day three weeks, and if we find G. S. Park or W. J. Patterson in this town then, or at any subsequent time, we will throw them into the Missouri river, and if they go to Kansas to reside, we pledge our honor as men to follow and hang them whenever we can take them."[14]

Though condemned by all in the North—and even by some in the South—the "wetting down of the Dog Star" was heartily endorsed throughout western Missouri. "The 'Freedom of the press' is not for traitors and incendiaries . . . ," warned the *Weston Platte Argus.* "These Northern scoundrels should be taught that they cannot come into a slave State and promulgate sentiments, which left unchecked, would soon lead our slaves to insurrection."[15] Elsewhere in the region, other "snakes in the grass" were flushed out and "obliged to leave."[16]

While the Missouri purge was in progress, incidents between free-state and proslavery Kansans were also increasing. At a "Southern Squatters" assembly in Leavenworth on April 30, several well-known "irruptionists," including free-soilers William Phillips and Cole McCrea, began to heckle the meeting's moderator, Malcolm Clarke. In the words of McCrea:

> I playfully called upon Clark [*sic*] for a speech; he frowned and came towards me, and addressed me as follows: "I don't want any God Damned abolition son of a bitch to speak to me." I answered Mr. Clark, "I did not wish to offend you; I did not know that you did not wish me to speak to you, or I certainly would not do it," he then said, "Well I don't; and the closer you keep to that resolution the longer you may escape a God Damn bruising which I have promised you and an other perjured abolition son of a bitch [Phillips]."[17]

"God damn your soul," yelled Lucian Eastin, editor of the *Leavenworth Herald*, "you and Phillips made affadavits against the election . . . and you went down . . . to defend that God damn abolition son of a bitch, Reeder."[18]

When McCrea shouted back that the meeting was a "rascally fraud," Clarke called him a "damned son of a bitch" and then, wrote a witness:

> Clark [*sic*] having no weapons, picked up a small stick of wood, and not being close enough to McCrea to strike him, threw it. . . . Shortly after they met . . . McCrea caught Clark by the shoulder, and Clark laid his hand on McCrea, and told him he must not use such language to him. . . . McCrea either drew a pistol, or some wretch handed him one from behind. . . . When Clark was in the act of leaving him, without making an attempt to strike or assault him, [McCrea] cowardly shot Clark, and not content, again fired, when Clark was in the act of falling. McCrea then started to run, but fearing the dead body of Clark might overtake him, wheeled and tried again to fire. . . . [H]e then ran and jumped into the river and got on a snag, when some of the citizens caught him. . . . [H]e professed to be dying—claimed to have been shot, and begged for mercy . . . ! [T]he blood running out of his mouth, the citizens supposed he would die, but all attention was turned to poor Clark. . . .[19]

As the crowd gathered round, Clarke lay in his blood, "struggling and writhing in the agonies of death." Within twenty minutes he expired.[20] According to a bystander:

> The people prepared a rope, and would certainly have at once hung the cowardly villain, but for the deception he played off,—and he was sent to the guard-house at Fort Leavenworth, for safe keeping. . . . It was soon found that the black-hearted wretch was not shot, but to prolong his miserable existence, and excite the sympathies of the people, bit his own tongue! so as to make it bleed, and pretended to be shot![21]

Although McCrea miraculously survived the mob and later escaped from prison, his friend William Phillips was not so lucky. Accused of handing McCrea the murder weapon, the young attorney was ordered to leave Leavenworth by a specified date.[22] When he stubbornly refused, then attempted to raise a bodyguard of free-soilers, a committee of twelve vigilantes, "armed to the teeth," arrested Phillips and marched him toward the levee.[23] Recorded one of the Southerners:

> On reaching the river we placed him in a boat, carrying him to the Missouri side, where we contemplated giving him a coat of tar and feathers. . . .

[A]fter a brief consultation [we decided] to take him to Weston, and
there to make a public demonstration of him. On our arrival at Rialto
Ferry, (one mile below Weston) we dispatched a messenger for a supply
of tar and feathers, which we procured without any trouble. In the
meantime Phillips was converted into an Ethiopean, and his hair cut in
the most inimitable style. The coat of tar and feathers was then given
him, which added very much to his personal beauty. . . . After having
"rigged him out" . . . we seated him upon a rail and bore him through
the public streets of Weston, much to the delight and merriment of its
citizens. After hawking him through the streets he was sold by a big
buck nigger, in front of the St. George Hotel, as a good hemp breaker, or
carriage driver. . . .[24]

"How much, gentlemen, for a full-blooded abolitionist, dyed in de wool,
tar[,] feathers and all?" the black shouted.[25] When only a cent and a half was bid,
Phillips was again ridden on a rail around Weston "to the music of old pans
and bells."[26]

"About four o'clock," concluded a spectator back in Leavenworth, "Phillips
was given over to his brother, who brought him immediately over here, where
after six hours of hard labor with sand and grease . . . Phillips was made to see
again his white skin. . . ."[27]

While some astute Missourians condemned the affair at Weston, as they had
at Parkville, rightly fearing the rich political fruit Horace Greeley of the *New York
Tribune* and others would reap from the incident, "fire-eaters" in Kansas were
elated.[28] "The joy, exultation and glorification produced by it in our community
are unparalleled," rang Lucian Eastin of the *Leavenworth Herald*.[29] Added John
Stringfellow of the *Atchison Squatter Sovereign*:

We can tell the impertinent scoundrels of the *Tribune* that they may
exhaust an ocean of ink, their Emigrant Aid Societies spend their millions
and billions, their representatives in Congress spout their heretical theories
till doomsday, and His Excellency Franklin Pierce appoint abolitionist
after free-soiler as our Governor, yet we will continue to lynch and hang,
to tar and feather, and drown every white-livered abolitionist who dares
to pollute our soil.[30]

Lending weight to his brother's words, tiny Ben Stringfellow stalked into
Governor Reeder's office at Shawnee Mission a short time later and, according to
one present, "struck him over the head, knocking him, with the chair on which he
sat, to the floor."[31]

To the dismay of proslavery men, however, and despite the violent efforts to gag their opponents, a small but ominous flow of free-soilers continued to "pollute" the Territory of Kansas. Even more surprising, not all who arrived were "chicken-hearted hirelings." As the McCrea-Phillips incident in Leavenworth demonstrated, an increasing number of Northerners were willing to give as well as receive. "Send us no more coxcombs and cowards, armed with big words," one such Yankee demanded of Eastern sponsors.[32]

At the free-soil enclave of Manhattan in "far western" Kansas, proslavery settlers were threatened with death and chased from their claims.[33] And Sam Wood, a headstrong Quaker from Lawrence, took abuse from no man, no matter the case. Remembered his friend Charles Robinson:

> One day, as he called for the mail for the citizens of Lawrence, at the post-office at Westport, while behind the boxes with the postmaster, some person in the crowd in the store used insulting language about him, which Wood overheard. When he had procured his mail he walked out from behind the screen and called for his insulter. He was pointed out, when Wood suddenly placed him upon the floor . . . and left him among his friends.[34]

Among the brave, none displayed more quiet courage than Robinson himself. Soon after the March election, the thirty-six-year-old doctor organized four companies of free-state militia, then sped east an urgent appeal for two hundred Sharps rifles and two cannons.[35] As he confided to Eli Thayer:

> If they give us occasion to settle the question of slavery in this country with the bayonet let us improve it. What way can bring the slaves redemption more speedily. Wouldn't it be rich to march an army through the slave holding states & roll up a black cloud that should spread dismay & terror to the ranks of the oppressors?[36]

While the radical in private differed greatly from the moderate in public, Robinson was cautioned by Thayer and a nervous Amos Lawrence that errors of violence must be left entirely to Southerners.[37]

In mid-May 1855, the steamboat *Emma Harmon* docked at the Lawrence levee, and among other items, five boxes marked BOOKS were unloaded. Word of the dreaded Sharps rifles reaching Kansas quickly spread to Missouri, causing great excitement. Fantastic rumors circulated about the killing capacity of the new, fast-firing weapon, and George Washington Brown, the catty editor of the *Herald of Freedom,* was not a man to let fortune fly by.

If it required a thousand men and two cannon . . . to reduce Lawrence to subjection on the 30th of March last . . . how many men, cannon, etc., will it require when we are prepared with five hundred Sharp's [*sic*] rifles, each capable of throwing ten balls per minute, with exact precision, a distance of one mile, and, it is said, will carry very accurately a distance of even three miles?[38]

Almost as terrifying to Missouri and Kansas slaveholders as advanced weaponry was the fear that their property might "take legs and run." Only two confirmed incidents had occurred since the arrival of New Englanders the year before, and in each instance the runaway had been recovered. In both cases, however, the fugitives had fled to Lawrence, and in both cases only the threat of violence had forced their surrender.[39] With understandable anxiety, the *Westport Frontier News* warned its readers:

We every day see handbills offering rewards for runaway negroes from Jackson and neighboring counties. Where do they go? There is an underground railroad leading out of western Missouri, and we would respectfully refer owners of lost niggers to the conductors of these trains. Inquire of Dr. Robinson, sole agent for the transportation of fugitive niggers.[40]

"We say . . . *officially*, that up to the present time, not the first rail has been laid of this road in Kansas," Robinson responded from Lawrence. "[B]ut the workmen are in readiness," he added menacingly, "and will commence operations with a will, if our affairs are again interfered with by foreign intruders."[41]

Meanwhile, the Territorial Legislature was laboring to ensure that the "first rail" of the underground railroad was never laid. Sitting initially at Pawnee, then Shawnee Mission, and finally settling down at Lecompton, the legislators enacted a rigid slave code that either imprisoned or put to death any who tampered with the system in Kansas.[42] Even the mere censure of slavery, "by speaking or by writing," was punishable by imprisonment "at hard labor for a term not less than two years."[43]

Not surprisingly, planters on the western border and elsewhere greeted the code with elation. "They now have laws more efficient to protect slave property than any State in the Union," cheered an Alabama newspaper. "These laws . . . will be enforced to the very letter and with utmost vigor."[44]

"It will not be long before the penitentiary of Kansas will stink with blue bellies," chortled another southern journalist.[45]

When the same news from Kansas reached the North, the reaction was explosive. "Hellish," hissed one nearly speechless Illinois editor.

Outraged, robbed, insulted, condemned to death for following the dictates of humanity; imprisonment for uttering manly words of truth, and all to please the slave power! Great God! Why is language so powerless! Why cannot we find words to express the thoughts and feelings that throng our heart and brain at such time as this . . . ? If this does not stir the freemen of Kansas up to civil war, then they deserve to wear the chains that the . . . Missouri mob have forged upon them. . . . The life of a free white man is thus made cheaper than the service of a negro slave . . . ! [I]t makes our blood boil to read such things! We shall rejoice when the first gun is fired in civil war in Kansas.[46]

"If the settlers in Kansas . . . hesitate an instant to take up arms . . . against the dastardly tyrants . . . ," raged the *New York Times,* "they are unworthy of their name and descent. The provocation of our forefathers to Revolution was trifling compared with that which these Kansas settlers have experienced."[47]

Few men in Kansas relished the opportunity to fight the foe more than Charles Robinson, as his earlier letter to Eli Thayer illustrated. And yet, as the wily Yankee well knew, it was a war the isolated and outnumbered Northerners could not think of winning. Only by following the "Fabian" policy of passive resistance might free-soilers hope to hang on and pray for a better day.

"We must be as independent and self-reliant and confident as the Missourians are," Robinson wrote to Amos Lawrence, "and never, in any instance, be cowed into silence or subserviency to their dictation. This course on the part of prominent Free-State men is absolutely necessary to inspire the masses with confidence, and keep them from going over to the enemy."[48]

With anger and impatience among free-soilers mounting, Robinson seized the opportunity before a July Fourth crowd in Lawrence to "set the ball in motion" for his plan of self-government and "open defiance" to the South.

What are we? Subjects, slaves of Missouri. We come to the celebration of this anniversary, with our chains clanking upon our limbs; we lift to Heaven our manacled arms in supplication; proscribed, outlawed, denounced, we cannot so much as speak the name of Liberty, except with prison walls and halters looking us in the face. We must not only see black slavery . . . planted in our midst, and against our wishes, but we must become slaves ourselves. . . . Fellow citizens . . . it is for us to choose for ourselves, and for those who shall come after us, what institutions shall bless or curse our beautiful Kansas. . . . Let every man stand in his own place, and acquit himself like a man. . . . Let us repudiate all laws enacted by foreign legislative bodies, or dictated by Judge Lynch over the way. Tyrants are tyrants, and tyranny is tyrany, whether under the garb of law or in opposition to it. So thought and so acted our ancestors, and so let us think and act.[49]

Among those circulating in the crowd that day were a number of men who, according to one observer, "were not residents" of Kansas; nor, they might have added, did they have any intention of ever so being. Young abolitionists, opposed to any peaceful solution of the territorial troubles, were drawn west in the hope that Kansas might provide a battleground on which to fight slavery as well as a clear field for plunder. Also in the audience that day was an individual eager to seize that reckless element and channel it toward violence at the first opportunity.

Like most settlers, James Henry Lane had come to Kansas with no higher ideal than to simply better his lot in life. After a lackluster stint as lieutenant governor and another in the U.S. House, his star in Indiana had seemingly set. A Democrat who had voted for the Kansas-Nebraska Bill, Lane was initially indifferent to slavery. "I look upon this nigger question just as I look upon the horse or the jackass question," he announced with characteristic color. "It is merely a question of dollars and cents."[50] And even after his alignment with the free-soil party, the tall, sandy-haired Hoosier declared that "if Kansas had been a good hemp and tobacco state [I] would have favored slavery."[51]

The glaring contradictions in Lane's life apparently troubled him not a jot, nor did it worry the rough settlers from Ohio, Illinois, and other western states who increasingly gravitated to him. A spellbinding stump speaker, at times comical, at times maudlin, often ribald and obscene, Lane had, as one listener discovered, a "magic faculty by which he controlled primitive assemblages, convincing them against their judgment and bending them against their will."[52]

Tireless, ambitious, and utterly unscrupulous, the agile politician quickly became an attraction and a leader second only to Charles Robinson. Wrote one keen student of both men:

> Robinson is cool-headed, cautious and calculative; just the man to plan and direct.—Lane is hot-headed, rash, regardless of consequences, but not wanting in bravery; just the man to carry out the plans and directions. Robinson looks ahead, counts the cost of everything, weighs every consideration, no matter how trifling, and comes to an unchangeable conclusion. Lane looks only to the present, acts only for to-day, never gives a thought about how his acts will appear in history. . . . Robinson is a great thinker, and we should judge, writes better than he speaks. Lane can't sit long enough to write at all.[53]

*James Henry Lane.* KANSAS STATE HISTORICAL SOCIETY, TOPEKA.

Soon, the two men, though outwardly cooperative, were in fact inwardly at war with one another. Each—the idealist and the opportunist—saw the other as the main obstacle to success: Lane, the ever-present powder keg, ready, willing and able to blast Robinson's methodical plan for peace and freedom in Kansas to bits; Robinson, the only force capable of frustrating Lane's quest for complete control of the free-state movement and certain high office.

Meanwhile, in their own quest for political power, the Pro-Slavery Party of Kansas had witnessed at least one irritating obstacle removed when Andrew Reeder was recalled. Although shady land speculation was the official explanation, many free-soilers felt Franklin Pierce had punished the governor for his increasing antipathy to slavery. To fill the void, the president sent Wilson Shannon, a congenial Ohioan who nevertheless promised to be a pliable proslavery tool. Already anxious over northern defiance, many militant Missourians saw the appointment of Shannon as a signal from Washington to crush out free-soilism before it spread.

The Southerners at Atchison hardly needed a cue. Named for the fiery Missouri senator, the turbulent town by the turbulent river was a hotbed of slavery sentiment and contained within its city limits as violent a population as the border could deliver. Nevertheless, J. W. B. Kelley, a "rabid" free-soil nomad from Ohio, refused to abide elsewhere, nor would he cease his "pointed remarks" against slavery. In early August 1855, when Kelley sharply criticized townsman Grafton Thomason because the latter had neglected to decently inter a dead slave he had owned, the big, burly Southerner located the little abolitionist and asked him to repeat his words.[54] According to a bystander, Kelley replied

> that he did not speak to men who owned negroes. Mr. Thomason did not wait for a further expression from him, but seized the independent individual and nearly wore him out against the ground. A friend [of Kelley's] attempting to interfere, was, by one blow from the powerful fist of Mr. Thomason, landed backwards, on the other side of Jordan.[55]

"Kelley was knocked down, and pounded with stones about the head and face," his friend continued, "until he was rendered entirely blind, and his head cut up in the most shocking manner!!"[56]

The following day Kelley was ordered to vacate town or suffer the consequences, a summons he promptly obeyed. "Other emissaries of [the] 'Aid Society' now in our midst, tampering with our slaves, are warned to leave," cautioned a circular, "else they, too, will meet the reward which their nefarious designs so justly merit—*hemp.*"[57]

Only days later, another Kelley—Robert S., junior editor of the *Atchison Squatter Sovereign*—was busily at work in his office. Like his partner, John Stringfellow, Kelley was a radical slavery man, and whatever he may have lacked in literary finesse he more than made up for in personal ferocity. Ran a typical Kelley screed:

> If we for a moment thought that a drop of Yankee blood ran through our veins, we should let it out even though our life were sacrificed in so doing. . . . We go in for a war of extermination against the lawless nullifiers and negro-stealers now infesting this Territory, and when occasion offers we will show our love for Northern blood by causing it to flow in profusion to enrich our soil.[58]

Thus it was that when the Reverend Pardee Butler rode into town that morning from his cabin on Stranger Creek and headed for the newspaper office, Robert

Kelley was in no mood to greet yet another loud and obnoxious abolitionist. The preacher, on his way east to bring back his family to the claim they would soon call home, was, like the victim who preceded him, a fanatical free-stater who "would, if need be, express his views in defiance of the whole community."[59]

> [T]he threats of the *Squatter Sovereign* had been so savage and barbarous, that I wanted to carry back to my friends in Illinois some evidence of what was going on. I went, therefore . . . to the *Squatter Sovereign* printing office to purchase extra copies of that paper. I was waited on by Robert S. Kelley. After paying for my papers I said to him, "I should have become a subscriber to your paper some time ago only there is one thing I do not like about it." Mr. Kelley did not know me, and asked: "What is it?" I replied: "I do not like the spirit of violence that characterizes it." He said: "I consider all Free-soilers rogues, and they are to be treated as such." I looked him for a moment steadily in the face, and then said to him: "Well, sir, I am a Free-soiler, and I intend to vote for Kansas to be a free State."[60]

Before checking into the hotel that night, Butler made several stops around Atchison, loudly proclaiming that his views were right, the town's wrong, and condemning as "infamous and unlawful" the brutal beating of J. W. B. Kelley.[61]

*Pardee Butler.* KANSAS STATE HISTORICAL SOCIETY, TOPEKA.

The following morning, Butler awoke to finish some correspondence before his downriver packet arrived. He cut short his letter-writing, however, when he heard someone enter the hotel.

> I . . . heard some one call my name, and rose up to go down stairs; but was met by six men, bristling with revolvers and bowie knives, who came up stairs and into my room. The leader was Robert S. Kelley. They presented me a string of resolutions, denouncing free State men . . . and demanded that I should sign them. . . . I felt my heart flutter, and was ashamed to speak, lest these men should notice that my voice trembled and should think I was afraid of them. . . . Sitting down I pretended to read the resolutions. . . . But these men were impatient, and said: "We just want to know will you sign these resolutions . . . ?" I said not a word, but going to the head of the stairs, where was my writing-stand and pen and ink, I laid the paper down and quickly walked down stairs and into the street. Here they caught me by the wrists, from behind, and demanded, "Will you sign?" I answered, "No," with emphasis. . . . They seized me and dragged me down to the river, cursing me for a damned abolitionist, and saying to me they were going to drown me. Arriving at the bank, Mr. Kelley went though the very interesting ceremony of painting my face with black paint—thus marking upon it the letter R. . . . This ceremony being ended, and the company having now grown to some thirty or forty persons (boys included) my trial began. . . . Loafers and gentlemen, old men and beardless boys, scarcely old enough to swear grammatically, drink whiskey or chew tobacco . . . , severally and together, they pitched in, every one on his own hook. For the space of about two hours I became a sort of target, at which were hurled all sorts of missles, in the shape of curses, imprecations, arguments, entreaties, accusations, and interrogatories.[62]

When a vote was suggested on whether to lynch Butler or not, a local dentist protested: "My friends, we must not hang this man; he is not an abolitionist, he is what they call a Free-soiler. The Abolitionists steal our niggers, but the Free-soilers do not do this. They intend to make Kansas a free State by legal methods. . . . I propose that we make a raft and send him down the river as an example." When the secret poll was taken, the preacher was saved by only one vote.[63]

While two logs were found and fastened together, Butler was offered his freedom, "provided I held my tongue."

> I said I would speak when I pleased. I told them I had done no wrong; that I had as good a right to come there as they had, and should do my duty

as I understood it, and they might do the same. I said, "you are many, I am but one man; dispose of me as you think best; I ask no favors of you. . . ." When the raft was completed I was ordered to take my place on it. . . . I said "Gentlemen, if you do not take my life, and Providence permits, I shall come back to Atchison." They said, "If you come back again to Atchison, we will hang you." They offered to show me the very tree on which they would hang me. . . . They took a skiff and towed the raft out into the middle of the Missouri River. As we swung away from the bank, I rose up and said . . . "[I]f I am drowned I forgive you; but I have this to say to you: If you are not ashamed of your part in this transaction, I am not ashamed of mine. Good-by."

Floating down the river, alone and helpless, I had opportunity to look about me. I had noticed that they had put up a flag on my raft, but had paid no attention to it; now I looked at it and it charged me with stealing negroes. . . . The picture on the flag was that of a white man riding at full gallop, on horseback, with a negro behind him. The flag bore this inscription: "GREELEY TO THE RESCUE: I HAVE A NIGGER. THE REV. MR. BUTLER, AGENT FOR THE UNDERGROUND RAILROAD." This flag I pulled down . . . and made a paddle of the flag staff. . . . The river was rapid, and there were in the river heaps of drift-wood, called "rack-heaps," dangerous places into which the water rushed with great violence; but from these I was mercifully saved, and though I could not swim, I landed a few miles below Atchison without harm or accident.[64]

Wrote later a satisfied Robert Kelley, who, by lying to the mob about the vote count, had, unbeknownst to the preacher, saved him from hanging:

Butler arrived in town with a view of starting for the East, probably for the purpose of getting a fresh supply of free-soilers from the penitentiaries and pest-holes of the northern states. . . . Such treatment may be expected by all scoundrels visiting our town for the purpose of interfering with our time-honored institutions, and the same punishment we will be happy to award all free-soilers, abolitionists, and their emissaries.[65]

Not all victims were as visible or vociferous as Pardee Butler and J. W. B. Kelley. Indeed, as proslavery anger mounted during the summer and autumn of 1855, almost any avowed free-stater was a potential target.

"I was at work one day on my cabin, when a body of about 150 mounted men came in sight . . . ," remembered a newcomer to Kansas, Samuel Walker. "[A]s they came nearer I saw that they were Border Ruffians. The leader advanced near me, and . . . wanted to know where in hell I was from. I told him I came from

Ohio. 'God damn you,' was his rejoinder; 'you had better go back there quick. . . .' He would give me two weeks to get out, as he was coming up at the expiration of that time to drive all the damned nigger stealers from the territory." [66]

Sam Walker had already suffered one serious run-in with Southerners several months before and was thus in no frame of mind to suffer yet another. Traveling west with his family in March, 1855, the free-soiler booked passage on a St. Louis steamer for the last leg to the Territory.

> We found . . . a number of Southern families with their slaves going to Platte county, Missouri. We had paid cabin fare, but we were not allowed to go to the first table with the Southern "ladies" and "gentlemen". . . . All kinds of insults were heaped upon us. At every landing a crowd of roughs would come aboard "to see the damned Yankees." On our arrival at Boonville a delegation of citizens came on board and held a consultation with the captain. What the delegation had to say may best be judged from the fact that the captain soon came to us and stated that his boat could not carry us any further up the river. . . . We demanded some of our passage money but could get none, of course. . . . [T]he moment we got ashore he backed off and headed up stream with the exultant Southerners all on board. [67]

Walker and several other northern castaways were able to buy oxen and wagons, but farmers on their route west refused to sell food or help in any way.

> As we were going down the hill near the crossing of the Big Blue it was sleeting and very slippery. One of my little girls jumped from the wagon, slipped, fell under the wagon, and one wheel passed over her leg, breaking it in two places. The nearest house to be found was the residence of a Baptist minister. I asked him to allow me to bring the child into his house. He refused, giving as his reason for objection that we were from the North and opposed to slavery. This lovely man of God was kind enough, however, to lend me a plank upon which to lay the little girl while the broken leg was being set. From this time until we reached . . . [Kansas] I could not get leave to take the suffering child into a house at night, though the weather was very cold. . . . [68]

Thus, still in a rage over this earlier treatment, Walker was more than ready to fight after the latest encounter. "As soon as the Missourians were out of sight, I dropped my ax and started around the settlement to let my friends know what was up. I traveled all night afoot, and the next day eighty-six men met at my cabin. We organized ourselves into a military company." [69]

The growing resolve of Sam Walker and other Kansas free-staters was not lost on those afar. Indeed, the *St. Louis Intelligencer* issued an ominous warning to its brethren along the border.

It has been a common opinion with thoughtless persons and thick-headed bullies of the West, that the Northern and Eastern men will not fight. Never was a greater mistake. The sons of New England and of the Middle States do not like to fight. They would rather work, plough, build towns, railroads, make money and raise families, than fight. But fight they will, if need be. Remember, the sons of New England shed the first blood in the American Revolution; and they were last to furl their flags in that terrible struggle. They have never disgraced their community by cowardice, and they will not. They are Americans, with spirit, courage, endurance, and deep love of liberty to animate them. The Free-State men in Kansas will fight before they will be disfranchised and trampled on. Mark the word.[70]

Almost as the St. Louis warning was being written, an embattled band of men were meeting, determined that, like those revolutionaries of old, they indeed would not be trampled upon. On September 5, with patient Charles Robinson and violent Jim Lane in the van, over three hundred free-soilers gathered midway between Topeka and Lawrence at the hamlet of Big Springs. What came from that convention was nothing more nor less than a second Declaration of Independence.

**Resolved,** That we owe no allegiance or obedience to the tyrannical enactments of this spurious Legislature—that their laws have no validity or binding force upon the people of Kansas. . . .
**Resolved,** That we will resist them primarily by every peaceable and legal means within our power, until we can elect our own Representatives and sweep them from the statute books. . . .
**Resolved,** That . . . as soon as we ascertain that peaceable remedies shall fail . . . we will endure and submit to these laws no longer . . . and will resist them to a bloody issue. . . .[71]

Meanwhile, as the nation, North and South, watched events taking shape in Kansas, and while men there and elsewhere were looking to their arms, a surprising number of settlers in the territory remained "entirely indifferent about the subject of slavery."[72] For the great majority of Kansas squatters, the political struggle swirling all about ran a remote second to the physical struggle with nature itself.

## CHAPTER FOUR

# I HAVE SEEN SUFFERING

Though slavery and violence made the headlines, it was the mundane that weighed most on the minds of Kansans. In a rough and raw land where even the basic tools of survival were often lacking, political debate was a luxury many could simply not afford. The first concern for new arrivals was, of course, shelter. While large numbers of women and children boarded in St. Joseph or Kansas City or remained east until the men of the family could stake a claim and raise a cabin, some wives insisted on sharing the hardships with their husbands. Except for a few small hotels run by Indians, accommodations in the territory were virtually nonexistent. And of those that were available, lodging was of the most primitive kind.

When Clarina Nichols of Vermont reached Lawrence in late 1854, she found the village hotel nothing more than an A-frame hut grandly dubbed the "Astor House." The structure was "all hay and poles," she wrote, "[that] reminds one of the straw roof of a huge warehouse. This pole roof is thatched upon the outside with prairie hay, and . . . cotton cloth covers the gable ends, which have doors of the same material nailed to pole frames." [1] Clarina continued:

> When I arrived . . . I was taken to a lodging-house and supplied with plenty of prairie hay for a bed. . . . [O]ur cooking area was the city "Levee". . . . [F]ancy breakfast-getting for some twenty families and companies which have kindled as many fires, some with two or three stones to hold up kettles and pans, and a very few with "stick cranes." The *cooks* are prominent in the scene and about as many of them are men as women. Yonder is a grave middle-aged man without crane or stones, toiling manfully to boil his tea kettle or fry his Missouri-cured "side pork," without upsetting the one or

burning the other, both of which he accomplishes in spite of his efforts
to the contrary. . . . There is a woman, her skirts burned full of holes . . .
and what remains of them converted into a sort of fringe by the prairie
stubble. . . . [S]he has a tear in either eye, for the smoke loiters near the
earth. Yonder breakfast—left to itself a moment for a crying baby has drawn
the mother into the tent, as it is called—has tipped over, and the beef soup
is flowing from the camp kettle into the spattering flame.[2]

Unlike Clarina, those who could not afford the "extravagance" of a hotel were
forced to shift as best they could, living in wagons, tents, or almost anything with
a roof. Sara Robinson visited a friend whose new home was nothing more than a
lean-to.

We find her in a little cabin of mud walls, cotton-wood roof, and with cloth
covering the inside. It is tent-shaped, and very small. There is an earthy smell
and a stifled feeling as I enter the low door; and, as I at a glance see the want
of comfort pervading all, I scarcely can find courage to ask how she likes
Kansas. A bed, standing crosswise, fills up one entire end of the cabin,
leaving only about eight feet square of space for the family, consisting of
father, mother, and four little girls under six years. Two rough benches,
about two feet in length, and two rude tables, make up the furniture.
The cooking is done out of doors. . . .[3]

Like this woman and many another, Miriam Colt also found that her first
Kansas kitchen was "natural."

I have cooked so much out in the hot sun and smoke, that I hardly know
who I am, and when I look in the looking-glass I ask, "Can this be me?"
Put a blanket over my head, and I would pass well for an Osage squaw.
My hands are the color of a smoked ham, and get so burnt that the skin
peels off one after another.[4]

While precut "balloon houses" were quick to construct, popular, and for as
little as $800, a structure could be delivered to Kansas from Cincinnati in a rela-
tively short time, the cost was well beyond the reach of most squatters. According
to one visitor, an impoverished homesteader at Wabaunsee experimented with
his own brand of balloon house.

Among the variety of dwellings found here, I notice one today occupied
by a very respectable man, which consisted of a box in which he brought

fruit trees into the territory—seven feet long, three feet wide and three deep—with a slight roof fixed over it, leaving one side entirely open. In this box is his bed, across the end of it his chest . . . and yet he pursues his daily toil, is cheerful and looks forward to better times. . . .[5]

Because much of the best hardwood stood on Indian reserves, many settlers were forced to build with any timber at hand. Most abundant was the great, towering cottonwood. When planed into boards, however, the green lumber upon drying had a tendency to twist and warp "like a cork screw." Initially, few squatters were concerned with the "airiness" of such homes. Indeed, because of fanciful reports from missionaries and early travelers, many newcomers to Kansas were expecting a semitropical paradise where cattle could graze on green grass all winter long and "flowers bloomed the whole year."[6] As a consequence, some settlers neglected to chink their cabins or even cover windows and doors.

The first hint that something was awry came in mid-November 1854. As one surprised squatter noted:

> Yesterday we were greeted by a pretty severe snow-storm, for which we were hardly prepared, our house being in no better condition to receive such a guest than an orchard with the bars down. This morning I crawled from under my buffalo skin, after having . . . [a] pile of snow . . . for a bed. I kindled a fire in our rough stone fire place, but the smoke rolled in upon us at such a rate, that we were compelled to remove the fire, not to the middle of the floor, but where the middle of the floor would be if we only had a floor. By doing this we could get to the windward of the fire and thus avoid the smoke. If you could only see a true picture of us now, as we are seated upon a trunk beside the fire, with our feet extended to keep them warm, and a large tool chest at our backs, with the lid raised to break the wind and a buffalo pelt drawn closely about us. . . .[7]

To the relief of all, the cold snap was brief and temperatures once more climbed, reaching 86 degrees the day after Christmas. "The weather has been . . . as clear, calm, warm, and beautiful as any I ever saw in June," sang an enrapt settler from Council City. "To-day—9th of January—is warm enough for one to sit comfortably in the shade without coat or hat. . . . I would not return to old Pennsylvania for half the State."[8] When the temperature again plunged, shivering squatters with visions of tropical warmth soon came to the grim conclusion that they had been "humbugged."

Snow and ice were not the only surprises awaiting the unwary emigrant. Indeed, without the buffer of mountain or vale the untamed Kansas wind could deliver some of the most ferocious weather anywhere on earth. "[S]uch winds as we have here you know nothing about . . . ," one woman wrote to an Eastern friend. "[I]t blows a perfect whirlwind for two or three days and nights, so that I can scarcely stand up when out of doors, and a cloud of dust fills your mouth and eyes. I never had any idea of dirt or dirty clothes, until my arrival here. . . . "[9]

"San Francisco can't hold a candle to the prairies of Kansas for wind," echoed a well-traveled latecomer to the territory, William Tecumseh Sherman.[10]

Few arrivals were prepared for Kansas winds. No one was prepared for Kansas storms. Recorded a stunned Sara Robinson in her diary:

14th.—The thunder rolls in deafening peals, reverberating across the hills, and the lightnings are one continual flash. . . . making the whole country as light as noon-day. Objects miles distant are as clearly seen as by the sun's light. The rains come down a pouring, tumultuous flood, and the winds blow wildly, threatening to overturn everything before them. . . .
15th.—The night brought another shower—if possible, more severe than that of last night.[11]

Added an equally awe-struck Miriam Colt from southern Kansas:

A most terrific thunder-storm came up last night . . . the fiery chains of lightning streaked the heavens from zenith to horizon. The rain came in torrents, and the wind blew almost tornadoes. . . . We all got wet, and were obliged to lie in our wet beds till morning. . . . [T]he rain had dissolved our mud chinking, and the wind had strewed it all over and in our beds, on our clothes, over our dishes, and into every corner of the house.[12]

After once witnessing the incredible force and fury of a Kansas storm, few forgot them and fewer still could find words to describe them. Exaggerations naturally occurred. Upon viewing a spectacular lightning display, one incredulous spectator thought it looked like "an immense ball of molten Silver burst in the high heavens," and Julia Lovejoy, in a dispatch to a New Hampshire newspaper, was almost breathless in her description.

But O our thunder-storms, Mr. Editor, you have need to witness them before you can conceive of their awful sublimity. On a sudden the heavens are overspread with black angry clouds, and seem for hours to be wrapped in a sheet of flame, heavy thunder, as if the whole artillery of heaven was at once discharged, when the rain not only falls in drops but in copious streams, deluging the earth.[13]

Tall tales aside, it wasn't long before newcomers came to realize that in Kansas, the heat could burn deeper, the cold could cut cleaner, and all could change quicker than anywhere else in America. "When I commenced this letter I said there was a thunder storm raging," Cyrus K. Holliday groused to his wife back east. "It is *now raining, hailing, snowing, blowing, thundering, & lightning* all at the same time. A great Country."[14]

As on any raw frontier, grim disease was waiting to welcome the pioneers with open arms.

> To day is the first day in thirteen weeks that we have been free from the Chill and Intermittent Fever. . . . I got so run down that . . . I have not been able to do any thing or sit up much of the time till to day. . . . I was so weak, so worn and exhausted that I could not see how I could ever build up again. . . . We were all three of us fearfully sick and nobody to take care of us. . . . Sometimes we feel well and strong and think within ourselves that the plague is stayed when suddenly the chills begin to run over us and in a few hours we find ourselves prostrated again.[15]

So spoke Sarah Everett, describing a malarial condition that ravaged the border for years. Though seldom fatal except to the very old or the very young, few, it seemed, were spared the debilitating effects of the ague, or, as it was more commonly called in Kansas, the "Shakes." In addition to the violent paroxysms a victim suffered, the illness could display a myriad of symptoms. Revealed Julia Lovejoy of her afflicted husband:

> When the thermometer ranged upwards of 100 deg., in July, and scarcely a breath of air he was shaking with ague. . . . stomach heaving, brain whirling, temples throbbing . . . nausea increasing, till with a violent retch the last particle of food is ejected therefrom, succeeded by a copious hemorrhage of bile, and the patient sinks away in a kind of dreamy unconsciousness, from which he is aroused by the reflection, "that in twenty-four hours, he must be put over the same rough road, with less strength to endure it!"[16]

As with Julia's husband, those suffering the shakes could expect not only a grueling gauntlet of symptoms, but also weeks, even months, of almost total incapacity.

Another scourge faced by homesteaders was cholera. Although less pervasive than ague, the results were vastly more lethal. Mere mention of a cholera epidemic was enough to ignite panic. When scores of troops at Fort Riley began dropping dead from the dreaded disease in the summer of 1855, several hundred civilian laborers defied the quarantine, raided the armory, then fled east. Efforts by the military to halt the men resulted in a pitched battle wherein four soldiers were slain. As word of the plague spread, entire communities were cleared. Though the deadly virus soon ran its course, settlers lived in constant fear of a new outbreak.[17]

While most large predators along the border—bears, wolves, and panthers— had long since been exterminated by resident Indian tribes and white travelers, arrivals to Kansas nonetheless found more than enough "wildlife" to hold their interest. Wrote a horrified Hannah Ropes, after she and her son moved into a "well-ventilated" cabin in Lawrence:

> Soon I see coming down the beam near me a cricket-looking body, *only* large as a half-dozen home crickets. I move suddenly, but say, very quietly, "Ned, what lodger is this?" He is intimately acquainted with them, for he points to quite a small army of them in another direction, and says, "Only crickets. They won't hurt you. Why, they lived here by right before we came." Verily the boy is more of a philosopher than his mother. Will she ever get rid of her fear of bugs . . . ? I watch the mice (not less than a dozen) play over the bridge of a floor, race over our baggage, climb up our nice shawl curtains; and, growing strong with the necessity for it, I drive them away only when they come too near the quilt.[18]

Upriver at Douglas, young Axalla Hoole of South Carolina could commiserate with Hannah.

> There are more insects about the house I live in than a little, crickets, spiders, cockroaches, granddaddies, &c. Yesterday Betsie and I burned and killed about a thousand of the last. They had got so troublesome that they were crawling over us at night; in the day they would collect in knots about the house, so I set a newspaper on fire and burned them.[19]

Even with a home seemingly free of pests, surprises in Kansas came one upon another. "The worms are working in the logs at the side & over head so that we have a continual dust dropping in every part of the cabin," Sarah Everett of Osawatomie moaned. "Sometimes it gets an inch thick on things that are not moved for two or 3 days. . . . "[20]

Of all insects, none caused more daily distress than mosquitoes. "During the months of June, July, August and September . . .," a Fort Scott editor complained, "myriads of the insects infested every house in town. Tobacco smoke, sulpher, and a thousand other exterminators, were tried repeatedly, or we might say unceasingly, but all in vain. Here they were, and here they stayed, until their murderous weapons were finally benumbed by the frosts of autumn."[21]

While fine nets over windows were not unknown, most settlers spent their working days out-of-doors. Recounted Miriam Colt from the humid Neosho Valley:

The mosquitoes have come upon us all of a sudden. They troubled us very much at the creek to-day while washing. After washing, Mrs. V and myself went down the creek into the embowered bottom lands to refresh ourselves with a bathe, and the mosquitoes came in such swarms upon us that we thought they would carry us off by tit-bits before we could protect ourselves with our clothing. . . . Our bed being short, in the night they have a good chance to nibble away at our protruding extremities. I lie awake—I can't sleep for their music and the pain and inflammation caused by their bites. I try to keep my children covered, so they wont eat them all up before morning. As for myself, I get so infuriated that I get up, descend the ladder, make my way out into the wet grass upon the run. . . . I then return from my dewy bath, lie down and try to sleep, but it is almost in vain.[22]

Much like Miriam, many a weary farmer, after a hard day in the field, found no haven at home. "[D]evil take the musquitoes . . . ," scribbled one assailed diarist. "[R]ead fiddled, & fought Musquitoes which are most confounded hungry to night. . . . Fought musquitoes nearly all night last night. . . . Lord! how I wish I was out of this."[23]

But of all the trials settlers had to endure—mosquitoes, spiders, storms, dust, even disease—none struck more horror into their hearts, especially those from cooler climates, than the silent, slithering peril underfoot—snakes! Rare indeed was that immigrant who remained indifferent on the subject. As letters home attest, many newcomers were almost frantic in their fear, stunned by the incredible size of the reptiles as well as their nightmarish numbers. Wailed Julia Lovejoy to a New Hampshire newspaper:

Oh, yea who breathe the air of our own native hills . . . ! When I . . . thought of your refreshing breezes, your cooling streams, amongst the mountains; oh, how we longed to bathe our fevered brow and throbbing temples in those little rivulets that issue from the mountain-side . . . or sit on the mossy bank and watch its ripplings over its pebbly bed, and not start with fear at every rustling leaf or moving spire of grass, lest a deadly serpant might be concealed beneath! Only one week ago we stopped to pick up (near our residence) some shavings where shingles had been made, and took up a serpant in our arms—a copperhead, we thought at a glance, but it escaped. Last May, the writer of this killed a monster of a rattlesnake, near our door-step, with ten rattles and a button, making it eleven years old.—No one else was on the premises at the time, but our little four-year-old boy.[24]

Horribly, as Julia and others soon discovered, a crude cabin in Kansas was a welcome mat to unwelcome guests. According to Miriam Colt:

We frequently see rattlesnakes crawling and hanging over the sills under the piazza where the floor is up. We hear a peculiar noise under the floor sometimes, have thought it was rats, but find it is the noise of snakes. My husband keeps a long hickory cane lying on the bed, so that when he hears that peculiar noise, he strikes on the floor near where some of the floor boards are gone, to drive the snakes away.[25]

"In houses whose floors were laid with green lumber, which in seasoning left broad openings," one Kansas traveler reported, "the inmates were occasionally startled to see one of these reptiles peer up through a crack, and stare about the room."[26] Once again, Julia Lovejoy, on "the bane of our life."

We can face a wild cat . . . [but] let a copper-head or a rattlesnake make their appearance, and our courage is all gone. We have never enjoyed a walk in the garden, or gathering plums, or, indeed, sleeping in our unfinished cabin in warm weather, on account of these intruders. . . . Mrs. Sanders . . . one extremely warm night, spread her bed on the ground inside their cabin, as they had no floor, took her babe and one or two other children, and lay herself down to sleep. In the night she turned herself over to nurse her babe, and felt something sting her under lip severly; the pain increasing, she called on her husband, who slept elsewhere, who got a light and went to a trunk to get some "pain-killer," and there coiled behind the trunk was a rattle-snake; her lip continuing to swell shockingly, he ran for some neighbors, and when he returned found two more rattlesnakes in his cabin, and his poor wife in awful agony—her lip turned black, and one who saw it informed me that it looked as large as her arm—her head and neck swelled to her shoulders—her eyes assumed the peculiar look of a snake's eyes, and as long as she could speak, in piteous tones, she begged "them to keep the snakes from biting her children." It was with great difficulty the physician could keep her from choking to death. . . . Another:—A young lady living about a mile from us, felt something crawling up her side, as she lay reclining . . . in bed, and supposing it to be her little "pet kitten," and not wishing to be disturbed in her slumbers, rudely pushed it away with her hand, when lo!

the ominous sound! she shrieked to her mother, "a rattlesnake!" and sprung for a light, and there lay his snakeship, who was soon . . . mauled to death. . . .

Mrs. Anderson, a lady 50 or more years of age, who lived on the opposite side . . . from us, threw her arms over her head in the night, as was her wont, when she felt a peculiar stinging sensation on her hand; she called for a light, and to her horror, saw a large copper-head over the head of her bed; she set up a terrific scream, supposing, probably, she had received her "death wound" . . . and though her arm swelled dreadfully, to her shoulder, she was soon entirely cured.[27]

*Julia Lovejoy.* KANSAS STATE HISTORICAL SOCIETY, TOPEKA.

Julia also had tales more personal to tell.

[A] huge rattlesnake was found, when the cover was removed, snugly coiled up under my bed, where I had slept sweetly a few hours before, and still another . . . peering with sparkling eyes from a cupboard, suspended over my bed, where my babe lay sleeping. . . . Our only daughter was bitten on the side of her foot, through a kid bootee, as she was walking in the grove near our dwelling; and . . . it devolved on us, ignorant as we were in such cases, to try and save her life. . . . We first tied a strong ligature tightly above the ankle, applied our lips to extract the poison as far as possible, and gave her as much whiskey as we could get her to take. . . .[28]

While many, like Julia Lovejoy, were never completely cured of the phobia, as always, some found sport in the fear of others. "In regard to snakes, they don't bother anyone here but Chet," wrote Peter Bryant of Holton to his brother. "Jove! you ought to see him jump when a garter' gets into the furrow. I think I have seen him leap 8 feet right straight up in the air at sight of one's tail. Rattlesnakes are about as thick here as in Illinois. I don't think we killed over twenty last summer."[29]

And, for James Stewart of Council City, familiarity ultimately bred indifference.

**June Sun 10.** Clear & beautiful, a good breeze. Killed a rattlesnake in the house this morning, wrote a letter . . . and read. . . .[30]

For young Stewart, at least, poisonous vipers sharing a cabin had obviously become a fact of frontier life almost too common to note.

Ill equipped to deal with the rigors of pioneer life, many men and women found the trials that beset them almost unendurable. As if her labors were not already great enough, one woman interrupted her grueling washday routine long enough to prepare yet another of an endless succession of monotonous meals. "Returning a half-hour later," her husband recalled, "she found that a drove of wild hogs had overturned the tubs and devoured the entire contents. The family had no under-clothing left."[31]

Assailed on every side, Miriam Colt also painted a dark and dismal picture from her drafty shack on the Neosho.

A cold, drizzling rain. The prairie winds come whizzing in. Have hung up an Indian blanket at the door, but by putting trunks and even stones on to the end that drags, can hardly make it answer the purpose of a door. It is dark, gloomy, cheerless, uncomfortable and cold inside. Have a fire out of doors to cook by. . . . It is not very agreeable work, cooking out of doors in this windy, rainy weather, or when the scorching sun shines. The bottoms of our dresses are burnt full of holes now, and they will soon be burnt off. . . . Our bill of fare is limited . . . over and over again: hominy, johnny cake, Graham pudding, some white bread. . . . Disappointment has darkened every brow. . . . We are 100 miles from a grist-mill, and 50 from a post office. . . . We are as much shut out from the world here as though we were on some lonely island in the ocean. . . .[32]

Like Miriam, many other women soon discovered that their homes, which fantasies had envisioned as happy and clean and warm and safe, were little more than nightmarish traps. "The family consisted of a man and wife and children of all sizes . . . ," remembered an overnight guest to a cabin in Kansas. "There was but one room for all of the outfit, with pigs taking up a big portion of the space. I thought it looked a little squally, for naturally everything was covered with dirt. . . . All the men and children slept on the floor, and with the comradeship of a few pigs all kept warm."[33]

"It is utterly impossible for you to understand anything about what we have suffered here . . . ," Sarah Everett admitted to a sister. "In a house that the meanest hovel you know would be preferable to. It's of no use to try to tell you anything about it, you dont want to know either."[34]

"I have seen more of human suffering since I came to this place than I have ever seen lifelong before," added Julia Lovejoy.[35]

The pressure was too great for many, and large numbers of men and women fled Kansas utterly demoralized. Among those who remained, some, like Miriam Colt, soon found themselves on the verge of insanity.

> The dark storm-clouds, (to my mind's eye,) are gathering in our horizon, and even now they flap their cold, bat-like wings about my head, causing my heart to tremble with fear. I am so impressed some nights with this feeling, that I sit up in bed for hours, and fairly cringe from some unknown terror. I tell my husband, "We are a doomed ship; unless we go away, some great calamity will come upon us. . . . " I call [my child] Willie to me, put my hand on his head, and weep and weep, and say, "O, Willie! Willie! Willie!" My husband says, "Miriam, don't feel so; I am afraid you will go crazy."[36]

But then, at times unexpected and from unexpected sources, bright bits of hope cut through the crushing gloom. Even a forlorn and sobbing Miriam Colt could view her lot in a new light.

> My Willie saw me weeping today; he asked, "What ails mamma?" I told him, "Mamma wants to go back to her old home." He then said, "Mamma, ain't the flowers pretty?"[37]

The smiling, innocent words were enough to break a mother's heart.

> My two precious children have not made the least complaint about hard fare, or even asked why they do not have the comforts they have been used to having. They have their tin cups filled with bouquets of fresh flowers every day. Innocent and trusting childhood; sipping enjoyment like bees, wherever it can be found.[38]

Almost immediately, Miriam began viewing her world anew.

> We have sunsets now that will do to look upon. The large, crimsoned, wheel-like sun approaches the horizon . . . [and] the whole western sky is enriched with his hue, until he is swallowed up without twilight in the depths beyond where the tall grass keeps waving. . . . Kansas moons have been described as equaling Italy's moons in lovliness. What Italy's moons are I know not by experience, but the moons here are lovely far beyond describing words.[39]

Although the splendor of prairie sunsets and Kansas moons were not enough to hold hundreds of disillusioned emigrants—including a bereaved Miriam Colt, who would soon bury her beloved little Willie—thousands more, like Cyrus K. Holliday of Topeka, showed a dogged determination to "stay and see the thing out," despite the tremendous adversities—or perhaps, because of them.

> You can't tell, Mary, how glad I am that you are not with me. What we have to endure is almost beyond belief and you never could have gone through it. It is a long time since I have seen anything in the shape of a bed. I have a Buffalo Robe and two blankets in which I roll myself and lay down to rest upon the bare ground with boots, hat, overcoat and all on. Our food is mush, molasses and bacon, mixed plentifully with dirt three times each day. Thus we live in Kansas. . . . [But] a more lovely country I certainly never saw. . . . And in a few years when civilization by its magic influence shall have transformed this glorious country from what it now is to the brilliant destiny awaiting it, the sun in all his course will visit no land more truly lovely and desirable than this. Here, Mary, with God's kind permission, we will make our home.[40]

Probably no more diverse population ever came together anywhere in America than that which converged on Kansas in the 1850s. Along with the normal flow of Irish, German, and English immigrants were added Puritan New Englanders, Deep South planters, yeomen from the Old Northwest, Border State hemp growers, Jewish merchants, African slaves, and reservation Indians. Among them all, however, none viewed the land and its occupants with more surprise, shock, and very often revulsion, and none were themselves seen as more alien to the new country, than the northeastern Yankees. Unlike most who came to Kansas, a sizable minority of New Englanders saw the territory as a temporary home at best; a brief battleground to be endured until Kansas had been "saved" from slavery and the scene of action shifted elsewhere. Consequently, it was with no small amount of irritation and impatience that the well-educated idealists "tolerated" their earthy neighbors.

With a cold, superior mien that could cut deeper than a Missourian's curse, the haughty New Englanders were at first contemptuous of the habits and mannerisms of their fellow free-soilers from Illinois, Indiana, and Ohio—their quaint mode of building homes with chimneys on the *outside*, their haphazard fencing of fields, their primitive concepts of democracy, their irreverent religious conduct, their vulgarisms and "rustic" language and phrases such as "powerful bad," "mighty weak," and "right smart." Eastern eyebrows raised at the "ungoverned appetites" of both sexes at the table, and fine ladies were shocked when young western women smoked, chewed, spit, and referred to their husbands as "the old man." In a paternal, impatient way, the Yankees were always quick to correct their ignorant, errant brothers and sisters on the "right" way of doing things.

The friction between East and West was most glaring in Lawrence, and one day Hoosier Josiah Miller, editor of the *Kansas Free State*, finally put flint to powder.

> We have no sympathy with that class of people who pin themselves to a small portion of God's footstool, and stick there, until . . . their whole souls and minds become contracted into the narrowness of a nut-shell. . . . [T]hey know nothing of human nature . . . outside their own selfish and contracted hearts. . . . [T]he Eastern emigration of this place. . . . come to Kansas for the purpose of instructing the western people how to build up a model New England State. They are advised, from head quarters, to avoid the use of all Western vulgarisms, and to cherish their New England habits and customs. . . . They like the Emigrant Aid Company because it sends out a large body of New Englanders, so that they can have their own society, &c. They work themselves into a belief that Western men, and especially Missourians, are of an inferior order of people, unfit for social intercourse; and unless a man agrees with them in all of their peculiar notions about building up a model State, he is charged as a "Missourian"—as this is the worst epithet, in their opinion, they can apply to any one they dislike.
>
> We would now sincerely advise these *wise* men of the East of the fact that the great majority of the settlers of Kansas are now and will be Western men. . . . This being the case, these *refined* gentlemen may just as well make up their minds, at once, to consider Western men as human beings, and conclude to associate with them. . . .[41]

As Miller made note, while they often maintained a reluctant relationship with their fellow free-staters from the Western States, it was the Southern settlers in Kansas, particularly those from Missouri, who merited the especial contempt and scorn of New Englanders. Missourians, wrote Bay Stater Hannah Ropes to a friend, are "a partially civilized race, fifty years behind you in all manner of improvements."[42]

"[They] put up a log or a rail pen for a shanty," Sarah Everett added, "split out a few oak boards to sleep under, and then pass the time fishing, hunting and lounging about."[43]

His hatred almost boundless, one Kansas correspondent to the *New York Tribune* considered Missourians little better than disgusting, degraded animals.

> They are a queer looking set, slightly resembling human beings, but more closely allied, in general appearance, to wild beasts. An old rickety straw hat, ragged shirt, buttonless corduroys with a leather belt and a coarse pair

of mud-covered boots constitute a "full dress." They never shave or comb their hair, and their chief occupation is loafing around whisky shops, squirting tobacco juice and whittling with a dull jack knife. They drink whisky for a living, and sleep on dry goods boxes. . . . They generally carry a huge bowie knife and a greasy pack of cards. . . . They are generally about six feet high, spindle-shanked and slab sided. It would be an insult to the brute creation to call them brutes. . . . They are "down on" schools, churches, and printing offices, and revel in ignorance and filth.[44]

When cholera struck a Missouri family south of Lawrence, there was no pity in the heart of Mrs. Charles Robinson. "They lived in the most abject filth, and drank of the stagnant water in the bed of the Wakarusa . . . ," sneered Sara. "The cabin was very small, untidy, and would of itself almost breed disease."[45]

The feeling amongst Missourians for New Englanders was mutual. "To him," one student of the former noted, "the Yankee appears the embodiment of all that is stiff and cold, calculating and selfish."[46]

"Have you ever seen one of them?" laughed a Kansas reporter for the *St. Louis Republican.* "I will draw you a small picture. . . . "

From five feet seven inches to six feet high, (or rather of an indefinate height, for they double up and stretch out, to suit occasion,) sallow complexion, lean and stringy, suspicious-looking, nervous movements, presumptuous, inquisitive, cold and hungry. . . .[47]

Echoed a Leavenworth editor:

We have little respect for any of the psalm-singing button-makers and tin peddlers of New England, and see enough of them about our own city whining and intermeddling with everybody's business, not to appreciate the feelings of contempt and abhorrence the people of Kansas must feel for the nest of thieving paupers and tract distributors of Lawrence. Here the better class of them come and "speculate" and "trade" and "dicker," calling themselves merchants and assume to be respectable and law-abiding citizens, but once give them a chance to cheat, or in any way act out their propensities, and they will rob their best benefactors.[48]

"Blue-bellies," "hirelings," "mud-sills," "pest-house paupers," cursed Missourians of their neighbors. "Scum," "white-trash," "rif-raf," "pukes," hissed New Englanders, returning the favor. Given the deep-seated hatred between the two groups and the tremendous stakes involved in Kansas, it was only natural that the name-calling would swiftly escalate into confrontations and bloody encounters.

## CHAPTER FIVE

# WHEN KANSAS BLEEDS . . .

[T]HE MOON . . . WAS NOW HIGH IN THE HEAVENS, THE AIR WAS CLEAR AS crystal, and perfectly still. . . . My eyes . . . watched that ridge closely. At last, fully two-thirds of a mile away, an object seemed to move, and then another, and another, and yet another. As they drew a little nearer and came higher on the ridge it was plain to be seen that it was a body of mounted men. . . . I must have gone against that door like a rock from a catapult, for it flew open with a bang. . . . I managed to gasp out, "They are coming." It was all I could say, but its effect was electrical. . . . Immediately after my announcement . . . the light went out. . . . [P]ell mell we rushed out of the house. . . . There, standing bunched up in the shadow of the building so we could not be seen by anyone approaching from the south, we awaited in absolute silence the coming of . . . [the] party.[1]

Thus wrote a suspense-filled sixteen-year-old, Charles Dickson. The boy and his companions along the Wakarusa had good cause to be suspenseful. Prior to this moonlit morning of November 27, 1855, the free-state response to the "bogus" territorial government had been confined largely to words. The time for talk had passed, however, and the hour of action was at hand. In a few moments the revolution, as young Dickson and his fifteen free-soil comrades knew, would begin.

The event that set these men in motion had come less than a week before. On November 21, a festering claim dispute near Hickory Point, a dozen miles south of Lawrence, finally erupted in gunfire, resulting in the death of one Charles Dow. On any other frontier the incident might have ended with the funeral. In politically charged Kansas, such an event could lead to civil war; the fact that Dow was a free-stater and his murderer, Frank Coleman, was a slaver almost guaranteed that it would.

Soon after the murder, proslavery cabins in the area were engulfed in flames, with frightened families fleeing toward Missouri for their lives. In response, a posse led by a former Westport postmaster and now Douglas County sheriff, Samuel Jones, swept into Hickory Point and collared one of the free-soil ringleaders, Jacob Branson. When word of the arrest reached Lawrence, members of the local militia sprang into action. Led by tough Sam Wood, the company struck south for Blanton's Bridge in the hope that Jones and his prisoner would there cross the Wakarusa on their way to Lecompton. And, as the excited young sentinel, Dickson, revealed, the guess had been correct.

"As they came near," another nervous free-stater recalled, "we . . . turned the corner of the house. Phillip Hupp was the first man to cross the road, next came Paul Jones, both armed with squirrel rifles; next came Capt. Hutchinson armed with a handful of large stones. J. R. Kennedy and myself were next, thinking it best to stay close to Capt. Hutchinson, as he was an old fighter. As they drew near we all closed together in front of them." [2]

*Sam Wood.* KANSAS STATE HISTORICAL SOCIETY, TOPEKA.

J. R. Kennedy continued:

> [We] all crowded rapidly up in front of the other party, when one of these said, "What's up?" Major [James] Abbott replied, "That is what we want to know,"—which remark was followed by a shot on our side. (The Major had a self-cocking revolver, and he had, in his excitement, pulled it a little too hard, causing it to go off.) Then the question was asked him again by the other side, "What's up . . . ?" I said to Major Abbott, "Ask them if Branson is there." He did so, and the answer was, "Yes, I am here, and a prisoner." Three or four of our men spoke at once . . . saying, "Come out of that," or "Come over to your friends. . . . " Branson replied, "They say they will shoot me if I do." Colonel Sam Wood answered quickly, "Let them shoot and be damned; we can shoot too." Branson then said, "I will come [even] if they do shoot," starting his mule. (The man who was leading it let the halter slip through his hands very quietly.) The rest of the proslavery party raised their shot-guns and cocked them. Our little crowd raised their guns. . . .[3]

Recorded Sam Wood:

> Guns were aimed and cocked upon both sides, but just as Branson left one of the opposite party lowered his gun with the remark, "I ain't going to shoot." Jones then advanced upon horseback, said . . . that he was Sheriff of Douglas County, Kansas, that he had a warrant to arrest the old man Branson, and he must serve it. He was told that we knew of no Sheriff Jones; that we knew of a postmaster at Westport, Missouri, by that name, but knew of no Sheriff Jones. We told him that we had no Douglas County in Kansas, and what was better, we never intended to have.[4]

"These armed men replied that they . . . knew no laws but their guns," one of the posse members later testified.[5]

J. R. Kennedy:

> About this time some one of them said, "Why, Sam Wood, you are very brave to-night; you must want to fight." Colonel Wood replied that he "was always ready for a fight." Just at this moment Sheriff Jones interposed, saying, "There is no use to shed blood in this affair; but it will be settled soon in a way not very pleasant to Abolitionists," and started to ride through those standing in the road. . . . Just as soon as he started, old Phillip [Hupp] set the trigger and cocked his old squirrel rifle quicker than he or any other

man ever did it before, and said to Sheriff Jones, "Halt! or I will blow your damned brains out. . . . " He stopped, and stayed right there, saying gently to Mr. Hupp, "Don't shoot."[6]

Following these tension-filled moments, the sheriff and his posse were allowed to resume their journey—minus the prisoner.

"After Jones left, and Mr. Branson realized he was safe . . . ," revealed Charles Dickson, "the brave old man . . . broke down and cried like a child. The reaction after the terrible nervous strain through which he had passed had come. To my boyish mind it was a strange sight to see tears rolling down his cheeks and his huge body shaking with sobs. . . . "[7]

But if Branson was overcome, Sam Wood and his men were overjoyed. The first act of aggression against the hated proslavery government had been committed. As the proud rebels marched back to Lawrence at dawn amid a roll of drums, the spirit of 1776 filled the morning air.

Word of the revolt spread swiftly.

To His Excellency
Wilson Shannon
Governor of Kansas Territory

Last night I, with a posse of ten men, arrested one Jacob Branson by virtue of a peace-warrant regularly issued, who, on our return was rescued by a party of forty armed men, who rushed upon us suddenly from behind a house upon the road-side, all armed to the teeth with Sharpe's [sic] rifles. You may consider an open rebellion as having already commenced, and I call upon you for three thousand men to carry out the laws.

Most Respectfully,
Samuel J. Jones
Sheriff of Douglas County[8]

At Leavenworth, Atchison, Lecompton, and other proslavery strongholds, riotous meetings were held within moments of the news. Wild-eyed "witnesses" described cabins wrapped in flames and screaming women and children fleeing in terror, while sidewalk firebrands demanded a traitor's fate for the "abolition reptiles and fanatics" of Lawrence.

"I would sooner my tongue should cleave to the roof of my mouth, or my right arm be severed from my body, than silently give over our beautiful country to ruthless abolitionism," declared editor John Stringfellow. "We must enforce the laws, though we resort to the force of arms; trust to our rifles, and make the blood flow as freely as do the turbid waters of the Missouri. . . . "[9]

When word of the rescue reached his office, Wilson Shannon wasted no time in calling out the militia.[10] Explained the governor to President Pierce the following day:

> The time has come when this armed band of men, who are seeking to subvert and render powerless the existing government, have to be met and the laws enforced against them. . . . If the lives and property of unoffending citizens of this Territory cannot be protected by law, there is an end to practical government, and it becomes a useless formality. The excitement along the border . . . is running wild. . . . This feeling and intense excitement can still be held in subordination if the laws are faithfully executed; otherwise there is no power here that can control this border excitement, and civil war is inevitable. . . . [W]e are standing on a volcano . . . and no one can tell the hour when an eruption may take place.[11]

Across the state line, emotions were even more explosive. "The excitement is up in Missouri," a spectator said. "The appeals of flying women and children, and the belief that the abolitionists have determined to expel the pro-slavery men from Hickory Grove [*sic*], has kindled a flame that no human power can control." [12]

Fueled by the fear that unless the free-soil movement was checked, all might soon be lost, Missourians rushed to aid their Kansas comrades. One bloodthirsty volunteer in Lexington, noted a shocked bystander, vowed he would not return until "every damned abolitionist . . . including women and children, were slain. He had no sympathy, no feeling . . . no more regard for them than a hyena." [13]

## TO ARMS! TO ARMS!!

> It is expected that every lover of Law and Order will rally at Leavenworth on Saturday, December 1, 1855, prepared to march at once to the scene of the rebellion, to put down the outlaws of Douglas County, who are committing depredations upon persons and property, burning down houses and declaring open hostility to the laws, and have forcibly rescued a prisoner from the Sheriff. Come one, come all! The laws must be executed. The outlaws, it is said, are armed to the teeth, and number 1000 men. Every man should bring his rifle and ammunition, and it would be well to bring two or three days' provision. Every man to his post, and to his duty.[14]

By the end of November 1855, the proslavery party of the western border was marching as one toward Douglas County—the territorial militia to Lecompton, their

Missouri allies to the Wakarusa. While this move was in progress, free-soilers were flocking to Lawrence.

After the cheers for Sam Wood and his rebels had faded, the commander-in-chief, Charles Robinson, realized Lawrence must gird for the storm. The town could not possibly stand against the combined proslavery might, so Robinson dispatched runners over the territory seeking succor. To the doctor's delight, free-staters responded. "Nothing could exceed the welcome given to the re-enforcements as they came with their Sharp's [*sic*] rifles from the different settlements," Robinson remembered. "Cheer upon cheer would go up till the whole town was enthusiastic. Especially was the arrival of one hundred men well armed, from Topeka. . . ." [15]

"The Free-State men came pouring in from all quarters," added another elated onlooker. Eventually, upwards of eight hundred men had joined the defenders. [16] "All the public buildings are turned into barracks, the preaching hall with the rest," reported the Reverend Richard Cordley. "[N]othing is thought of but the best means of defense." [17]

When the first Missourians appeared in early December and set up camp six miles southeast of town, near Franklin, the besieged Northerners accelerated their preparations for war. Circular earthworks were thrown up at either end of the town's main thoroughfare, Massachusetts Street, while another fort was rising atop barren Mount Oread. Watching the stir below from her home upon the hill, an apprehensive Sara Robinson jotted in her journal:

> The men were at work on a part of the forts, while . . . entrenchments were being thrown up on each side of Massachusetts-street; the soldiers were drilling through the centre of the broad street; ladies were standing in the doorways looking on; while little boys, having caught the general spirit of a resort to arms, were marching about in martial array, with feathers in their paper cocked-hats and imitation guns. . . . The howitzer has just arrived, and several men are guarding it in one of the lower rooms. Some ladies go in to look at the grape and bomb-shells. [18]

Many women did more than stand in doorways or admire artillery. Indeed, "the Lawrence belles . . .," noted a newsman for the *New York Herald*, "are strong politicians, and even more belligerent in their Wakarusa War notions, than their Free State 'lords and masters.'" [19] Although "repeatedly" asked to flee the city for safer ground, the females refused, devoting their time instead to making cartridges and bandages. [20]

Some bold women went a step further, as one correspondent made clear.

> Forty ladies enrolled themselves secretly with the determination of fighting by the sides of their husbands and sons as soon as the combat

commenced. Many of them had previously practiced pistol shooting for the purpose of giving the invaders a suitable reception if they came. . . . One young girl—a beauty of nineteen—told me that she dreamed last night of shooting three invaders.[21]

While many men jocosely referred to the female company as "Breast-works," the gravity of the situation was beyond dispute.

With a well-publicized record in the Mexican War, Robinson's second-in-command, James Lane, took charge of defense and discipline. During the daily drills, wrote a witness, "Lane walked beside the companies, in an easy, swinging military gait, and gave orders in his short, shrill voice. . . . Lane would sometimes make a speech. . . . On such occasions [he] was fiery and his remarks were calculated to rouse up the men to the fighting point."[22]

Heartened as he was by the spirit of his command, yet anxious lest Lane's words wreck his plan for a defensive action only, Robinson was quick to step in.

Men of Lawrence, and free-state men, we must have courage, but with it we must have prudence! These men have come from Missouri to subjugate the free-state men, to crush the free-state movement. . . . They . . . will wait at least for a plausible excuse before commencing to shed blood. This excuse must not be given them. . . . If the Missourians, partly from fear and partly from want of a sufficient pretext, have to go back without striking a blow, it will make them a laughing-stock. . . . This is the last struggle between freedom and slavery, and we must not flatter ourselves that it will be trivial or short. . . . These may be dark days, but the American people and the world will justify us, and the cause of right will eventually triumph.[23]

Meanwhile, the Missouri bivouac along the Wakarusa swelled with additional volunteers. Most came with little more than "a shot-gun and a jug," but all were determined to march on Lawrence and "not leave one stone standing upon another."

"[T]he man of seventy winters stood shoulder to shoulder with the youth of sixteen," penned a correspondent from the camp.[24] Noticing one such old man with an ancient flintlock standing in the crowd, the reporter strolled over.

He was Pro-Slavery . . . to the back bone. With him to hate the Abolitionists was to "do God service." So the old man was not only among the first to take the field himself, but literally carried out the assertion of the Governor by bringing with him not only his son but his grandson to join. . . . "Gentlemen [*sic*] . . . this hyar old firelock war carried by my father through thar dark days of thar Revolution—the days that tried men's souls—as I heerd a chap say when he war a makin' a stump speech down in Arkansaw;

but I'll be (here the old man ripped out a very English oath, and brought down the butt of the piece with a crash to the ground); yes, I'll be derned, gentelmen, ef she war ever carried in a better cause than this." [25]

"We have a force sufficient to put down the outlaws, with several pieces of cannon, capable of battering down every house in Lawrence . . . ," boasted Kansas Secretary of State, Daniel Woodson, from the Wakarusa. "Every thing looks war like now. . . . A day or two will tell the tale." [26]

Soon after, the opponents began learning the art of war. Although, for the time being, most on both sides remained confined to their camps, there was a spattering of picket fire whenever the two made contact. Stumbling within range of one marksman, Robert Kelley of the *Squatter Sovereign* experienced the unpleasant sensation of having a ball whiz through his hair, "making us feel for awhile," said the shaken editor, "as though we were beheaded." [27] Patrols also sallied forth to scout and watch the movements of the enemy. On the California Road between Lawrence and Topeka, free-state guerrilla bands terrorized southern settlers.

"My house is a fortification. I am compelled to keep a guard with sentinels all night . . . ," wrote a nervous George Clarke near Lecompton. "The outlaws have marked our men. . . . [O]nly two days ago ten armed men surrounded a member of my family with threatening language, and ended the interview with a threat to dispose of myself." [28]

Proslavery patrols were equally active, and two free-soilers were overtaken after leaving Lawrence. Reported a witness:

They were compelled to go to the camp at Lecompton, and were put into the custody of Sheriff Jones. . . . They were taken into a small room, kept as a liquor-shop, which was open and very cold. That night Jones came in with others, and went to "playing poker at twenty-five cents ante." The prisoners were obliged to sit up all night, as there was no room to lie down when the men were playing. Jones insulted them frequently, and told one of them he must either "tell or swing." [29]

"They then carried us down to their camp," continued one of the prisoners. "Kelly, of the *Squatter Sovereign* . . . came round and said he thirsted for blood, and said he should like to hang us on the first tree. [My friend] was very weak, and that excited him so that he became delirious." [30]

Around noon on December 6, another three men—brothers Thomas and Robert Barber and their brother-in-law, Thomas Peirson—slipped from Lawrence and headed home to chop winter wood for their families. According to Peirson:

We followed the California road [west] for three miles or more, when we turned off the highway to take a cross-road which led to the left, towards our homes. Just before doing so, and while still in the California road, I saw a party of from 12 to 15 mounted men to the right of the trail, and some half a mile or mile distant, they appeared to be coming towards the California road. In a few minutes I saw two men detach themselves from the main body and ride forward at a quicker gait, as if to cut us off. We were riding fast at the time, but immediately slackened our speed to a walk, so as to give these people no excuse for interfering with us. . . . We had ridden about a mile in the cross-road, when these two men who had taken a shorter cut, got ahead of us, and came in from the right, at a trot. . . . One of them halted directly in front of us in the road, and within a few feet of our horses' heads. He was [George Clarke] a stout, thick-set man. . . . He was riding a grey horse. His companion. . . . was riding a sorrel horse.[31]

In the words of Robert Barber:

After halting us, the rider of the grey horse asked, "Where are you going?" My brother Thomas . . . replied, "We are going home." He then asked us, "Where are you from?" My brother answered, "We are from Lawrence." "What is going on in Lawrence?" was the next question. "Nothing in particular," said my brother. "Nothing in particular, hey?" replied the man. He then added, "We have orders from the Governor to see the laws executed in Kansas." Thomas . . . then asked, "What laws have we disobeyed?" Upon hearing this, the rider of the grey horse raised his hand and pointed towards his party, at the same time exclaiming, "Then, turn your horses' heads and go with us." My brother then said, "We won't do it." "You won't, hey?" said their spokesman, at the same time starting off with his horse so as to bring him on the right side of my brother. . . . The man drew his pistol as he started. . . . [My] attention was at that moment taken up with drawing my own pistol. . . . As I was changing it into my right hand to fire, I saw . . . the man on the gray horse—discharge his pistol at my brother.[32]

Returning to Peirson:

I saw Thomas settle down in his saddle as the pistol was discharged. I thought he was hit. The man on the sorrel horse fired immediately, the reports of the two pistols were almost simultaneous. . . . Robert . . . fired three times without success. I was trying, but without success, to draw my pistol. . . . [W]hen I finally got it out, our opponents had wheeled and were galloping off towards their party. Thomas then said "Let us be off." We started accordingly at the top of our horses' speed, the Barbers riding almost in front of me, and I following in their rear.[33]

Once again, Robert Barber:

After riding in this manner for about a hundred yards, my brother said to me, "That fellow shot me;" he smiled as he said so. I asked him, "Where are you shot?" He pointed to his right side. I then remarked, "It is not possible, Thomas?" To this he replied, "It is," at the same time smiling again. . . . After uttering these . . . words—he dropped his rein, and reeled in his saddle; seeing that he was about to fall, I caught hold of him by the left shoulder, grasping the loose overcoat which he wore. I held him thus for nearly a hundred yards; I could then hold him no longer, and he fell to the ground; as he did so, I slipped from my horse. . . . I bent over my brother, and found that he was dead.[34]

As Barber and Peirson made good their escape, George Clarke and his companions continued to the Wakarusa camp. "I have sent another of these damned abolitionists to his winter-quarters," bragged Clarke to the Missourians assembled there.[35]

Meanwhile, the remains of the murdered man were discovered and carried into Lawrence. "Young Barbour's [*sic*] body was . . . laid away in one of the rooms of the new hotel, stretched out upon a seat, with his usual clothes upon him," Hannah Ropes recounted. "He looked like one asleep; for the wound, though bleeding most profusely, did not disfigure him; it drew the color from his cheeks, that was all." [36] The following morning, Barber's grief-stricken wife reached town. Said Sara Robinson:

"Words can never convey the mingling emotions which moved the crowd, or the heart-crushing agony of the young wife. There were no children in the household, and all the affections had twined around this one idol. All of life, all of happiness, were centered in him. . . . It seemed as though her heart must break, and, in her distress and shrieks, the brave, strong-hearted men mingled tears and muttered imprecations of vengeance upon the murderers. . . .[37]

Soon after the widow's arrival, Lawrence was paid another visit. In an effort to end the crisis and prevent civil war, Governor Shannon left his temporary capital at

Shawnee Mission and journeyed to Douglas County. Though the governor had requested the intervention of troops from Fort Leavenworth—which included a visiting Lt. Col. Robert E. Lee—it was doubtful whether they could arrive in time or even if the federal government would allow them to.[38] Thus, Shannon set off on his own. The governor first spoke with David Atchison, Albert Boone, grandson of the famous woodsman, and other proslavery leaders bivouacked around Lawrence. While Shannon was hopeful that the rebellious free-staters had learned their lesson and would henceforth obey the territorial laws, the governor was aghast at the warlike mood among the Missourians he met.

> I found in the camp at Wakarusa a deep and settled feeling of hostility against the opposing forces in Lawrence, and apparently a fixed deter-mination to attack that place and demolish it and the presses, and take pos-session of their arms. It seemed to be a universal opinion in the camp that there was no safety to the law and order party in the Territory while the other party were permitted to retain their Sharp's [*sic*] rifles, an instrument used only for war purposes.[39]

As Shannon implied, while the proslavery host feared the fortresslike Free State Hotel and its heavy stone walls and gunports, it was the fast-firing, long-range Sharps that gave them most cause to pause and consider. Rumors fed rumors until the weapon became in the minds of many Missourians a "diabolical gun," capable of killing with accuracy at several miles. Although some leaders were anxious to pull back and avoid war, most insisted that the rebels must obey the laws and surrender the deadly rifles. Dubious of success, yet determined to do his duty, Shannon stepped into the waiting carriage and traveled to Lawrence.

When the governor and his retinue, which included Albert Boone, drew up beside the hotel, they were met by Charles Robinson, James Lane, and rows of free-state militiamen. Also on hand was Sara Robinson.

> The governor is a gray-haired man, tall and well-proportioned. He has coarse features and a hard-looking face, generally. Nature must bear a part of the blame, but the weather and bad whiskey, doubtless, come in for a share. . . . Gen. Robinson and the governor went through the halls, and up the unfinished stairways to the council-chamber. As the eyes of the governor fell upon the rigid limbs, and the death-pallor of [Thomas Barber], who yesterday was so full of life, hope, and strength, he gave a perceptible shrug of his shoulders. The governor's suite also entered, and as they passed the silent dead, Col. Boone . . . said, "I did not expect such a thing as this."[40]

As the "low, continued wailings" of Mrs. Barber echoed through the hotel, the men discussed conditions for peace. Though Robinson insisted that most in Lawrence did not condone the rescue of Branson, and the many should not be held accountable for the few, the doctor pledged that his followers would henceforth obey any "legitimate" officer of the law. Regarding the surrender of weapons, particularly the Sharps rifles, Robinson absolutely refused—on this score there would be no debate. After dining with his hosts, a dismayed Wilson Shannon returned to the Wakarusa bearing the peace proposals as set forth by Robinson.[41]

If any free-soilers were in the least worried that their commander would surrender the arsenal of Sharps, their fears were groundless. "I would propose a compromise measure," Robinson joked with his men, "keep the rifles, and give them the contents."[42] As the doctor well knew, the much-feared weapon was perhaps all that stood between Lawrence and disaster.

"I have only time to thank you and your friends who sent us the Sharp's [*sic*] rifles . . . ," scratched Robinson in a hasty note to Amos Lawrence. "[T]hey will give us victory without firing a shot."[43]

Indeed, with each passing hour the fortunes of the free-staters rose. Not only did a number of Indians from the powerful Shawnee and Delaware tribes offer support, but reinforcements continued to arrive.[44] Midday on December 7, a strange, solemn wagonload of men entered the town.[45] "To each of their persons was strapped a short heavy broad sword," remembered George Washington Brown of the *Herald of Freedom*. "Each was supplied with a goodly number of fire arms, and navy revolvers, and poles were standing endwise around the wagon box with fixed bayonets pointing upwards."[46]

Although the group was received with "great eclat," as were all arrivals, it soon became clear that the old man in charge had come not merely to defend Lawrence from attack, but "to draw a little blood."[47] Wrote a witness:

> From that moment he commenced fomenting difficulties in camp, disregarding the command of superior officers, and trying to induce the men to go down to Franklin, and make an attack upon the pro-slavery forces encamped there. The Committee of Public Safety were called upon several times to head off his wild adventure. . . .[48]

Emboldened by the old stranger, as well as proslavery procrastination, other voices joined the cry to attack. "[W]ith one round the Missourians would fly like frightened hares," argued some.[49] Saner counsel prevailed, however, and a serious mutiny never matured. Angered by the "cowardice" of the Lawrence leadership, yet sure of what the future would bring, John Brown "retired in disgust."

Meanwhile, six miles to the southeast, a situation similar to that stirred by "Old Brown" was occurring along the Wakarusa. When Wilson Shannon revealed the terms by which the free-staters would agree to peace, most proslavery leaders were outraged. So long as the rebels remained armed with Sharps rifles and cannon, the Southerners argued, so long would they resist territorial laws.

"I was advised by a prominent man," Shannon later wrote, "that unless the citizens of Lawrence gave up their arms, the place would be attacked, and I had better consult my own safety and keep out of danger." [50]

The governor desperately worked to defuse the situation. When a face-to-face meeting between contending parties was proposed, the Missourians surprisingly agreed. A short time later, Robinson, Lane, and other free-state leaders confronted their opposites between the lines at Franklin. After some heated debate, the antagonists finally agreed upon peace terms—the Northerners would keep their guns but would henceforth obey the territorial laws. Although Shannon was heartily pleased with his efforts and some Southern leaders seemed satisfied, a wave of anger erupted once the rank and file learned of the agreement. Many were for "raising the black flag" and marching at once to Lawrence. David Atchison quickly stepped in.

"The position the Lawrence people have taken is such that it would not do to make an attack upon them . . . ," reasoned the Missourian. "But, boys, we'll fight some time, by God!" [51]

*Wilson Shannon.* KANSAS STATE HISTORICAL SOCIETY, TOPEKA.

Despite Atchison's prestige and the power in his plea, an assault on Lawrence by mutineers seemed likely. Then, that evening, December 8, a ferocious winter storm blew into Kansas. "It came down with icy keenness, and driving a snowy sleet . . . ," recalled one of those in the sprawling camp. "The wind blew almost a hurricane. . . . Cold and more bitter grew the night, and the . . . fires had to be put out, as the furious flames were blown about so as to endanger all of those near them." [52]

As the shivering Missourians huddled around one another, talk of war abruptly ceased. The following morning, the host on the Wakarusa, as well as that at Lecompton, began falling back, bringing the almost bloodless "Wakarusa War" to an inglorious and anticlimactic end. In addition to the death of Charles Dow, which ignited the trouble, and that of Thomas Barber, which worsened it, three Southerners died during the campaign—one by his own sentry, another from a falling tree, and yet another in a drunken row.[53] As everyone understood only too well, however, a violent precedent had been set, but nothing had been resolved.

"Shannon has played us false!" cried Dr. John Stringfellow when the news reached Lecompton. "The Yankees have tricked us. The Governor of Kansas has disgraced himself and the whole proslavery party. . . . When this difficulty comes up again, we should leave our chicken-hearted commanders at home."[54]

Meanwhile, the free-staters of Lawrence and Kansas celebrated. With an almost perfect blend of bluff and diplomacy—and the timely arrival of winter—the proslavery horde had been forced to retire without so much as a skirmish. What earlier had seemed like certain war and certain defeat was now clearly seen as the first major victory of freedom in Kansas, or, as Eli Thayer had hoped for, an "opening wedge."

After witnessing for himself the departure of the Missourians, Wilson Shannon reentered Lawrence to proudly announce that the terms of the agreement had been fulfilled. "In the evening," related the governor, "I was invited to attend a social gathering of ladies and gentlemen of the town. . . . "

> There were but two rooms finished in the hotel . . . and were, therefore, very much crowded by the company assembled. The time was spent in the most friendly and social manner, and it seemed to be a matter of congratulation on every side that the difficulties so lately threatening had at length been brought to a happy termination. In the midst of this convivial party, and about ten o'clock at night, Dr. C. Robinson came to me, in a state of apparent excitement, and declared that their picket guard had just come in and reported that there was a large irregular force near the town . . . who were threatening an attack; adding that the citizens of Lawrence claimed the protection of the Executive, and to this end desired me to give himself and Genl. Lane written permission to repel the threatened assault. . . . [He] wished me to give him written authority . . . so that it might appear . . . that they were not acting against, but with the approbation of the Territorial executive. With this view, amid an excited throng, in a small and crowded apartment and without critical examination of the paper which Dr. Robinson had just written, I signed. . . .[55]

When the threatened assault failed to materialize, the drunken governor soon realized he had been hoodwinked into granting an "air of legality" to the rebel free-state government. According to Shannon:

It did not for a moment occur to me that this pretended attack upon the town was but a device to obtain from me a paper which might be used to my prejudice. I supposed at the time that I was surrounded by gentlemen and by grateful hearts, and not by tricksters, who . . . were seeking to obtain an advantage over me. I was the last man on the globe who deserved such treatment from the citizens of Lawrence. For four days and nights, and at the cost of many valuable friends, whose good will I have forfeited by favoring too pacific a course, I had labored most incessantly to save their town from destruction and their citizens from a bloody fight.[56]

Deceived and duped by the one, reviled and cursed by the other, well-meaning Wilson Shannon had become an object of pity and contempt to all.

Another incident that cast long shadows over the future of Kansas occurred on the following day when Sheriff Jones naively accepted a similar invitation to attend a "peace jubilee" in Lawrence. "Several speeches were made," recounted Charles Robinson, "and all would have passed off pleasantly had it not been for an attempt to excite hostility to Jones. . . ."[57]

In the forefront of those working for war was Robinson's second-in-command, James Lane. Wrote a witness, Hannah Ropes:

Any reader of human faces can never study his without a sensation very much like that with which one stands at the edge of a slimy, sedgy, uncertain morass. If there is any good in him, I never . . . have been able to make the discovery. . . . Lane's voice could be heard in different rooms, detailing to eager listeners the most painful circumstances of poor Barbour's [*sic*] death, and, with wonderful ingeniousness, keeping up the wicked spirit of vengeance among those over whom he exercised any power.[58]

Fearing that the already ugly mood might lead to violence against Jones, Robinson quickly intervened. "He not only stemmed the tide," Hannah concluded, "but rolled back the surging emotions of the crowd. . . ."[59]

Because of these and similar incidents, it soon became clear to the proslavery party of Kansas and Missouri that the free-staters had no intention of adhering to the recent treaty. "I do not see how we are to avoid civil war . . . ," David Atchison confided to a friend in Georgia. "Twelve months will not elapse before war—civil war of the fiercest kind will be upon us. . . . I was a peace maker in the difficulty lately settled by Governor Shannon . . . but I will never again counsel peace."[60]

"There is no settlement of the difficulty," agreed Sara Robinson. "It is only the present lull of the late storm, gathering, it may be, greater fury."[61]

While the rumblings from Missouri increased and while Lawrence bolstered its defenses, "Generals January and February" swept down the border to ensure that the contestants remained apart. Indeed, the icy gale that ended the confrontation along the Wakarusa inaugurated one of the most intense and prolonged winters in border memory.[62] As Sara Robinson scribbled in her diary on Christmas Day:

> Thermometer ranging between twenty and thirty degrees below zero. The water freezes in the tumblers at breakfast, and everything eatable, or intended to be eaten, is frozen hard. The bread can only be cut as we thaw it by the fire, setting the loaf down and cutting one piece at a time. Potatoes, squashes, pumpkins, citrons, and apples, are as hard as rocks. . . .
>
> **Dec. 26th.**—It is no warmer yet. What will the poor settlers do who have no floors in their cabins?[63]

"I never saw so many people suffering with chilled feet and hands before in my life . . . ," admitted another from Lawrence. "Full one half of those who walk our streets limp as they go, and are obliged to wear buffalo over-shoes, or something very loose upon their feet. I know of some women who are obliged to use crutches for a similar reason." [64]

Added Sarah Everett from Osawatomie:

> Some families had to abandon their houses & go to their neighbors who were fortunate in having warmer ones. . . . A lady who called here yesterday told me that two of her daughters during that week froze their feet so that they are now unable to walk a step, and said there were large running sores two thirds the size of the palm of her hand on them now. Two more women told John that they froze their feet sitting right by the stove.[65]

While Julia Lovejoy bundled her baby in furs and blankets to prevent him from freezing, stunned slaveholders, lured to Kansas by reports of the "very mild climate," found their chattel an utter liability. At Tecumseh, Judge Rush Elmore passed the winter chopping wood to keep his nineteen slaves warm, and his harried wife spent much of her time cooking to keep them fed.[66]

Although most movement was restricted during the long, cruel winter, the bitter cold did little to slacken the torrid war of words. "Kansas, and 'the vile Abolitionists,' are in everybody's mouth," noted *New York Herald* reporter Douglas Brewerton as he struggled through western Missouri. "They are shouted in the bar-rooms, they are sounded in the streets. . . . Old men shake their heads and express decided opinions while young Missouri, yet more determined, looks revolvers, and talks bowie-knives, as he openly declares that 'the boys ought never to have left an infernal Abolitionist alive in Lawrence.'" [67]

Tales told by Southerners returning from the Wakarusa War left listeners gaping in disbelief. One Kansas sheriff related to a village editor an incident that occurred during the siege of Lawrence.

> The Sheriff . . . came upon a hut which contained one woman and child; both barefooted and the former sitting with a book in her hand, and tears stealing down her cheeks, with a mournful face and ever anon she would bring a long sigh. The house was made of plank turned edgewise, the cold wind whistling through the cracks, and the only comfort was to be found by a stove made of sheet iron. The Sheriff . . . became solicitous for the welfare of the distressed woman. . . . [H]e discovered that the woman was reading "Uncle Tom's Cabin," and weeping in sympathy for the negroes of the South. . . . This woman is a fair sample of the abolitionists that the Southerners have to contend against. She was almost without a house, but few household comforts, barefooted, the weather freezing cold, and yet she was weeping bitter tears in sympathy for the slaves of the South; while they were clad in warm habiliments and blessed with comfortable houses and enough to eat.[68]

"We expect to visit Lawrence in a short time to see the curiosities of that place," the astonished editor concluded; "it is worth more than a monkey show." [69]

In the meantime, free-state letter writers were busy harassing proslavery neighbors and threatening territorial officials.[70]

> SHERIFF JONES—You are notified that if you make one more arrest by the order of any magistrate appointed by the Kansas Bogus Legislature, that in so doing you will sign your own Death Warrant. Per order.
>
> SECRET TWELVE.[71]

When word spread that even proslavery livestock and dogs were being poisoned, Lucian Eastin of the *Leavenworth Herald* was livid: "And these are the kind of people that want to rule this Territory. They are not fit to live and too mean and corrupt to die. . . . "[72]

"Come one! Come all! Slavocrats and nullifiers," goaded the *Lawrence Herald of Freedom* in return. "[W]e have rifles enough, and bullets enough, to send you all to your (and Judas's) own place. . . . If you're coming, why don't you come along?"[73]

Although the ink occasionally froze on pen points, abolition propagandists were also busily engaged, trying with every word to tilt Eastern public opinion their way. When a free-stater in Topeka was slightly stabbed by an "uncouth backwoodsman" who resented being the brunt of the former's jibes and jokes, the incident was transformed with a wave of the pen into a hideous proslavery atrocity. The Northerner was, reported a breathless Ohio editor, "assaulted by a gang of Missourians, and most shockingly beaten. His face and head were horribly mangled; his face was cut open from mouth to ear, and his neck was partially cut off. He was rescued before he was quite killed." [74]

While little could halt the spread of lies and distortions abroad, punishment was swift and sure for transgressions closer to home. When a free-soil editor in Leavenworth suggested that the Kansas Militia had marched on Lawrence with no higher resolve than to "Ravish the women, and kill the children," a mob, led by the hatchet-wielding "Kickapoo Rangers," destroyed the newspaper's office and tossed the press into the river. [75]

One of the most astute and unbiased writers circulating in Kansas was Douglas Brewerton. After but a day or two on the border, the New York newsman was appalled by the flaming rhetoric on both sides.

> Kansas Territory has already been the theatre of too many windy battles, in which words—words—words—bad words—harsh words—devilish words—have been rattled down like hail-stones, night after night, and day after day, by interested *talkers* upon either side, who didn't care a brass farthing whether the true interests of the people went to Pandemonium or not. . . . Would to God that this great . . . country, had some vast lunatic asylum, located . . . amid the wilds of the Rocky Mountains, where tried and convicted demagogues from all quarters of the Union, could find a home. . . . [L]et the citizens of the United States take it to heart, that this disturbance in Kansas means something. . . . [W]hen Kansas bleeds, Georgia must open her veins, and Massachusetts too, for when this comes to pass it requires no prophet to foretell a struggle which will crimson alike the Missouri and the Hudson. [76]

As the new year began, defiance to the territorial laws became more flagrant each day. Despite the death threats, Sam Jones was determined to do his duty. When the sheriff attempted one day in Lawrence to arrest a woman's husband for common "breaking and entering," a glimpse at the difficulties he faced is quickly gained. Recorded a witness:

> The little lady, with true Yankee grit, at once informed Sheriff Jones that he would not be permitted to arrest her husband. . . . [D]isplaying on her person . . . two enormous Colt revolvers, and brandishing another in his face . . . [she] threatened to relieve him of the cares of office and Douglas County, while the mob gathered round, armed to the teeth, ready to take

advantage of any pretence to attack the Sheriff. . . . [S]he at once paraded her husband through the streets of our young city with as much pomposity as a militia officer. The crowd insulted the Sheriff, by telling him to "pitch in now," it was only a woman resisting the laws, and not the people of Lawrence. . . . The Sheriff got a couple of friends to aid him, and watching his opportunity, one of them seized the lady by the wrists, while the Sheriff seized the prisoner, forced him into a wagon and drove off to Leavenworth, to put him in jail. But the lady was not satisfied—pluck to the last, as soon as the gentleman released his hold she drew a revolver and snapped it at his head, and when he turned to run, she fired at him, just grazing his temple and cutting off a large lock of his hair. She fired four times, but without effect.[77]

In addition to everyday acts of sedition, the free-staters pressed ahead with a scheduled January 15 election to choose officers for their own government. In isolated or heavily free-soil districts the polling passed peacefully. At strongly proslave Leavenworth, however, the mayor forbade a vote. When a scattering of free-staters in the area decided to reschedule the election for January 17 at nearby Easton, the Kickapoo Rangers rode out to seize the ballot box. Soon after the two sides met, gunfire erupted, resulting in the retreat of the rangers with one of their number dead.[78] The following day, eight of the free-soilers, including local leader Reese Brown, climbed into a wagon and headed for home. According to one account:

[They] had proceeded about half way when they were met by the Kickapoo Rangers, consisting of thirty mounted men, and about the same number in wagons. They surrounded the wagon of the Free State party, and yelling and shouting like demons ordered them to surrender. Brown and his companions jumped from the wagon, and some of the party were for fighting, but a moment's reflection convinced them of the hopelessness of a conflict. . . . The guns belonging to Brown's party were immediately seized, and everything in the wagon also. One of Brown's party was knocked down, and his head twice saved from the hatchet of a fiend. . . .[79]

A correspondent of the *New York Tribune* continued.

The prisoners were taken back to Easton; but Brown was separated from them, and put in an adjoining building. A rope was purchased at the store, and was shown to the prisoners, with the intimation that they should be hanged with it. . . . It was fiercely discussed for hours what should be done with them; and meanwhile liquor was drank pretty freely. . . . Unwilling that all of these men should be murdered, the Captain allowed the other prisoners to escape. . . . Then followed a scene of atrocity and horror. Captain Brown had surrendered his arms, and was helpless. . . . When they began to strike him, he rose to his feet, and asked to be permitted to fight any one of them. He challenged them to pit him against their best man—he would fight for his life; but not one of the cowards dared thus to give the prisoner a chance. Then he volunteered to fight two, and then three; but it was in vain. . . . These men, or rather demons, rushed around Brown, and literally hacked him to death with their hatchets. One of the rangers, a large, coarse-looking wretch named [Robert] Gibson, inflicted the fatal blow—a large hatchet gash in the side of the head, which penetrated the skull and brain many inches. . . . Brown fell, and his remorseless enemies jumped on him, while thus prostrate, or kicked him. Desperately wounded though he was, he still lived; and, as they kicked him, he said, "Don't abuse me; it is useless; I am dying." It was a vain appeal. One of the wretches . . . stooped over the prostrate man, and, with a refinement of cruelty exceeding the rudest savage, spit tobacco juice in his eyes.[80]

"God damn you, I want to see you gasp your last before I leave you," snarled one of the attackers as he delivered another sharp kick.[81]

Some in the crowd soon took pity and tried to bind the victim's wounds. With brains oozing from his skull, however, Brown's case was hopeless, and the belated rescuers opted to carry the dying man home to his wife. "He was not able to tell us much about his cruel treatment," a mourning Martha Brown wrote her father. "He said they beat him like a dog. He said: 'I am not afraid to die; if I have done wrong in any way, I hope God will forgive me; I die in a good cause; I am sorry to part with you and our little children but I want you to meet me in heaven.'"[82]

Hardly had the news from Easton been received when word came down from Atchison County that a proslavery settler there had been severely beaten and his leg nearly hacked away by ax-weilding free-staters.[83] This "dastardly outrage," as well as the bloody violence at Easton and elsewhere convinced an already excited editor of the *Kickapoo Pioneer* that a new northern reign of terror had begun.

Rally! Rally! Forebearance has now ceased to be a virtue; thereupon we call upon every proslavery man in the land to rally to the rescue. The war has again commenced, and the abolitionists have commenced it. Proslavery men, law and order men, strike for your altars! strike for your firesides! strike for your rights! Avenge the blood of your brothers who have been cowardly assailed but who have bravely fallen in defence of southern institutions. Sound the bugles of war over the length and bredth of the land, and leave not an abolitionist in the territory to relate their treacherous and contaminating deeds. Strike your piercing rifle-balls and your glittering steel to their black and poisonous hearts! Let the war cry never cease in Kansas again until our territory is wrested from the last vestige of abolitionism.[84]

Across the river in Platte City, David Atchison, equally concerned at the return of violence, sent off an urgent appeal to a friend in Georgia.

We are in a constant state of excitement here. . . . The very air is full of rumors. . . . [I]f Georgia intends to do anything, or can do anything for us, let it be done speedily. Let your young men come forth to Missouri and Kansas. Let them come well armed, with money enough to support them for twelve months, and determined to see this thing out . . . ! We must have the support of the South. We are fighting the battles of the South. . . . You far southern men are now out of the nave of the war, but, if we fail, it will reach your own doors, perhaps your hearths. We want men, armed men.[85]

*George Washington Brown.* KANSAS STATE HISTORICAL SOCIETY, TOPEKA.

As the proslavery party of Kansas and Missouri seemed poised for yet another descent on the town, Lawrence prepared for yet another siege. For his part, bellicose George Washington Brown—a man who habitually wore two pistols and a bowie knife in his belt—was in no mood for still another static, defensive "war." [86] Seething at the unpleasant vision of slavers, "these monsters . . . these wild beasts," pressing free-soilers to the wall again, the *Herald of Freedom* editor at last lashed out.

> The people of Kansas have been menaced for a long time; we have observed preparations for months to destroy us; they have invaded our Territory; robbed us of every legal right; and now they seek our utter extinction. In law a person is not required to wait until he is knocked down before he is justified in resorting to force to disable his assailant. . . . We feel as we write, and believe the time is rapidly approaching for action. If others wish to remain silent when threatened with extermination they may do so, but they shall not censure us for pursuing that policy which we believe the times demand. [87]

While he commiserated with Brown and a growing chorus of angry voices, Charles Robinson was determined to hold the line that he and his emigrant aid associates felt would most surely, if not swiftly, bring victory. Commit no act, Amos Lawrence reminded Robinson, "that w[oul]d put you in the wrong before the country. . . . The Fabian policy is the true one, i.e., the greatest forebearance, total discouragement of all aggressions; a deadly tho smiling quiet. This you must adopt, or rather have only to keep on as you have done. You must gain time, & so strength." [88]

As free-staters once more marshaled to Lawrence and manned the works, Robinson and James Lane alerted President Pierce that Missourians were again preparing to invade Kansas "for the avowed purpose of . . . demolishing our towns, and butchering our unoffending Free-State citizens." [89] The two men demanded that the president call out troops to halt the invasion.

Franklin Pierce was well aware that the war of words in Kansas was escalating and that the malignant propaganda spewing from the West was infecting the East. With every edition, newspapers North and South engaged in acrimonious duels over freedom and slavery. That the contest, left to itself, would lead to war not only in Kansas but elsewhere was graphically demonstrated several days after Robinson sent his letter. On January 23, in the streets of Washington, Horace Greeley was thrashed by an irate southern congressman because of the editor's antislavery diatribes in the *New York Tribune*. [90]

"[H]e struck me a stunning blow on the right side of my head," the surprised journalist said, "and followed it by two or three more, as fast as possible." [91]

Prompted by a spiraling situation, the president, as Robinson and Lane had hoped, issued a proclamation vowing to use troops should an invasion of the territory take place. At the same time, Pierce made it clear that he would not hesitate to employ those very same soldiers to squash any "attempted insurrection" within Kansas. Pleaded the president: "I call on the citizens, both of adjoining and of distant States, to abstain from unauthorized intermeddling in the local concerns of the Territory. . . ."[92]

Unfortunately, Pierce's proclamation had almost no impact on either side. Charles Robinson was committed heart and soul to his rebel government, and David Atchison was just as committed to crushing it.

"I say, prepare yourselves," the Missourian warned a Platte City crowd. "Go over there. Send your young men, and if they attempt to drive you out, then damn them, drive *them* out. Fifty of you, with your shotguns, are worth two hundred and fifty of them, with their Sharpe's [*sic*] rifles. Get ready—arm yourselves; for if they abolitionize Kansas, you lose $100,000,000 of your property."[93]

Meanwhile, the people of Lawrence readied for the coming storm. From a room in the Free State Hotel, an anxious correspondent for a Boston newspaper described the scene.

> As I write, the heavy and measured tread of the sentinel, as he paces his beat on the roof above my head in the midst of a blinding snow storm, reminds me that I am at the very focus towards which all eyes are now turned. And well that may be. This nation, at least the northern portion of it, are not aware that they are standing on the very brink of a volcano, just ready to belch forth its destructive torrents. . . . Gen. Robinson does not sleep at his own house, but takes his quarters here in this fort[r]ess, and sleeps sometimes in my room, while a company of soldiers are quartered in another near by. The roof of the building, three stories in height, has a parapet running all around it, pierced with loop holes, from which in a street fight there could be poured a most destructive volley of rifle balls.—The thorough look-out which is being kept, will, we think, prevent us being taken by surprise and . . . hacked to pieces by demons with wood hatchets. . . .[94]

Rumors, never lacking in Lawrence, kept nerves on edge. "Letters from our friends . . . state that there is something threatening in the undercurrent, and their advice to us is to prepare for the worst . . . ," whispered one resident. "[Y]esterday half a ton of lead arrived, and nearly as much powder. Two other teams are on the way with the same 'material aid.'"[95]

Much "material aid" had long since reached the territory. Indeed, by February 1856, Kansas had become a vast arsenal with thousands of swords, knives, revolvers, shotguns, an estimated three thousand Sharps rifles, and several field pieces circulating on the land—and all this in free-state hands alone.[96] "Pistols lie around the room loaded, and rifles are standing in safe places," noted prim and proper Sara Robinson. "How strange to our eastern friends would seem this familiarity with fire-arms, and stranger yet the necessity of carrying them to our sleeping apartments. . . . "[97]

At least one eastern friend would not have found the colony's fascination with firearms strange. Revealed Sara's husband Charles:

> At the time when the clouds were the most threatening a letter was received from Eli Thayer describing a new gun he was making of about an inch and a half calibre, which would carry several miles as accurately as the best rifle at a shorter range. This was to be breech-loading and with it every officer of the enemy's forces could be picked off before the battle should begin by the rank and file. This letter was read and re-read to squads and individuals, and it inspired great confidence in the drooping spirits of the despondent.[98]

As Robinson well knew, though, Thayer's murderous invention—actually a small-bore, swivel cannon—would take time to perfect. In the meantime, free-soilers could count only upon themselves, their Sharps, and above all, the bitter Kansas winter.

"I believe it is that alone which keeps our opponents from pouncing upon us," speculated one free-stater. "It would be impossible to conduct a campaign successfully while the cold is so severe."[99]

And so it was. January and February passed, and, despite the shrill threats and deep rumblings, no Missouri mob marched on Kansas, much to the relief of Charles Robinson and his free-soil followers.

One old man was not happy with the quiet situation, however. As he sat shivering in his cold cabin near Osawatomie, waiting out the winter, biding his time, John Brown warmed his soul with sweet visions of what was to come: of Missouri cities wrapped in flames; of streets littered with slaughtered men, women, and children; of a torch-lit army of pike-wielding slaves marching from there throughout the South to repeat the bloody process a thousand times over. As an instrument of God's will, the old man had come west to do everything in his power to ensure that this terrifying specter came to pass. "It is infinitely better that this generation should be swept away from the face of the earth," he declared, "than that slavery shall continue to exist."[100] The time had not yet arrived for him to begin that terrible sweeping, but the day would come. Of that he was certain.

## CHAPTER SIX

# JERUSALEM
# IN HEAPS

THOUGH THE HARSH WINTER OF 1855–56 KEPT MISSOURIANS AT BAY, IT DID NOT keep them idle. Always nervous over the flow of eastern immigration into Kansas, John Stringfellow of the *Atchison Squatter Sovereign* suggested in February 1856 that Lexington, Missouri, serve as a port of entry, "where all steamboats may be searched and the infectious political paupers be prevented from tainting the air of Kansas Territory with their presence." [1] Acting in part on the advice, "respectable and reliable citizens" of Lexington began boarding boats to hunt for "contraband of war." Although most suspicious cargo proved nothing more than farm implements, tools, or pianos, the search occasionally uncovered crates of weapons bound for free-soil settlements. [2]

To Stringfellow's disgust, though, Yankees who minded their manners had no trouble traveling to Lexington and beyond. For those who ignored this simple rule of the river, there were dire consequences. After entering into a theological debate with several passengers aboard the steamer *Polar Star*, the Reverend William Clark warmed to the topic.

"I frankly admitted that I was opposed to the extension of slavery, and in favor of Kansas becoming a Free State . . . ," the New Englander later wrote.

> I walked out of the cabin, on the fore deck, where some twenty or thirty were discussing the affairs of Kansas. . . . Immediately a man, who had been looking intently at me, to whom I had not spoken during the passage, asked me what I said. As a matter of courtesy, I repeated my words. . . . [3]

Listening nearby as Clark and the Missourian named Childs spoke, a curious bystander recorded:

Childs asked Clark what he would do if a black man wanted to marry his daughter. Mr. Clark replied: "I would advise her to reject him, but if she was resolved upon it, and I could not persuade her to the contrary I suppose I should be compelled to submit to it." Upon this Childs struck Clark in the face, repeating his blows, while the crew were crying "Kill him! kill him! kill the God damned abolitionist! kill him . . . !!" After Childs had succeeded in beating Mr. Clark's face all to a pummace [*sic*], and it was covered with gore the Captain came and commanded the peace, and told Clark he must leave the boat. Being still under way, and breakfast being called, Childs took a seat at the table.—A moment after Mr. Clark came in and took a seat by the side of Childs, when the latter arose, clinching his chair, broke it to pieces over Clark's head. The boat immediately stopped at a wood yard. . . . The Captain ordered Clark to leave the boat, which he did, without his money being refunded to him, and the last . . . [we] saw of him he was going up the bank with his carpet sack on one arm and his overcoat on the other, and his face all beat to pieces and bleeding badly.[4]

As Clark and many another abolitionist quickly discovered, an unguarded word on the uneasy Missouri could earn them a brutal beating and a long walk on a muddy riverbank. "Should my friends wish to know my present views on peace," said the sore and suddenly militant preacher, "I would say Peace principles are the best for all classes of *men*; but as to [the] wild beasts . . . of Missouri, who walk upright, wear men's clothes, vote for the people of Kansas, and hang around steam boats—nothing but Colt's revolvers have any influence with them. . . . "[5]

As Clark inferred, much of a Border Ruffian's time was spent either on a steamboat or on a steamboat landing. Because the main thoroughfares of Missouri river towns were commonly adjacent to the levee, and because each such street counted a plenitude of groggeries and "gambling hells," it was guaranteed that the Border Ruffians would be found there. Sketched one free-soiler:

Imagine a man standing in a pair of long boots, covered with dust and mud and drawn over his trousers, the latter made of coarse, fancy-colored cloth, well soiled; the handle of a large bowie-knife projecting from one or both boot-tops; a leathern belt buckled around his waist, on each side of which is fastened a large revolver; a red or blue shirt, with a heart, anchor, eagle or some other favorite device braided on the breast or back, over which is swung a rifle or carbine; a sword dangling by his side; an old slouched hat, with a cockade or brass star on the front or side, and a chicken, goose or turkey feather sticking in the top; hair uncut and uncombed, covering his neck and shoulders; an unshaved face and unwashed hands. Imagine such a picture of humanity, who can swear any given number of oaths in any specified time, drink any quantity of bad whiskey without getting drunk, and boast of having stolen a half dozen horses and killed one or more abolitionists, and you will have a pretty fair conception of a border ruffian. . . .[6]

Formed largely from a floating frontier population that included teamsters, trappers, hunters, and scouts, the wild and reckless "borderers" spent much of their free time loafing about the levees of Lexington, Leavenworth, Kansas City, Weston, Atchison, and St. Joseph, drinking "red-eye" whiskey that could "kill round a corner at forty rods," brawling with one another, and telling tall tales to any who cared to listen.[7]

Newsman Douglas Brewerton reported on a conversation he overheard one day.

> **First Borderer.**—Jim, what are yeou [i.e., y'all] doing now—busy, hey?
>
> **Second Borderer.**—Busy, thunder; I'm just that busy, that I have to keep a jumping round like a toad under a harrer.
>
> **First Borderer.**—How's Bob?
>
> **Second Borderer.**—Oh, Bob's flat broke, as flat as a nigger baby's head, rolled under a saw-log.
>
> **First Borderer.**—Why, I thought the ole man would have kep him up.
>
> **Second Borderer.**—So he would; but Bob's such a no-account cuss that the ole man jest gin him up, and now he's so poor, that if steamboats war a dime a-piece, Bob couldn't buy a yawl.
>
> **First Borderer.**—How about that fight you had tother day with Parsons?
>
> **Second Borderer.**—Wael, I allow it wasn't much of a fight, no how; we didn't reckon nothin' on it, down our way; it war jest a difficulty about a claim that me and some of Parsons' boys got inter; so ole man Parsons jumped me up—but I reckon he didn't size my pile.
>
> **First Borderer.**—Did you drop him?
>
> **Second Borderer.**—Well, I did; but he's a mean cuss; for I hed him down far, and war a gougin' him, when he got this hyar right thumb of mine inter his dog-gaun ugly mouth, and I'll jest allow ole man Parsons hes got teeth like a bar; for while I war a gougin' him, he kep a chawin' away, as ef my thumb war hog meat; an' now I'll be dog-gauned ef I kin strike nary lick with it, without hollerin' like a wild Ingin, with thar pain.
>
> **First Borderer.**—Wael, ole man Parsons is some—but come, Jim, let's licker.
>
> **Second Borderer.**—Well, now yeou air talkin'; for hyar's a child that air a heap dryer nor a powder-horn.[8]

Brewerton continued:

> Never mind our Borderer's rough-setting. He is a diamond of the purest
> water for all that. An honest single-hearted sort of creature, rather Indian
> in his nature, who loves and hates with equal zeal. He'd cut your throat if
> you insulted him, and his idea of an insult includes any disparagement of
> the South or her peculiar institutions; but on the other hand, he would share
> his last dollar with you if you needed it, and if a woman or a child be in the
> case, he is one of the tenderest hearted fellows in the world.[9]

To the shock and surprise of easterners, the derisive epithet they so sneeringly
fastened on Missouri frontiersmen in 1854 was quickly adopted by the state's gentry.
Steamboats, omnibuses, newspapers, horses, dogs, even newborn babies, suddenly
appeared bearing the proud title "Border Ruffian."[10] While aghast at some of their
excesses, West Missourians would all agree that the Border Ruffians were the rough,
raw edge in the fight for a way of life.

Slavery had existed in Missouri among the Spanish and French long before
statehood in 1820. With the arrival of Americans, the system flourished. Just as
Kentucky was a mirror of Virginia, its eastern matrix, so, too, had Missouri reflected
the customs and social values of Kentucky. Prior to 1854, small concern was felt
for Kansas. Despite antislavery agitation, few on the border doubted that when the
void was finally filled, Kansas—like Missouri and Kentucky before it—would
become, if not a Slave State, at least sympathetic to slavery. But then, with passage
of the Kansas-Nebraska Bill and the organized effort to people the territory with
free-soilers, Missouri slaveholders viewed the action as a disruption of the natural
flow of events and a direct attack on a cherished institution that had existed for
generations. As everyone so correctly understood, with Iowa and Illinois already
ringing the state on the north and east, slavery in Missouri could not survive a free
Kansas to the west.

Because of the border's lush and low river valleys, a large percentage of Missouri
slaves were located in the western third of the state. In the dozen or so counties
edging Kansas, roughly fifty thousand bondsmen worked the rich, black bottoms
of the Missouri, Platte, Grand, Osage, and Blue Rivers, raising prodigious crops
of hemp, corn, wheat, and tobacco.

"In no part of the Union is slavery more profitable," commented the *New York
Tribune* on western Missouri, "and in no part of the Union do slaves bring more
in the market, either to sell or hire. . . . "[11]

"Instead of log-cabins plastered with mud," a traveller through the region
added, "[there] appeared generous frame and brick dwellings surrounded by natural
parks of oak and elm. On all sides were fields . . . [and] the slaves were fat and
comfortable-looking."[12]

Though only a fraction of West Missourians were actually masters, their owner-ship of slaves represented a vast investment of between fifty and one hundred million dollars. Additionally, the prestige and power wielded by the slaveholders far out-weighed their paltry numbers. Consequently, while few in western Missouri actually owned slaves, a great many aspired to join the ranks of those who did. In turn, this slaveless segment of society could be counted on in a crisis to preserve and perpetuate the system.[13]

Despite the arguments of abolitionists and their hypercriticism of slavery as cruel and inhuman, most Missourians could only smile. What may have been true of the steaming sugar plantations of the Gulf Coast rang hollow along the western border. "[B]ein' slave is may-be mighty hard on white folks," chortled one Missouri black, "but it's dreadful good for nigga."[14] Indeed, many northerners, whose knowl-edge of slavery came only through a perusal of abolition tracts or Harriet Beecher Stowe, were surprised by the benign face the "peculiar institution" cast in Missouri. Unlike the large and impersonal operations further south, many of the relatively small planters of Missouri viewed the slave as an extension of their family who worked the fields side-by-side when out-of-doors and often lived and socialized with one another when indoors. Additionally, and as more than one amazed visitor discovered, Missouri slaves often enjoyed a standard of living that differed little from that of whites.[15]

Pausing one day near Lexington, Douglas Brewerton of the *New York Herald* queried a planter about the care and conduct of his eighty slaves.

> We give our hands, both male and female, two full suits of clothes per annum, with under-clothing in proportion; these suits are made of a coarse, but very warm and durable fabric, which costs between one and two dollars per yard. When one of our slaves desires to marry, he goes to his master, confesses the "soft impeachment," and asks his consent. If the object of his adoration belongs to another plantation, the master of the girl is waited upon for the same purpose. These requests are scarcely ever refused. As the negro has a great idea of doing things like "quality folks," their weddings are state occasions. . . . [I]t is usual for the planter to present the newly-married pair with a four-poster and mattress, or it may be a new brass kettle with which to set up house-keeping.
>
> The slave has also his little garden, which he may till with self-interest; as an incentive, the proceeds are his own, to be disposed of as he thinks proper. He is also permitted to keep a hog, and, if he desires to do so, chickens. There is, probably, no slave who might not purchase his freedom, if he were so inclined and would exert himself sufficiently to obtain the requisite means (for we are told that when such an intimation is made to the master, he is generally willing to value his servant at a much lower

rate). . . . Slave women differ very much in their affection for their children; some exhibit great solicitude for the welfare of their offspring, while others seem perfectly reckless as to their fate. The old women are, for the most part, employed in looking after the children and cabins during the absence of the negroes in the field; this is the more necessary, as the young darkeys are wonderfully mischievous, as much so as juvenile monkeys. . . . When the youngsters get large enough, they are frequently taken into the planter's house, where they do light work, stuff themselves with eatables, and, in many instances, get petted until they become completely spoiled.

Singular as it may appear, we find it very difficult to obtain good house-servants; for the negro seems better fitted for outdoor employment. This is even the case with those who are brought up in our houses, for as they approach the age of fifteen or sixteen years, they grow restless and discontented, and begin to envy what they consider the greater amount of freedom which falls to the share of the field-hands, who have their stated and regular hours for work, and are, at liberty when their labor is done, to enjoy themselves . . . in any way they please. . . .

If one of my negroes falls sick, he sends word to the house, when my wife usually goes down to visit the patient, and if it be a simple matter, within the reach of our family medicine-chest, she prescribes, and treats the case herself. But if the symptoms are violent, or, the disease assume a graver character, we send immediately for a physician, the best that can be obtained. . . . As regards our method of slave discipline the whip is but seldom resorted to, and then only in extreme cases. An increase of labor, or a deprivation of some customary privilege, will usually suffice to bring the offender to his senses. A negro rarely suffers for an offense which he has not committed, for though the circumstantial evidence against him be ever so strong, when it comes to the moment of punishment, one of your old darkeys, of known character and discretion, will generally step out with some such expostulation as this:

"Massa John, what you gwyne whip dat nigga for? he no do it. More like to be dat lying nigga, Pete, Massa. . . . "[16]

Although swift and terrible fates did indeed befall slaves who committed murder, rape, and other violent crimes, the punishments were seldom, if ever, more severe than that of white transgressors. Nevertheless, it was this last aspect of slavery that evoked the greatest outcry from abolitionists. In turn, it was this antislavery response to punishment that drew the ire of southerners and their charges of hypocrisy. Editorialized Lucian Eastin of the *Leavenworth Herald*:

If one thing is disgusting or repugnant to our feelings above all others, it is to see the inconsistency of Abolition sympathy. In cases where the sufferer is a negro, their feelings of sympathy are exceedingly sensitive; but where the aggrieved party is white, their feelings of sympathy are at once obtunded. Only let a negro be punished—however just and deserved the punishment may be—and you at once hear the most sincere expressions of sympathy and commisseration for him; but let the most brutal and unparalleled outrages be practiced upon a white man, you will never hear an utterance of sympathy or compassion from the lips of an Abolitionist.[17]

It was this glaring contradiction in emancipationist philanthropy that was most revolting to slavers. After viewing both systems close up, New Yorker Douglas Brewerton had reached a verdict: "[T]he relation between the master and his slave is, in nine instances out of ten, a more kindly one than that which exists between the Eastern manufacturers and his sickly, pale-faced operative."[18]

Rather than travel afar waging war on slavery in Missouri, some Southerners—and not a few Northerners—suggested that New Englanders stay home and root out bondage in their own backyard. Reported a Lowell, Massachusetts, newspaper:

Observing a singular-looking long, low, black wagon passing along the street, we made inquiries respecting it and were informed that it was what we term a "slaver." She makes regular trips to the north of the states, cruising around Vermont and New Hampshire, with a "commander" whose heart must be as black as his craft, who is paid a dollar a head for all he brings to market, and more in proportion to the distance—if he brings them from such a distance that they cannot easily get back. This is done by "hoisting false colors," and representing to the girls that they can tend more machinery than is possible, and that the work is very neat, and the wages such that they can dress in silks and spend half their time in reading. Now is this true? Let the girls who have been thus deceived answer.[19]

Some ships that docked in northeastern ports were themselves little better than slave galleys, unloading a cargo of Scottish, Irish, or English girls bound for the sweat shops of the textile industry. "These poor children," raged one southern editor, "torn from the paternal roof and from . . . native land and home, and sold to New England cotton-spinners . . . [are] 'forwarded to their destination' without the special wonder of a single philanthropist in Boston. If they had only been destined to raise cotton instead of spinning it, what an uproar there would have been in Faneuil Hall and the Fish Market."[20]

Despite the obvious inconsistencies, abolitionists would not be shaken from their course. Indeed, to many a stunned southerner, abolition fanaticism seemed boundless. Not only was the radical John Frémont soon to be chosen as the "Black Republican" candidate for president, but words such as the following by an Ohio clergyman were becoming increasingly common.

> O, God! We pray that Thou wilt curse the slaveholder in all his under
> takings, confound all his plans, and spread terror, horror and dismay
> throughout the entire South. Curse, O, God, we ask Thee, with a blighting
> curse, all the Democrats in the Union; may they in an especial manner feel
> the weight of Thy great displeasure. We entreat Thee, O, Lord, to go to
> Washington and kill Franklin Pierce; show him no mercy, but strike him
> down. . . . We ask Thee, O, Lord, to afflict every pro-slavery man with
> the leprosy or small pox; and may they, after feeling the pains of a thousand
> deaths, be tumbled headlong into Hell without a trial, there to feel ten
> thousand strokes on their bare backs, daily inflicted by each and every one
> of the slaves in the United States. Our Heavenly Father, we ask Thee to
> strengthen us in our resolves to make Kansas a free State at the peril of the
> Union; we ask Thee to interpose Thy mighty hand in our behalf and help
> us to shiver the Union into atoms rather than to concede to the Southern
> demons . . . one inch of the disputed Territory.[21]

Surprisingly, although a large number of "practical" abolitionists had suddenly materialized in Kansas, efforts to lure slaves from Missouri had proven notoriously unsuccessful. Part of the reason, no doubt, was that with the Fugitive Slave Law still binding—in Kansas as elsewhere—a runaway could, and must, be returned to his master. Another factor that kept slaves at home was the natural human fear of the unknown. Perhaps the greatest explanation why so few bondsmen "stole themselves" and fled to Kansas was simply that many slaves were not entirely convinced that freedom was better for them than slavery.

Asked if he would prefer to go to Kansas and live in Lawrence, one border black only shook his head: "No! s'pect not. . . . [B]een raised 'mong quality—couldn't think of gwine thar, sir; drather stay at home 'mong white folks."[22]

"[D]is nigger ain't a gwyne to 'stress himself bout politics," added another slave. "[D]on't reckon much on dese Abolitionists, no how; but jest know dis, massa, dat dis nigga's jest as happy and 'joys himself as much as if he owned de whole town of Lexington."[23]

"Some do seem happy in their midnight ignorance," one Yankee grudgingly admitted.[24]

Since most Missouri slaves could not be coaxed from the state, some abolitionists began decoying and even kidnapping them to freedom. One "conductor" caught with four blacks near the Iowa line, confessed that the emigrant aid society had paid him forty dollars per month for his work.[25] Then, too, there were the professional agitators—men like reporter James Redpath, a "hired scavenger" who came to Kansas from England to stir slave revolt in Missouri. Redpath, hissed the editor of the *Kansas City Enterprise*, "is but a recent importation of British fanaticism—a minion puked upon our shores for the purpose of abusing and misrepresenting a class of people who have never harmed a hair of his head. . . . It is enough for Americans to abuse Americans; but for a fresh British mercenary to come here and assume that right, we hold it is beyond toleration."[26]

"Now we will be equally candid . . .," the ever-ready *Squatter Sovereign* added, "for every negro stolen, we will hang ten abolitionists, for it will take at least that many to get one negro off. So, gentlemen negro thieves, you can commence the war as soon as you choose."[27]

All in all, and despite the apparent indifference of their bondsmen, Missouri masters realized only too well that if abolitionists ever seized control of Kansas, it was but a matter of time before slavery, with all its investments, "went up." As the spring 1856 immigration season approached, there was concern in southern circles that the sheer weight of northern numbers would doom Kansas to free-soil. The proslavery pens of David Atchison, John Stringfellow, and others went to work, urging Deep South planters to join the fray. A circular from the "Kansas Emigration Society of Missouri" ran a typical appeal:

> The western counties of Missouri have for the last two years been heavily taxed, both in money and time, in fighting the battles of the South. Lafayette County alone has expended more than $100,000 in money, and as much more in time. . . . But the abolitionists, staking their all upon the Kansas issue, and hesitating at no means, fair or foul, are moving heaven and earth to render that beautiful Territory a "Free State." Missouri . . . has done her duty. . . . But the time has come when she can no longer stand up single-handed, the lone champion of the South, against the myrmidons of the entire North. . . . We repeat it, the crisis has arrived. The time has come for action—bold, determined action. Words will no longer do any good; we must have men in Kansas, and that by tens of thousands. A few will not answer. . . . We tell you now, and tell you frankly, that unless you come quickly, and come by thousands, we are gone.[28]

Understandably, many slaveholders were wary of risking their valuable chattel in a territory infested with abolitionists. "We can assure them," soothed John Stringfellow, "that their property is just as safe here as in S. Carolina, and the negro thief is as closely watched, and severely punished, as in the most distant Southern State. We again repeat there is no risk or danger in bringing slaves to Kansas."[29]

To the great relief of Stringfellow, Atchison, and others, when traffic opened on the river in the spring, a goodly contingent of Southerners did indeed step ashore. Arriving in bands of a handful to a hundred, many were given a hero's welcome with parades, speeches, even gifts. And with the Southerners, slaves, according to one account, were also "pouring" into the territory.[30]

"Strange as it may seem . . . ," remarked a youthful Virginia master after he landed on the Leavenworth levee, "my young darkies went with me cheerfully . . . and were quite as much excited at the prospect of the new life in the West as I was myself."[31]

Heartened by the southern response, many felt the tide had finally turned. "[T]here can scarcely be a doubt," waxed John Stringfellow, "that the pro-slavery men will compose an immense majority of the voters at the next election. The Northern Emigrant Aid Societies do not appear to be so active as formerly. . . ."[32] One cause for the noticeable decrease in free-soil immigration was a well-publicized report that the Missouri River was undergoing a virtual blockade. Another reason Northerners hesitated to enter the territory were the newspaper articles describing the fate of some of those who did.

Despite the threats of death should he return, Pardee Butler once more strode boldly up the streets of Atchison on April 30. "I spoke to no one in town save two merchants . . . ," Butler recalled. "Having remained only a few minutes, I went to my buggy to resume my journey." Unfortunately for the home-bound preacher, his nemesis of old, Robert Kelley, was ready and waiting.

> I was . . . dragged into a grocery, and there surrounded by a company of South Carolinians. . . . They yelled, "Kill him! Kill him! Hang the _____ Abolitionist." One of their number bristled up to me and said, "Have you got a revolver?" I answered, "No." He handed me a pistol and said, "There, take that, and stand off ten steps; and_____, I will blow you through in an instant." I replied, "I have no use for your weapon. . . . " The fellow was furious; but his companions dissuaded him from shooting me, saying they were going to hang me. They pinioned my arms behind my back . . . [and] obtained a rope. . . . They dragged me into another building, and appointed a moderator, and got up a kind of lynch law trial. Kelley told his story. I rose to my feet, and calmly and in respectful language began to tell mine. . . . But these men . . . savagely gagged me into silence by rapping my face, choking me, pulling my beard, jerking me violently to my seat, and exclaiming, "Damn you, hold your tongue!"[33]

Only through the intervention of a sympathetic Missourian was Butler saved from hanging yet a second time. Though Kelley, too, had a change of heart, the editor insisted that in lieu of death the hardheaded preacher should be tarred and feathered. Remembered Butler:

> One little, dark visaged, thin featured, black eyed South Carolinian, as smart as a cricket, and who seemed to be the leader of the gang, was particularly displeased. "Damn me," said he, "if I am come all the way from South Carolina, and have spent so much money to do things up in such milk and water style as this." They stripped me naked to the waist, covered my body with tar, and then for the want of feathers, applied cotton wool. . . . [T]hey tossed my clothing into my buggy, put me therein, accompanied me to the suburbs of the town, and sent me naked out upon the prairie. . . . The first mob that sent me down the Missouri River on a raft . . . were courteous gentlemen compared with this last one. When I was towed out into the middle of the stream, I do not remember to have heard a word spoken by the men on shore. This last mob, when they left me on the border of the town, shrieked and yelled like a pack of New Zealand cannibals. . . . I adjusted my attire about me as best I could, and hastened to rejoin my wife and two little ones, on the banks of the Stranger Creek.[34]

"The time is past," growled Robert Kelley, "when such cowardly and contemptible abolition rascals, can hold up their heads in Atchison."[35]

This and like tales of outrage brought northern blood to the boiling point, and many were determined to reach the western battleground, blockade or no. "I perpose to take sixty or so good men, well-equipped and mounted and garilla as long as there is a Ruffian left in Kansas," a Maine farmer wrote to Amos Lawrence. "My plan is not to show quarter and consequently take no prisoners. . . . [I will] butcher them clean by the board."[36] Another down-easter, E. Z. C. Judson, better known as Ned Buntline, announced that he, too, was rounding up two hundred free-state fighters and heading west.[37] Other companies of "Rifle Christians" formed and struck for the territory while the Reverend Henry Ward Beecher of New York passed the plate and armed recruits with Sharps rifles—or, as they came to be called, "Beecher's Bibles."

Even as the explosive national situation escalated, the rebels of Kansas showed no signs of abandoning their illegal government. Indeed, with renewed vigor the "outlaws" pressed ahead. While the free-state legislature met in March at Topeka, in defiance of both federal and territorial authorities, the newly elected "governor," Charles Robinson, drew up his plan of attack. To bring the proslavery government to its knees, Robinson urged his followers to resist any territorial officer trying to enforce the laws. Additionally, taxes were to be withheld, courts disrupted, and judges harassed and intimidated. To avoid a confrontation with the U.S. government and thereby jeopardize the propaganda war, federal troops acting as posses for local officials were to be simply evaded, not resisted.[38]

Although Robinson's strategy was beginning to bear fruit, the increasingly violent proslavery response ignited increasingly violent reactions. Dozens of free-soil militias sprang up with many leaders bristling to take the offensive.

"They chose me . . . as their captain . . . ," said Thomas Bickerton of his artillery unit.[39]

> I accepted the office on condition that they would obey every order, and that if the President himself should stand in our way he must receive our fire. . . . I taught the men how to load and fire the piece; also, the art of fencing with light swords, and soon had them well drilled in these exercises. My company now increased so fast that I divided them up into squads, and armed a part with rifles. . . . I told them what was expected of them, and if any one had any scruples about shooting a U.S. officer they had better leave the company.[40]

"We had a thousand times rather see the bowie-knife and revolver called into requisition for the adjustment of differences than to see the Courts," fumed another impatient Northerner.[41]

While reinforcements continued to trickle in through Iowa and Nebraska, free-staters continued their persistent, though vain, attempts to lure reservation Indian tribes to their side. Sneered the *Squatter Sovereign*:

> The "border ruffians" have probably as little fear of the one set of barbarians as the other. It is an unnatural alliance, however, that of abolitionists and Indians, and degrading to the red men, who have generally no objection to slaveholding, and are not deficient in manhood and generous qualities. . . . [T]he low and thieving class of paupers that compose the Abolition party of Kansas, are characters, despised alike by the Indian and White man.[42]

Despite the determination of free-soilers to resist the territorial laws, as sheriff of Douglas County, Samuel Jones was just as determined to enforce them. Since the rescue of Charles Branson five months before, Jones had bided his time, waiting for an opportunity to bag Sam Wood and the other offenders. Described by his enemies as a "tall, muscular, athletic loafer," a man who "seldom looks those with whom he is conversing full in the face," to friends the sheriff was "high-minded, honorable, and brave;" "rather a fine-looking young man," offered a neutral observer.[43] Whatever he may have seemed to others, Sam Jones was, in fact, a tenacious, serious-minded law officer who was destined to do his duty, regardless of the consequences.

On April 19, hearing that Sam Wood had returned to Lawrence, Jones made his move.[44] Spotting the fugitive chatting with friends on a street, the sheriff stepped in. In the words of Sara Robinson:

> He said to Wood, "You are my prisoner."
> "By what authority?" was the very natural reply.
> "As Sheriff of Douglas County."
> "I do not recognize such authority," said Wood, adding, however, that he would go with him if he would allow him to go to his house, only a few steps distant, first.
> This the sheriff refused, and Wood declared, "Then I'll not go with you at all!" and very cooly walked away.[45]

When Jones tried to follow, a jeering mob rushed in, stole his pistol, then "jostled" him until Wood had escaped. "The whole affair only lasted two or three minutes," Sara recalled.[46]

The next day Jones returned with a posse of four men. But again, when the "sham sheriff" attempted to arrest one of the Branson rescuers, a mob swarmed in, and during the scuffle Jones was struck in the face. As the posse left town once more empty-handed, the free-soilers, according to a witness, "threw their hats in the air, and clapped their hands."[47]

Several days later, Sam Jones entered Lawrence for yet a third time. On this occasion, however, a file of U.S. dragoons under the command of Lt. James McIntosh came along as escort. Wrote Lieutenant McIntosh:

> From that time until sundown he succeeded in arresting six of the offending individuals. While making these arrests a large crowd was assembled in the streets; and, although no resistance was made or violence resorted to, public excitement was great, and Mr. Jones and the Territorial Government were freely and bitterly denounced. About sundown, the Sheriff having pointed out to me a room for the prisoners, I marched them to it, and placed my tents immediately in rear of the house. I at once placed two sentinels in the room with the prisoners, and one walking around outside of the house. . . . I cautioned Mr. Jones, and advised him to sleep . . . in the same house occupied by the prisoners, where he would be under the protection of my guard. Mr. Jones, apparently not apprehending danger, came to my tent during the evening, and after being seated a while, I asked him to give me a drink of water, and I went with him to a barrel near the house for the purpose of getting it, and while standing at the barrel a shot was fired from a crowd of about twenty persons. Mr. Jones immediately said, "I believe

that was intended for me;" but having heard several other shots during the evening, which I thought were fired in the air . . . I told him I thought he was mistaken; he then returned to my tent. . . . In about five minutes I went to the tent, when Mr. Jones said, "That was intended for me, for here is the hole in my pants." Greatly incensed at this cowardly act, I immediately joined the crowd, and while speaking to them, I heard another shot, and at the same time some of my men exclaimed, "Lieutenant, the Sheriff is dead." I went to the tent immediately, and found Mr. Jones lying upon the floor, and [saw] that he was still alive. . . .[48]

While the victim rolled on the ground in agony, shouting free-staters nearby beat pots and pans to the tune of "Let the Union Slide."[49] The sheriff was severely, though not mortally, wounded, but news of his "assassination" caused a violent chain reaction along the western border. Shrieked the *Atchison Squatter Sovereign*: THE ABOLITIONISTS IN OPEN REBELLION—SHERIFF JONES MURDERED BY THE TRAITORS. . . . SHOT DOWN BY THE THIEVING PAUPERS![50]

"Oh, murder most foul!—cold blooded assassination, blacker than hell!!" cried the *Union* from the sheriff's hometown, Lecompton. "A public officer, in discharge of his official duties to be shot down in cold blood."[51]

Stunned by the incident, nervous over national opinion, Charles Robinson called for a mass "indignation" meeting the following morning to denounce the shooting and pledge his complete cooperation in bringing those guilty to justice. One eyewitness was not fooled, however. The gathering was held, relayed the spy, "to blind the whole affair by offering prayers and shedding torrents of crocodile tears over the attempted murder."

Robinson . . . said "that he did not believe the deed was committed by any Free State man, but that Jones went into the tent for the purpose of being shot at by some of his own friends, and then have an excuse for saying that he was assassinated by Free State men!" Just think of it . . . Robinson having the cold-heartedness to speak such malicious falsehood over the death-groanings of the assassinated! And he is loudly cheered in his heathenish remarks.[52]

This, announced the *Kansas City Enterprise*, was "the most cold-blooded, heartless and criminal exhibition of feeling, we have ever known uttered in a public assembly. . . . [Robinson] is a murderer, lacking only the courage to strike."[53]

Whatever Robinson's hope, nothing could mollify Southerners following the assault on Jones. "HE MUST BE AVENGED. HIS MURDER SHALL BE AVENGED, if at the sacrifice of every abolitionist in the Territory . . . ," roared

*Samuel Jones.* KANSAS STATE HISTORICAL SOCIETY, TOPEKA.

John Stringfellow. "We are now in favor of levelling Lawrence, and chastizing the Traitors there congregated, should it result in the total destruction of the Union." [54]

Once again, but with a wrath in their hearts unlike anytime in the past, the proslavery party of the border prepared to march on Lawrence. Sensing that no amount of bluff, deceit, trickery, or lies could stop the storm bearing down on them, Charles Robinson, Andrew Reeder, and other free-soil leaders quietly packed their bags and slipped from the territory. Some did not get far. George Washington Brown was nabbed just over the line by a Westport mob and hustled off to jail by a triumphant Robert Kelley of Atchison. "[Brown] felt . . . as though he was in a powder magazine, smoking a cigar," Kelley laughed. "Had we meted out justice to the culprit, he would at this time be *done Brown*. As it is, we think the hemp is already grown that will soon adorn his neck!" [55]

Another fugitive soon cornered was Charles Robinson. Pulled from a boat at Lexington, the doctor was led away to Leavenworth. Though treated surprisingly well, it was only through the personal efforts of several Southerners—notably William Martin, captain of the dreaded Kickapoo Rangers—that the free-state general was spared from hanging. "[S]urely no man could have acted more honorably than he did while he held [me] as prisoner," Robinson later wrote. "It is doubtful if there was another pro-slavery man who would or could have saved [me] from the wrath of the excited mob." [56]

Nevertheless, with the cry for his blood almost unanimous, Robinson's life hung by a thread. Raged one local editor:

[He is] a treacherous traitor, and deserved to be hung until dead, dead. . . . If he has justice done him he will be sure to stretch hemp without a foot hold. When Robinson, Reeder, and a few other traitors are dealt with as the law directs, and their vile bodies buried in silence and covered with clods of disgrace, then the people of Kansas will have peace.[57]

With their leaders either captives or flying fugitives, the free-staters of Lawrence watched as the proslavery circle closed tighter and tighter. Since the shooting of Sheriff Jones, southern patrols had scoured the land, seeking victims.[58] Divulged one witness:

Camps were formed at different points along the highways and on the Kansas River, and peaceful travellers subjected to detention, robbery, and insult. Men were stopped in the streets and on the open prairie, and bidden to stand and deliver their purses at the peril of their lives. Cattle, provisions, arms, and other property were taken whenever found, without consent of the owners. Men were choked from their horses, which were seized by the marauders, and houses were broken open and pillaged of their contents.[59]

On May 15, a band of Border Ruffians surrounded the village of Benicia, seven miles upriver from Lawrence. "I now want to give you a piece of advice," the leader warned after the Northerners had been herded into a cabin.

You have been offering resistance to the laws of the territorial Legislature. . . . The President has declared it legal; Congress has declared it legal; and resistance to those laws is Treason! What did you come here for? Why did you not go to Minnesota, or Nebraska? It is not half settled, and is as good country as this. But, no; you must come here. You want to get the whole of the territory. . . . This territory belongs to the South, and, by God, the South will have it . . . ! God damn you, if you are ever caught here again you shall be strung up! Go to Nebraska, damn you! You have no right in Kansas![60]

Four days later, near Blanton's Bridge on the Wakarusa, a young free-soiler was mortally wounded by rifle fire when he failed to halt as ordered. On the following day, near the same spot, a comrade was shot through the head and also killed.[61]

As the violence spread and a showdown neared, South Carolinian Axalla Hoole scratched out a tension-filled letter from his cabin at Douglas.

> While I am writing, guns are firing in the camps of the different companies of soldiers who are gathering to attack Lawrence. . . . [T]hey are shooting in every direction. I expect before you get this Lawrence will be burnt to the ground. . . . I don't think that they will show any fight, though they are preparing. But I hear they are very much frightened and have sent to the Governor for protection. . . .[62]

Understandably, the people of Lawrence were indeed frightened. And, as Hoole had correctly overheard, in an effort to prevent the coming retribution, several city leaders petitioned Wilson Shannon, as well as U.S. Marshal Israel Donelson, to summon federal troops. Pleaded the citizens:

> [W]e now . . . declare our willingness and determination, without resistance, to acquiesce in the service upon us of any judicial writs against us by the United States Marshal for Kansas Territory, and will furnish him a posse for that purpose, if so requested. . . . We declare ourselves to be order-loving and law-abiding citizens, and only await an opportunity to testify our fidelity to the laws of the country, the Constitution, and the Union. . . . [W]e ask protection of the constituted authorities of the Government, declaring ourselves in readiness to co-operate with them. . . .[63]

Responded Marshal Donelson:

> May I ask, gentlemen, what has produced this wonderful change in the minds of the people of Lawrence? Have their eyes been suddenly opened, so that they are now able to see that there are laws in force in Kansas Territory which should be obeyed . . . ? You say you call upon the constituted authority of the Government for protection. This, indeed, sounds strange coming from a large body of men armed with Sharp's [*sic*] rifles and other implements of war, bound together by oaths and pledges to resist the laws of the Government they call on for protection.[64]

Now ruing their earlier decision to refuse reinforcements in the hope that it might defuse the situation, those in Lawrence could only await helplessly the imminent onslaught.[65]

"We are in a bad fix," admitted Sam Walker. "Things look bad, very bad, at present."[66]

At dawn on May 21, early risers in Lawrence were startled to see hundreds of Border Ruffians silhouetted on the crest of Mount Oread. Even more menacing, a four-cannon battery also glared down, ready to open fire. Throughout the morning more Southerners arrived, until by noon a vast array stood poised above the town.[67] With several horsemen serving as escort, a U.S. deputy marshal rode quietly into Lawrence, arrested two free-soil fugitives without incident, then, after lunch at Shalor Eldridge's just-finished Free State Hotel, he pushed back up the hill. Once there, the officer transferred the waiting army to Sam Jones. Detailing a company to act as his posse, the partially recovered sheriff stepped into a buggy and rode into town.[68] Pulling up beside the hotel, Jones spoke first with Samuel Pomeroy.

> General Pomeroy, I recognize you as one of the leading citizens here, and as one who can act for the people of Lawrence. I demand that all the arms in Lawrence be given up, or we will bombard the town. . . . I give you five minutes to decide on this proposition, and half an hour to stack the arms in the street.[69]

Though Pomeroy was quick to reveal the hiding place of the brass howitzer, as well as several swivel guns, the hapless "general" lamely insisted that the Sharps were private property. Wrote witness Shalor Eldridge:

> While this was transpiring couriers were hastily passing between the sheriff and the headquarters on the hill. The arms that had been surrendered were sent away, and the activity among the forces betokened some further purpose. Jones now made a demand on me for the evacuation of the hotel, giving two hours for the removal of the furniture. It was obviously impossible to remove in two hours what it had taken as many weeks to place; and with no storage spaces obtainable, it was useless to attempt to do more than remove our families with such belongings as we could carry away.[70]

At one o'clock, Jones sent another messenger to Mount Oread, requesting that the proslavery army march into town forthwith. A tremendous shout went up at the summons, and the force moved down to the base of the hill. Once there, a euphoric David Atchison momentarily quieted the crowd.

> Boys, this day I am a Kickapoo Ranger, by God! This day we have entered Lawrence with Southern Rights inscribed upon our banner, and not one damned abolitionist dared to fire a gun. Now, boys, this is the happiest day of my life. We have entered that damned town, and taught the damned abolitionists a Southern lesson that they will remember until the day they

die. And now, boys, we will go in again, with our highly honorable Jones, and test the strength of that damned Free-State Hotel, and teach the Emigrant Aid Company that Kansas shall be ours. Boys, ladies should, and I hope will, be respected by every gentleman. But, when a woman takes upon herself the garb of a soldier, by carrying a Sharpe's [*sic*] rifle, then she is no longer worthy of respect. Trample her under your feet as you would a snake . . . ! If one man or woman dare stand before you, blow them to hell with a chunk of cold lead.[71]

With wild shouts shattering the air, and with red and blue flags flapping in the wind, the Border Ruffians swarmed into town. Terrified by the sight, the people of Lawrence scrambled for cover. "Almost every man, woman and child ran and left their houses open completely panic stricken," one of those fleeing recalled.[72]

Another who viewed the onset and knew his office would be one of the first stops was Josiah Miller of the *Kansas Free State*. "Well, boys, we're in for it!" yelled the editor when a large group pulled up and prepared to storm the building.[73] Shalor Eldridge was watching from across the street.

The ruffians ascended the stairs cautiously as if fearing an ambuscade, but once in the room they vied with each other in the work of destruction. The press and fixtures were broken up with axe and sledgehammer. Files and exchanges, with a six months' stock of paper and a half-printed edition of the *Free State* were tossed through the windows into the street and scattered by the winds over the prairie for a mile around. Cases of type were carried to the river and thrown in. Boxes of books, constituting a library of 300 volumes, were hacked to pieces with sabers; and when the destruction was complete the company marched back . . . each member carrying a mutilated book on the point of his bayonet. Another company entered the office of the *Herald of Freedom* . . . and the work of destruction began. Everything pertaining to the office was reduced to complete ruin.

While the destruction of the printing offices was going on a detail was engaged in removing the furniture from the hotel.[74]

When a cannon was wheeled up and aimed at his new and costly hotel, Shalor Eldridge staggered in disbelief. Reported the *Lecompton Union*:

[A]ppeals were made to Sheriff Jones to save the Aid Society's Hotel. This news reached the company's ears, and was received with one universal cry of "No! no! Blow it up! Blow it up!" About this time a banner was seen fluttering in the breeze over the office of the *Herald of Freedom*. Its color was a blood-red, with a lone star in the centre, and South Carolina above. . . . The effect was prodigious. One tremendous and long-continued shout burst from the ranks.[75]

"Mr. Jones listened to the many entreaties [of Eldridge]," the *Union* continued, "and finally replied that it was beyond his power to do anything, and gave the occupants so long to remove all private property from it."[76]

Inside the hotel, all was bedlam. Little Mary Eldridge was helping her frantic mother haul valuables from the building when she looked up to see a familiar face.

[W]e recognized [him] as being the same man who came up from St. Louis with us, accompanied by his mother. The boat on which we came . . . brought the furniture and provisions for the hotel . . . and one of the nicest sofas was unpacked for this old lady's use. . . . [G]reat was our indignation when we saw this man enter our home to destroy it. He said he was sorry . . . but he went right on with the destruction just the same. He did offer to carry out some furniture, and mother said she would like to save two pieces, as they came from our old home in Massachusetts. While we were preparing to get out, word was sent in several times that if we did not hurry they would fire. . . . Finally they sent word to mother

*Shalor Eldridge and family.* KANSAS STATE HISTORICAL SOCIETY, TOPEKA.

that they would give her just ten minutes longer, and then if she did not come out they would fire anyway.[77]

When the hotel was finally cleared, the cannon match was lit. Remembered Mary's distracted father:

Atchison claimed the honor of directing the first shot; but being somewhat unsteady, presumably from indulging too freely in the contents of the hotel cellar, he aimed too high and the ball passed over the top of the building, and, screaming through the air like a steam whistle, lit in the western portion of the town. Some thirty shots were fired more accurately, producing no more effect than perforating the concrete walls. Despairing to destroy it in this way, two kegs of powder were placed in the basement and exploded, but produced no serious effect. Piles of paper from the printing offices were then brought in and fired, when soon the whole interior was ablaze . . . the flames bursting through the windows and shooting through the roof.
. . . While the flames were at their height, Sheriff Jones, who had been all the while complacently watching the destruction, raised himself in his saddle and addressed his posse:
  "Gentlemen, this is the happiest day of my life. I determined to make the fanatics bow before me in the dust and kiss the territorial laws. I have done it, by God. You are now dismissed."[78]

"The dismissal of the posse," Eldridge concluded, "was accepted by them as an invitation to plunder."[79]

Although several shouting officers tried to halt the pillage, they were not successful. Stores, stables, and vacant homes were entered and their contents stolen.[80] Some returning residents tried, without much luck, to save their property. "I saw a young man . . .," one witness later wrote, "[and] a ruffian came up to him and demanded his Sharp's [*sic*] rifle & revolver. Said he, 'I haven't a rifle, & my revolver I bought and paid [for] & you can't have it.' 'We'll see, you God damned son of a bitch . . . whether I'll have it or not,' at the same time calling 5 or 6 of his men to him, they put their bayonets to his breast & thus forced him to give it up & demanded his money."[81]

The looting went on until dark, when most of the Border Ruffians, many drunk and reeling, finally stumbled from town. Part of their route home was lighted by flames from the home of Charles and Sara Robinson, high atop Mount Oread. Only one person had been killed in the sack, and he a Southerner, struck dead by a stone falling from the hotel.[82]

At Lecompton, Leavenworth, and other proslavery hotbeds in the territory, the returning militiamen were hailed as conquering heroes. Missourians were no less joyous, and at Westport, Weston, and Platte City, the Border Ruffians celebrated with cheers, gunfire, and round after round of rotgut whiskey. To his horror, Thomas Gladstone, a traveling Englishman, suddenly found himself caught in the revel at Kansas City. Recorded the abolitionist:

> Looking around at these groups of drunken, bellowing, blood-thirsty demons, who crowded around the bar of the hotel, shouting for drink, or vented their furious noise on the levee without, I felt that all my former experiences of border men and Missourians bore faint comparison with the spectacle presented by this wretched crew, who appeared only the more terrifying from the darkness of the surrounding night. . . . Men, for the most part of large frame . . . still reeking with the dust and smoke of Lawrence, wearing the most savage looks, and giving utterance to the most horrible imprecations and blasphemies; armed, moreover, to the teeth with rifles, cutlasses and bowie-knives. . . . Some displayed a grotesque intermixture in their dress, having crossed their native red rough shirt with the satin vest or narrow dress-coat pillaged from the wardrobe of some Lawrence Yankee, or having girded themselves with the cords and tassels which the day before had ornamented the curtains of the Free-state Hotel.[83]

"Thus fell the abolition fortress," concluded an elated *Lecompton Union*, "and we hope this will teach the Aid Society a good lesson for the future."[84]

Beaten, humbled, humiliated, a goodly number of free-soilers had indeed learned a valuable lesson and were ready to call it quits. The "lesson" learned by others, however, was that freedom for Kansas could not be won by political or "Fabian" means alone. Indeed, when word of the attack on Lawrence reached the outside world, many in America for the first time came to the grim realization that the sectional crisis had become an "irreconcilable conflict," wherein only by war could the issue be settled. And while her husband sat a prisoner in the enemy's camp, Sara Robinson toured the East, trying to the best of her ability to convince the nation that this war had already begun.

> So, now, the slave power, blood thirsty, and still crying [for] more victims, had sent its own tools,—ragged, ignorant, debauched, semi-savages, the very offshoot and growth of its peculiar institution,—to destroy a quiet town, to steal, destroy, and outrage its inhabitants. The work has been accomplished. The first time in the history of the American people has an American town been besieged and its inhabitants robbed, by forces acting under the instructions of U.S. officers.[85]

Having escaped the fate of Sara's husband, James Lane, too, stumped the North, throwing all his incredible oratorical talent into the breach to raise money and men in the fight for Free Kansas. On May 31, before a torchlit Chicago crowd of ten thousand, Lane stalked to the podium. "Before the applause had subsided sufficiently for his voice to be heard," noted a chronicler, "the fascinating spell of his presence had already seized upon the whole vast audience, and for the next hour he controlled its every emotions—moving to tears, to anger, to laughter, to scorn, to the wildest enthusiasm, at his will. No man . . . possessed such magnetic power over . . . men as he." [86]

"[A]s he detailed the series of infamous outrages upon the freemen of Kansas," a reporter for the *Chicago Tribune* continued, "the people were breathless with mortification and anger, or wild with enthusiasm to avenge those wrongs." [87]

Added yet another spellbound listener:

The grass on the prairie is swayed no more easily by the winds than was this vast assemblage by the utterances of this speaker. They saw the contending factions in the Territory through his glasses. The Pro-slavery party appeared like demons and assassins; the Free-State party like heroes and martyrs. He infused them with his warlike spirit and enthusiastic ardor. . . . Their response to his appeals . . . was immediate and decisive. [88]

While Lane, Sara, and northern editors everywhere beat the drums of war, the violence from "bleeding Kansas" spilled onto the steps of the nation's capitol itself. On May 22, one day after the sack of Lawrence, Charles Sumner sat writing at his desk in the U.S. Senate, lost in correspondence. Several days before, the senator from Massachusetts had delivered a scathing, intemperate speech from the floor of the upper chamber, mercilessly flailing Southerners and slave-owners for their "Crime Against Kansas." Missourians, sneered the tall, stately senator, were "hirelings, picked from the drunken spew and vomit of an uneasy civilization." [89] Sumner then lowered his sights to a chamber colleague, an aging Andrew Pickens Butler of South Carolina.

The senator from South Carolina has read many books of chivalry, and believes himself a chivalrous knight, with sentiments of honor and courage. Of course he has chosen a mistress to whom he has made vows, and who, though ugly to others, is always lovely to him; though polluted in the sight of the world, is chaste in his sight. I mean the harlot slavery. [90]

Of all the many millions who were shocked and incensed by the speech, none took the words more personally than Butler's nephew, Congressman Preston Brooks.

I felt it to be my duty to relieve Butler and avenge the insult to my State. . . . To punish an insulting inferior one used not a pistol or sword but a cane or horsewhip. I . . . speculated somewhat as to whether I should employ a horsewhip or a cowhide, but knowing that the Senator was my superior in strength, it occured to me that he might wrest it from my hand. . . .[91]

According to Charles Sumner:

While thus intent, with my head bent over my writing, I was addressed by a person who approached the front of my desk: I was so entirely absorbed, that I was not aware of his presence until I heard my name pronounced. As I looked up with pen in hand, I saw a tall man . . . standing directly over me, and at the same moment caught these words: "I have read your speech twice over, carefully; it is a libel on South Carolina, and Mr. Butler, who is a relative of mine.' While these words were still passing from his lips, he commenced a succession of blows with a heavy cane on my bare head, by the first of which I was stunned so as to lose my sight. I saw no longer my assailant, nor any other person or object in the room.[92]

"Every lick went where I intended . . . ," Brooks later admitted. "[He] was reeling around against the seats, backwards and forwards. . . . I . . . gave him about 30 first rate stripes. Towards the last he bellowed like a calf. I wore my cane out completely. . . . "[93]

When several senators tried to step in, others interfered. "Let them alone, God damn you," cried one of those savoring the punishment.[94] At last, Sumner went down in a heap, "as senseless as a corpse," said an onlooker, "his head bleeding copiously from the frightful wounds, and the blood saturating his clothes."[95]

"I could not believe that a thing like this was possible," the senator whispered when he finally revived.[96] But as Sumner so savagely discovered, in the increasingly angry climate spreading east from Kansas, violent words could quickly beget violent deeds. While southerners cheered Brooks's action and sent him dozens of canes, Sumner's bloody shirt was sent north for viewing by infuriated New Englanders.[97]

"The news of the most foul, most damnable and dastardly attack . . . perfectly overwhelmed me with indignation and rage," cursed a Chicagoan on word of the flogging.[98]

"I can think and speak of nothing but the outrages of slaveholders at Kansas, and the outrages of slaveholders at Washington," declared another man.[99]

A Connecticut schoolgirl said ominously:

> I don't think it is of very much use to stay any longer in the High School, as the boys would better be learning to hold muskets, and the girls to make bullets.[100]

In the wake of the Sumner affair, and with Lawrence emblazoned in everyone's mind, northern and southern legislators came daily to the Capitol wearing pistols and knives under their coats, expecting war to erupt at any moment. "Everybody here feels as if we were upon a volcano," confided one congressman.[101] Meanwhile, as the scattered and leaderless free-soilers of Kansas fled from proslavery aggression, a sense of isolation and hopelessness sapped their resolve. "This is . . . the darkest hour that Freedom has ever seen in Kanzas," penned a despondent Lawrence clergyman.[102]

"Kansas has now I think reached its turning point," agreed Edward Fitch from the same town. "If the North doesn't now arouse and do more than she has done yet, Kansas will be a slave state and we . . . shall be wiped out."[103]

While the Lawrence disaster did indeed "arouse" the North and help was on its way, for the time being Kansans were on their own and almost totally at the mercy of their Missouri masters. Of all the free-staters in Kansas, however, there was one who refused to be cowed by recent events. Nor was it in his nature to lie back and wait for others to act. And as for masters, he knew only the One. As a soldier of God, his duty was to wage war with evil wherever it was found—even

*Ruins of the Free State Hotel.* KANSAS STATE HISTORICAL SOCIETY, TOPEKA.

if it meant fighting alone, even if it meant fighting unto death. While those about him were flying in fear and confusion or abandoning the cause in despair, he would stand his ground like a rock. Indeed, he would do more than that; he would not merely wait for the enemies of God to strike at him but would instead strike at them. He would spread terror in the ranks of the foe. He was brave and bold, yet he was also as cruel and cold as a sword slash. Now his moment had arrived; now he would act!

## CHAPTER SEVEN

# ORDAINED FROM ETERNITY

"WE ARE GOING DOWN TO MAKE AN EXAMPLE. ARE YOU COMING WITH US?" WITH ice in his voice, with death in his eyes, John Brown searched the faces of his followers. Only moments before, he and the stunned group of men around him had learned of Lawrence. Like many others from the Osawatomie region, Brown and his sons, as well as several neighbors, had hied north in hopes of reinforcing the threatened town. A few miles south of Palmyra, however, the old man heard to his grief that he was far too late. When word arrived a short time later that Charles Sumner had been beaten half to death on the floor of the U.S. Senate, Brown "went crazy," remembered one of his sons, "crazy."[1]

"Something must be done to show these barbarians that we, too, have rights," the angry father announced.[2]

In the words of John Brown Jr.:

It was now and here resolved that they, their aiders and abettors who sought to kill our suffering people should themselves be killed, and in such a manner as should be likely to cause a restraining fear. Father . . . proposed to return with several of my men. . . . I assisted in the sharpening of his navy cutlasses. . . . No man of our entire number could fail to understand that a retaliatory blow would fall.[3]

When one of the party protested, Brown stared him into silence. "I have no choice," muttered the old man. "It has been ordained by the Almighty God, ordained from eternity, that I should make an example of these men."[4]

John Jr. chose not to join the "secret expedition," but his brothers Fred, Salmon, Owen, Watson, and Oliver, as well as his brother-in-law, Henry

*John Brown.* KANSAS STATE HISTORICAL SOCIETY, TOPEKA.

Thompson, did. Neighbors James Townsley and Theodore Weiner also agreed to go. Except for Weiner, who mounted a horse, all stepped into a heavy wagon and started slowly south.[5] Later that day, near the confluence of Mosquito and Potta-wotomie creeks, the men pulled up and hid in a deep ravine. "We stayed there all that night and all of the next day until late in the evening," Salmon Brown recalled.[6] Near ten o'clock, that dark, windy night of May 24, Salmon and the others buckled on their broadswords, tucked in their pistols, and quietly followed John Brown.

He was a strange old man, a man outwardly simple, yet inwardly complex. Despite his fifty-six years, he was lean and wiry and tough as leather; men half his age could seldom match him in strength and stamina. "Generally," wrote one who knew him, "he carried his head pitched forward and a little down, and shoved his right shoulder forward in walking." Another also noticed "a certain nervous twitch of the head."[7] Except for the black throat stock he habitually wore to hide his aging neck, there was nothing noteworthy or vain in his dress: dark coat, dark vest, dark pants, dark hat. Although his exterior was dour, John Brown was often lively in private, and when conversing with friends and relatives, humor was not an unknown trait to him. "When he laughed," said a stunned acquaintance, "he made not the slightest sound, not even a whisper or air intake of breath; but he shook all over and laughed violently. It was the most curious thing imaginable to see him, in utter silence rock and quake with mirth."[8]

It was the eyes of John Brown that most people noticed, though. To some, there was a chilling, reptilian quality in them, something that suggested an inner unbalance—of a mind diseased or deranged.[9] Others saw in those same steady lights a glint of the fierce soul flickering within. Those who would see Brown's eyes this night would witness a terrifying mixture of both. And his sharp, crackling voice would hold no hint of humor or mirth.

"We started, the whole company, in a northerly direction, crossing Mosquito creek . . . ," revealed James Townsley. "Soon after crossing the creek some one of the party knocked at the door of a cabin, but received no reply. . . . The next place we came to was the residence of the Doyles."[10]

Like most of his neighbors in the Pottawatomie Valley, James Doyle was a proslavery man. Also like most of his neighbors, Doyle was not noisy or aggressive about it. Though friends had tried to cajole him into serving as their territorial legislator, the Tennessean was more intent on raising a cabin, working the claim, and minding his business. "I came to the territory to secure a home for my family, not for political purposes," responded the farmer. "I wish nothing to do with politics."[11]

Mahala Doyle:

[A]bout eleven o'clock at night, after we had all retired . . . we heard some persons come into the yard and rap at the door and call for . . . my husband. . . . [He] got up and went to the door. Those outside inquired for Mr. [Allen] Wilkinson and where he lived. My husband told them that he would tell them.[12]

"About this time," remembered James Townsley, "a large dog attacked us. Frederick Brown struck the dog a blow with his short, two-edged sword, after which I dealt him a blow with my saber, and heard no more of him."[13]

Mahala Doyle continued:

[M]y husband, opened the door, and several came into the house, and said they were from the army. . . . They told my husband that he and the boys must surrender, they were their prisoners. . . . They first took my husband out of the house, then they took two of my sons—the two oldest ones, William and Drury—out, and then took [them] . . . away. My son John was spared, because I asked them in tears to spare him.[14]

Remembered James Townsley:

The old man Doyle and two sons were . . . marched some distance from the house . . . where a halt was made. Old John Brown drew his revolver and shot . . . Doyle in the forehead, and Brown's two youngest sons immediately fell upon the younger Doyles with their . . . swords. One of the young Doyles was stricken down in an instant, but the other attempted to escape, and was pursued a short distance by his assailant and cut down.[15]

"I heard two reports [of gunfire]," the terrified mother recounted, "after which I heard moaning, as if a person was dying; then I heard a wild whoop."[16]

Now past midnight on Sunday, May 25, Brown and his men moved down the creek until they reached the cabin of Allen Wilkinson, a local postmaster and member of the Territorial Legislature. In the words of Wilkinson's wife, Louise:

We were disturbed by [the] barking of the dog. I was sick with the measles, and woke up Mr. Wilkinson, and asked if he "heard the noise, and what it meant?" He said it was only some one passing about, and soon after was again asleep. It was not long before the dog raged and barked furiously, awakening me once more; pretty soon I heard footsteps as of men approaching; saw one pass by the window, and some one knocked at the door. I asked, "Who is that?" Some one replied, "I want you to tell me the way to Dutch Henry's." He commenced to tell them, and they said to him, "Come out and show us." He wanted to go, but I would not let him; he then told them it was difficult to find his clothes, and could tell them as well without going out of doors. The men out of doors, after that, stepped back, and I thought I could hear them whispering; but they immediately returned, and, as they approached, one of them asked my husband, "Are you . . . opposed to the Northern or free soil party . . . [?]"

When my husband said, "I am," one of them said, "You are our prisoner. Do you surrender?" He said, "Gentlemen, I do." They said, "Open the door." Mr. Wilkinson told them to wait till he made a light; and they replied, "If you don't open it, we will open it for you." He opened the door against my wishes, and four men came in, and my husband was told to put on his clothes. . . . I begged them to let Mr. Wilkinson stay with me, saying that I was sick and helpless, and could not stay by myself. My husband also asked them to let him stay with me until he could get some one to wait on me; told them that he would not run off, but would be there the next day, or whenever called for. The old man . . . looked at me and then around at the children, and replied, "You have neighbors." I said, "So I have, but they are not here, and I cannot go for them." The old man replied, "It matters not," and told him to get ready. My husband wanted to put on his boots and get ready, so as to be protected from the damp and night air, but they wouldn't let him. They then took my husband away. One of them came back and took two saddles; I asked him what they were going to do with him, and he said, "Take him a prisoner to the camp. . . ."

After they were gone, I thought I heard my husband's voice. . . . [I] went to the door, and all was still.[17]

"Wilkinson was taken and marched some distance south of his house," Townsley recalled. "[He was] slain in the road with a . . . sword by one of the younger Browns. After he was killed his body was dragged out to one side and left."[18]

Moving south one mile, the murderers waded Pottawatomie Creek at Dutch Henry's Crossing. Upon climbing a steep bank, they stood before the home of James Harris.

[A]bout two a.m., while my wife and child and myself were in bed . . . we were aroused by a company of men who said they belonged to the Northern army. . . . They came into the house and approached the bedside where we were lying, and ordered us, together with three other men who were in the same house with me, to surrender; that . . . it would be no use for us to resist. . . . When they came up to the bed, some had drawn sabres in their hands, and some revolvers. They then took into their possession two rifles and a bowie-knife . . . and afterwards ransacked the whole establishment in search of ammunition. They then took one of these three men, who were staying in my house, out. . . . He came back. They then took me out, and asked me if there were any more men about the place. I told them there were not. . . . They asked me if I had ever taken any hand in aiding proslavery men in coming to the Territory of Kansas, or had ever taken any hand in the last troubles at Lawrence; they asked me whether I had ever done the Free State party any harm, or ever intended to do that party any harm. . . . They then said if I would answer no to all the questions which they had asked me, they would let me loose.[19]

Not surprisingly, Harris did indeed answer no to all the lethal questions. One of his guests, William Sherman, was not as lucky. "[We] marched him down into the Potawatomie Creek [*sic*]," concluded James Townsley, "where he was slain with swords by Brown's two youngest sons, and left lying in the creek." [20]

At last, it was over. Like some evil mist, Brown and his band dissolved with the dawn, leaving in their wake shattered wives and children to stumble upon the corpses of fathers and sons. Word of the atrocity raced along the Pottawatomie. Within hours, horror-struck proslavery settlers had cleared the valley "almost entirely," fleeing the midnight monsters moving in their midst—monsters who not only massacred innocent men and boys before the eyes of their screaming families but who also "chopped them into inches." [21]

Like a violent earth tremor, shock waves of terror rolled over the border. While many southern settlers fled the territory without a backward glance, not a few free-soilers, fearing retaliation, packed their bags and left as well. For those who remained, life became a horrifying hour-by-hour ordeal. "I never lie down," one proslavery man admitted, "without taking the precaution to fasten my door, and fix it in such a way that if it is forced open, it can be opened only wide enough for one person to come in at a time. I have my rifle, revolver, and . . . pistol where I can lay my hand on them in an instant, besides a hatchet & axe." [22]

"Osawatomie is in much fear & excitement . . . ," reported a resident from that New England colony. "All work is nearly suspended, the women are in constant fear." [23]

"All here is excitement and confusion," echoed a dweller in Paola to the north. [24]

When details of the slaughter reached the largest town in the territory, Leaven-worth, the "already crazed" population were swept by a fury of hate and revenge. George Washington Brown later spoke with a woman there.

> She said a body of armed men marched through the streets, visiting each dwelling, and ordered every Free-State man, woman, and child to go at once to the levee. They would not allow her even to close her house; but with her children she was marched to the river, where she found hundreds of others. All were forced upon a steamer lying at the levee, including her husband, whom she found there. The Captain was ordered to take these involuntary passengers to Alton [Illinois] and there leave them. [25]

Still a captive in the city, Charles Robinson counted his life not in hours, but seconds. "It was all that active proslavery men . . . could do to save him from violent death," Brown continued. "Indeed, the people were wrought up to such a furious frenzy that his death was expected at any moment." [26]

Wild with excitement, those downriver in Kansas City were whipped to madness with each new report. "The killing of the five men, harrowing enough in its true details," declared a witness, "was magnified as to numbers and exaggerated in atrocity as the rumors were repeated. . . . With every fresh rumor the papers were issuing inflammatory extras. These were scattered throughout the crowds and on the steamboats as they landed. . . ."²⁷

Despite the distance, anger was fully as great at Atchison. Raged John Stringfellow:

> The abolitionists shoot down our men without provocation wherever they meet them. Let us retaliate in the same manner. A free fight is all we desire. If murder and assassination is the programme of the day, we are in favor of filling the bill. Let not the knives of the Pro-slavery men be sheathed while there is one Abolitionist in the Territory. As they have shown no quarter to our men, they deserve none from us. Let our motto be written in blood upon our flags, *"Death to all Yankees and Traitors in Kansas!"*²⁸

Though troops from Forts Leavenworth and Riley were dispatched to prevent civil war, bands of guerrillas from both sides cautiously began hunting one another. For a great many men, the reins that had held them in check during the past two years were now let slip, and the war so long talked about opened in earnest. Those in the middle—that great body of quiet, indifferent individuals who had not taken a stand on either side—were first to suffer.

"[I]n such a conflict there cannot be and will not be any neutrals recognized," warned John Stringfellow prophetically. " 'He that is not for us is against us' will of necessity be the motto; and those who are not willing to take either one side or the other are the most unfortunate men in Kansas. . . ."²⁹

When free-staters came calling, Martin Bourne suddenly discovered that he was just such an "unfortunate man."

> I own slaves, and have a crop of corn and wheat growing. Have never taken any active part with the proslavery party. . . . These men said I must leave in a day or two, or they would kill me. . . . I left for fear of my life and the lives of my family. They said that the war was commenced, that they were going to fight it out, and drive the proslavery people out of the Territory. . . .³⁰

Standing in Joab Bernard's store two days after the massacre, John Miller was another who found out firsthand that his middle ground had vanished.

> [A] party of thirteen men came to the store on horseback, armed with Sharp's [*sic*] rifles, revolvers, and bowie-knives. They inquired for Mr. Bernard. I told them that he had gone to Westport. One of them said to me, "You are telling a God damned lie," and drew up his gun at me. . . .

They called for such goods as they wanted, and made Mr. Davis and myself hand them out, and said if we "didn't hurry" they would shoot us. . . . After they had got the goods . . . they packed them upon their horses and went away. . . . They on the next day came back with a wagon, and took the remainder of the goods in the store . . . as well as two fine horses. . . .[31]

Meanwhile, as guerrillas preyed on neutrals, newspaper reporter James Redpath set off in search of the men whose actions had triggered war. After stumbling about for several days, the Englishman finally entered the woods along Ottawa Creek, just south of Palmyra.

[S]uddenly, thirty paces before me, I saw a wild-looking man . . . with half a dozen pistols of various sizes stuck in his belt, and a large Arkansas bowie-knife prominent among them. His head was uncovered; his hair was uncombed; his face had not been shaved for many months. We were similarly dressed—with red-topped boots worn over the pantaloons, a coarse blue shirt, and a pistol-belt. . . .

"Hullo!" he cried, "you're in our camp!"

He had nothing in his right hand—he carried a water-pail in his left; but, before he could speak again, I had drawn and cocked my eight-inch Colt. I only answered . . . "Halt! or I'll fire!" He stopped, and said that . . . he was Frederick Brown, the son of old John Brown; and that I was now within the limits of their camp. After a parley of a few minutes I was satisfied that I was among my friends, put up my pistol, and shook hands with Frederick. He talked wildly, as he walked before me, turning round every minute, as he spoke of the . . . recent affair of Pottawatomie. His family, he said, had been accused of it; he denied it indignantly, with the wild air of a maniac. His excitement was so great that he repeatedly recrossed the creek, until . . . I refused to listen to him until he took me to his father.[32]

Already deemed a "half-wit" by others, young Brown had been driven over the edge by the events of the past few days and the blood on his hands.[33] Unlike Fred Brown, his brother Jason had not been privy to the slaughter; yet when he heard the news, he, too, suffered "the most terrible shock . . . in my life. . . . The thought that it might be true, that my father and his company could do such a thing was terrible. . . ."[34]

Another son innocent of the butchery but who became unhinged by the enormity of the crime was John Jr. As a friend disclosed:

[A]fter intelligence was received in camp of the massacre . . . John . . . immediately mounted his horse, in the greatest possible excitement, ordered his company to disband, and rode towards Osawatomie. . . . The reports of the awful murder of his neighbors, the consciousness that his father . . . had been guilty of that terrible outrage, and the treatment he received at Osawatomie from his own political friends, crazed him. He sought the woods, and wandered about for days, with only an occasional gleam of recollection. He became tangled in the brushwood, waded streams, some-times out upon the open prairie, and imagining crowds pursuing him. . . . A severe storm of rain and lightning came on, and he thought, in the flashes, he could see his pursuers.[35]

When Fred Brown finally finished his lunatic ravings, Redpath followed him through the woods.

[A]fter many strange turnings, [he] led me into camp. As we approached it, we were twice challenged by sentries, who suddenly appeared before trees, and as suddenly disappeared behind them. I shall not soon forget the scene that here opened to my view. Near the edge of the creek a dozen horses were tied, all ready saddled for a ride for life.... A dozen rifles and sabres were stacked against the trees. In an open space, amid the shady and lofty woods, there was a great blazing fire with a pot on it; a woman, bareheaded, with an honest, sun-burnt face, was picking blackberries from the bushes; three or four armed men were lying on red and blue blan-kets on the grass; and two fine-looking youths were standing, leaning on their arms, on guard near by. . . . Old Brown himself stood near the fire, with his shirt-sleeves rolled up, and a large piece of pork in his hand.

*James Redpath.* KANSAS STATE HISTORICAL SOCIETY, TOPEKA.

He was cooking a pig. He was poorly clad, and his toes protruded from his boots. The old man received me with great cordiality, and the little band gathered about me. But it was for a moment only; for the Captain ordered them to renew their work.[36]

Another newsman looking for Brown was Henry Clay Pate. Unlike the sympathetic Redpath, however, this *St. Louis Republican* reporter and his proslavery posse were hoping to track the old man down and see him and his bloody band dangling from tree limbs. Ironically, of all the Browns running loose on the land, it was the crazed John Jr. and the hapless Jason who first fell into Pate's hands. After burning their homes near Osawatomie, as well as a store owned by Theodore Weiner, Pate marched the two brothers away.[37] Although he personally felt that death on the spot was a fit reward, when a cavalry column soon overtook his posse, Pate delivered the Browns and other free-state prisoners into federal custody. The culprits were led away in chains, "like a gang of galley slaves," and the posse set off once more in search of Old Brown.[38]

On Saturday night, May 31, Pate and his twenty-five men reached the Santa Fe Road and bivouacked in a grove near the hamlet of Black Jack. The following day six scouts were sent prowling west toward Palmyra. When the riders reached the village and found it deserted, they paused to plunder the homes before moving on to nearby Prairie City.[39]

George Griffith and his wife were attending church in Prairie City, listening to the words of the parson.

[D]uring the course of his sermon an excitement in the congregation suddenly broke out. Many men jumped up and ran for their guns which they had deposited in the corner as they came in. . . . [O]n going to the door I saw six men riding up, armed and in line. . . . [W]hen the men rushed out with their guns cocked four of these men surrendered, but two in the rear turned and fled as fast as their horses could run, with bullets from our churchmen's guns tearing up the dust in their front, rear and sides. . . .[40]

From the prisoners Griffith and the rest learned of Pate's proximity and immediately sent word to John Brown. When the old man and a handful of fighters arrived that evening, Samuel Shore and nineteen others joined, and together the Northerners set off in search of the Southerners.[41]

"We were out all night, but could find nothing of them until about six o'clock next morning . . . ," Brown later wrote. "[W]e prepared to attack them at once, on foot, leaving Frederick and one of Captain Shore's men to guard the horses. As I was much older than Captain Shore, the principal direction of the fight devolved on me. We got to within about a mile of their camp before being discovered by their scouts, and then moved at a brisk pace. . . ." [42]

According to abolitionist August Bondi:

Captain Brown called out, "Now follow me" and down hill he and his company started in a run. We had not yet come down half the hill when we were greeted with shots of the Missouri pickets [and] at the same time we heard the guns of Shore's men replying behind us. Soon the Missourians sent whole volleys against us, but on charged Brown's company; when we arrived at the foot of the hill we saw before us the old Santa Fe road. . . . Captain Brown jumped into the old washed out trail and commanded "Halt, Down." His companions followed his example; now we saw that not a man of Captain Shore's company, except for Captain Shore himself, had followed down hill. Most of them had already disappeared, a few were yet on the brow of the hill wasting ammunition and very soon those also retired in the direction of their comrades. [43]

Now outnumbered two to one, the grim old man decided to dig in rather than retreat. "Captain Brown passed continually up and down the line," remembered Bondi, "sometimes using his spy glass to inspect the enemy's position and repeatedly cautioning his men against wasting ammunition." [44]

Having seen enough of war himself, Samuel Shore, like his men, soon "got up and dusted." Nevertheless, and despite one of his own men being shot through the lungs and carried to the rear, Brown and his dwindling force continued the fight. By sheer weight of will, the free-staters eventually drove Pate and his posse back into a ravine. Sensing a trap, several Southerners also slipped from the fight, leaving five wounded comrades to roll on the ground in agony. One Missourian received a bullet through the mouth that tore away his upper lip and shattered four teeth. [45]

Wrote August Bondi:

It might have been about nine o'clock in the forenoon when Captain Brown stopped near me and Weiner, and after having looked through his spy glass at the enemy's position for quite a while, he said, "It seems the Missourians have also suffered from our fire, they are leaving one by one, we must never allow this, we must try and surround them, we must compel them to surrender." He then walked down our line, spoke with some of the men and returned with the Moore boys to where Weiner and myself were posted and beckoned us to follow him. . . . [We] ran up a hill south of the Missouri camp. As soon as we had gained a commanding position within two hundred yards of the enemy, Captain Brown ordered the two Moores to aim with their carbines at horses and mules exclusively. . . . The Moore boys with four shots killed two mules and two horses which we could perceive created great consternation in the Missouri camp and we saw several leaving.

Now Captain Brown drew and cocked his revolver, and declared that he would advance some twenty yards by himself and if then he would wave his hat, we should follow. . . .[46]

Before the charge could begin, however, Brown's unbalanced son, Fred, galloped over the prairie in full view of both parties. "Father, we have them surrounded and have cut off their communications," the boy screamed deliriously as he swung his sword in the air. The strain of battle followed by the strange apparition was simply too much for Pate.[47] From the ravine a white flag went up, and the Missourians marched out to surrender.

It was only then, when the bloody and beaten Border Ruffians were disarmed, that they learned to their horror into whose hands they had fallen. Much to the prisoners' great surprise and relief, though, they were given water, had their wounds attended to, and were "kindly treated" in general. Soon, some captives even felt safe enough to engage in banter. Remembered free-stater Luke Parsons:

I said to [a wounded Southerner] as he lay in the grass: "You had better let me have those spurs as you wont need them any more." He said: "You will have to take them off." I stooped down and took one off, and asked him where the other was. He replied: "I go on the principle that if one side of the horse goes, the other must; if you will adopt this plan, you wont need but one."[48]

Nevertheless, as he was led from Black Jack and spent the following days under Brown's watchful eyes, there was never a doubt in Henry Pate's mind that the fate of him and his men hung by a thread.

Brown told me he would take the life of a man as quick as he would that of a dog. . . . He said if a man stood between him and what he considered right, he would take his life as cooly as he would eat his breakfast. . . . Always restless, he seems never to sleep. With an eye like a snake, he looks like a demon.[49]

Luckily for Pate and his companions, Col. Edwin Sumner and a column of U.S. cavalry—which included a daring young officer, Lt. J. E. B. Stuart—soon overtook Brown and forced the release of his prisoners. And just as fortunate for Brown's band, Sumner that same day dispersed a body of over two hundred Border Ruffians who were bearing down on the abolitionists.[50] Successful on this occasion, the outmanned military found itself wholly unable to deal with a guerrilla situation that grew more serious daily. Indeed, while trying to rescue a proslavery family south of Lawrence, a squad of soldiers were themselves fired upon by free-staters, and one of the troopers was severely wounded.[51]

As Brown and his followers spread terror along the Marais des Cygnes, other Northerners were fighting back on the Kaw. Two days after Black Jack, on June 4, a company of Lawrence men staged a predawn raid on nearby Franklin. After "riddling" the town with bullets and injuring several defenders, including one who soon died, the attackers were at last beaten back by a cannon loaded with nails.[52]

Three days after the fight at Franklin, a large force of Missourians rode into Osawatomie. Though horses and guns were rounded up and a few trifles were taken, the raiders, to the surprise of all, soon remounted and left. When a townsman later read reports of the raid in eastern newspapers, he was dumbstruck. "[T]hey seem like accounts of different events," he admitted.[53] Wrote one imaginative "eyewitness," one who had never set foot in Kansas, much less Osawatomie:

> There were but few men in town, and the women and children were treated with the utmost brutality. . . . Even rings were rudely pulled from the ears and fingers of the women, and some of the apparel from their persons. . . . Having completely stripped the town, they set fire to several houses. . . . There are hundreds of well-authenticated accounts of the cruelties practised by this horde of ruffians; some of them too shocking and disgusting to relate. . . . The tears and shrieks of terrified women folded in their foul embrace failed to touch a chord of mercy in their brutal hearts; and the mutilated bodies of murdered men hanging upon the trees, or left to rot upon the prairies or in the deep ravines, or furnish food for vultures and wild beasts, told frightful stories of brutal ferocity, from which the wildest savages might have shrunk with horror.[54]

Because of incredible tales such as the above, as well as the fierce propaganda of James Redpath, Sara Robinson, and others, hundreds of outraged free-state fighters were determined to reach the territory and enter the fray. Border Ruffians, however, were just as determined to keep them out. The Missouri River, already closed to arms, was now shut entirely to Northerners with no visible means of support. Hundreds of abolitionists who tried to run the gauntlet were halted at Waverly, Lexington, Kansas City, Leavenworth, and Weston and shipped back down the river. One large group from Chicago that thought it had an "understanding" with a sympathetic steamboat owner soon learned otherwise. Grumbled a member of the party:

By some misunderstanding that arrangement had failed to be effected, and we found ourselves on board of a Border Ruffian steamer, manned by a Border Ruffian crew from captain to deck-hands, and in company with a large number of Border Ruffian passengers. . . . [B]efore we were hardly aware of it, the [main] cabin was filled from one end to the other by many of the best citizens of Lexington, intermingled by a number of the most fiendish devils the infernal regions ever puked up.[55]

With three brass cannons trained on the craft, there was no question of resistance.[56] Another group of Northerners miraculously advanced all the way to Leavenworth only to fall just short when a mob, led by the ax-wielding city postmaster, greeted them on the levee. "[I'll] kill any God Damn Yankee who dares land from the Steam Boat," threatened the murderous official.[57]

After witnessing one abolitionist band after another being turned back thusly, Robert Kelley of the *Squatter Sovereign* at last exploded.

We do not fully approve of sending these criminals back to the East to be reshipped to Kansas—if not through Missouri, [then] through Iowa and Nebraska. We think they should meet a traitor's death, and the world could not censure us if we, in self-protection, have to resort to such ultra measures. We are of the opinion, if the citizens of Leavenworth City or Weston would hang one or two boat loads of abolitionists it would do more toward establishing peace in Kansas than all the speeches that have been delivered in Congress during the present session. *Let the experiment be tried.*[58]

As Kelley intimated, many free-soilers who failed to reach Kansas by water turned their sights north to Iowa and Nebraska and the slower but surer land route. By the first of July, only a trickle of emigrants had entered the territory via the trail but hundreds now viewed it as their only option. Fearful of soon being trampled by numbers, the desperate proslavery party of Kansas again beseeched the South.

"Heaven and earth are being moved in all the Free States to induce overwhelming armies to march here to drive us from the land," ran one such appeal. "We are able to take care of those already here, but let our brethren in the States take care of the outsiders—watch them, and if our enemies march for Kansas, let our friends come along to take care of them, and if nothing but a fight can bring about peace, let us have a fight that will amount to something."[59]

Though relief from the Deep South was slow in coming, aid from neighboring Missouri could always be counted on. "For many days the ferry-boat had been plying busily backwards and forth across the river, bringing over the Clay County boys," noted Sara Robinson from Kansas City when she returned to rejoin her imprisoned husband. "As they landed . . . ," Sara continued, never letting slip an opportunity to cut the enemy, "I saw their besotted, rough, unintelligent faces. . . . The intellectual was blotted out, the animal, the sensual part of human nature alone remaining. . . . Every day at Westport armed bands of infuriated, drunken men, were marshalled in the streets." [60]

Together with their comrades in Kansas, the Border Ruffians moved to smash the revolt and run the remaining rebel leaders to earth. After skulking from one hiding place to the next, ex-Governor Andrew Reeder finally fled the border clad as a woodchopper. Although Albert Searle, too, made an escape, his flight was not without adventure. Creeping quietly into Kansas City just prior to the proslavery march on Lawrence in May, the free-soil militia leader finally found a haven at a riverfront inn.

"On June 5 the mob searched every room in the hotel for free-state men . . . ," the culprit recalled. "I escaped by being in my sister's room, secreted between the mattresses of her bed, she lying on the outside feigning sickness. . . ." [61]

It was getting to be very uncomfortable quarters for me, and on June 6 I left there with Martin Gaylord, intending to return to Lawrence . . . by traveling in the woods on the south side of the Kansas river. . . . We got lost and came out to the edge of the prairie, near the Quaker mission, about ten miles from Kansas City, and attempted to cross the California road and reach the mission. The first thing we knew we were met by a gang of fifteen or twenty Border Ruffians and captured, almost on the very spot where I had spent the first night I camped on Kansas soil. . . .

In the confusion caused by our capture, the following is in subtance the language addressed to us: "Where do you live? Where are you from? What are your politics? How much money did that damned Emigrant Aid Company give you to come out here? What the hell did you come here for? Did you come to make Kansas a free state? Why didn't you go to Nebraska . . . ?" After other profanity they called out: "The rope, boys; the rope! Let's hang the God damn Yankees. . . ." Arrangements were being made for hanging us, and I expected to be hung as much as I ever expected anything, but on searching me preparatory to hanging they found a quart bottle of good whisky in my coat pocket. . . . I asked them to take a drink, which they did, after insisting that I should drink first, which under the existing circumstances I was very willing to do. . . . One of the men, who seemed to be a leader and quite an intelligent looking fellow, and one who had been eyeing me very closely, at once claimed to recognize me. . . . He said he believed I was a gentleman . . . and that my whisky was good and I should not be hung. . . . [Later that night] he shook hands, and, bidding us good night, told us to "get"—and we "got."

Gaylord, who was religiously inclined . . . objected to my profanity, even in this trying ordeal, and said our escape was very "providential." I did not think Providence had anything to do with the matter, and claimed that our escape was due to the whisky, a little lying, some profanity and our good luck.[62]

Meanwhile, those free-state leaders who had not slipped the net were herded to Lecompton and prison. Selected as the site for the territorial capital, Lecompton lay cradled among the woods and bluffs midway between Topeka and Lawrence. "[C]omposed of a few dwelling-houses, many land-offices, and multitudenous whiskey saloons," the southern stronghold on the Kaw catered to a roving host of lawyers, loafers, and adventurers who drank and brawled a little or a lot on a daily basis.[63] Joining Charles Robinson and other prisoners in Lecompton was George Washington Brown, who was led through town by a band of Border Ruffians.

"[T]he streets were filled with the cowardly desperadoes," said the editor, "who, as we passed, cried out: 'There is that God damned abolitionist Brown, of the *Herald of Freedom*. Shoot him! Shoot him! Why don't you shoot the damned nigger thief? Loan me a gun, and I'll shoot him.'"[64]

Fearing the drunken rabble might do just that, especially when details of the Pottawatomie bloodbath were made known, U.S. Marshal Donelson promised to place arms in the prisoners' hands the moment a mob appeared.[65] Despite the well-grounded fears, however, and despite Sara Robinson's tearful appeal to the East stating that her husband was suffering "in durance vile," the prisoners were treated surprisingly well. "[T]he people of Lawrence came in carriage-loads to see the 'traitors' . . . ," as Sara herself admitted. "They came bringing books, strawberries, gooseberries, figs, lemons, prunes, ice-creams, and early vegetables. . . . [N]one came empty-handed."[66] In addition to holding regular church services and choir practice, the prisoners were guarded only loosely and allowed considerable freedom as the days of their captivity passed.[67] All the same, caught in an unstable situation, surrounded by drunken Border Ruffians, the captives' lot was a precarious one. Another name added to the growing list of prisoners was that of John Brown Jr.

"He became an occupant of my tent, and remained with me some time after he was brought into camp . . . ," remembered editor Brown. "[H]is mind seemed continually running on the Potawatomie [*sic*] massacre. . . . During the entire period he was with us . . . whenever that event was mentioned in his hearing his eyes would flash and sparkle like a mad man's. He would exhibit the wildest excitement, and express himself in the severest terms at the enormity of the outrage." Because it was rumored Old Brown would attempt to rescue his demented son, orders were issued to kill the captives in case of attack.[68]

Despite the chaos in Kansas, and the clear warnings of both federal and territorial governments, the leaderless rebel legislature, as planned, began assembling in early July at its capital, Topeka. Dismayed that the thousands of free-state fighters had not materialized as promised, those in the territory responded with alacrity to the military summons.[69]

"[M]en are crowding into Topeka by hundreds . . . ," exulted Cyrus K. Holliday on July 2.[70]

"[N]ot to celebrate their independence," a comrade continued the same day, "but to win it."[71]

Another man fired by the notion of igniting a second American revolution on July 4 was John Brown. Since the battle at Black Jack, he and his men had remained almost constantly on the move, dodging dragoons and Border Ruffians alike. "We have, like David of old, had our dwelling with the serpents of the rocks and wild beasts of the wilderness," wrote Brown to his wife in New York.[72]

*John Brown Jr.* KANSAS STATE HISTORICAL SOCIETY, TOPEKA.

"Our clothes readily showed the effects of [the] bushwhacking business . . . ," August Bondi added. "[W]e had come down to wearing ideas, suspicions and memories of what had once been coats, pants and hats. . . ."[73]

Ragged though they were when they neared Topeka, Brown and his band were eager to close with the foe, "and fight, if necessary, even the United States troops."[74] As the old man hinted, the possibility of a clash between federal soldiers and free-soil rebels grew with each passing day. With orders from Governor Shannon to scatter the Topeka outlaws, "peacefully, if you can, forcibly if necessary," Edwin Sumner, with five companies of cavalry and two field pieces, reached the town on July 3, then bivouacked on the outskirts.[75]

The following day, Topeka was astir with ominous excitement. A cannon shot from the nearby army camp announced the dawning of America's eightieth anniversary, and from windows and rooftops the colorful national flag floated on the breeze. "Some half a dozen military companies, in handsome uniform, paraded about," penned a participant. "Ladies promenaded, with little banners flying from their parasols. . . . In spite of the apparent indifference, many hearts throbbed anxiously for . . . [i]t was well known that nearly all the military force in Kansas was concentrated within a few hundred yards in Topeka. . . ."[76]

While a band filled the morning air with patriotic tunes and women presented to one of the militia companies a flag inscribed OUR LIVES FOR OUR RIGHTS, inside the capitol scores of men went through the motions of exercising self-government. Sam Walker was there.

> Fiery speeches were made and grand resolutions passed. They would willingly die on the altar of freedom, but would never retreat or surrender. One fine speaker was especially eloquent and brave. He soared aloft like the eagle, and in words of burning patriotism exclaimed: "The eyes of the world are upon us. We represent a great cause, and must be true to it. I know not what others may do, but as for me, I will never leave this hall except at the point of the bayonet."[77]

"It was nearly twelve o'clock," another man recounted; "the sun was blazing down, and the thermometer stood at 100, when we learned that Col. Sumner . . . [was] approaching Topeka in full military array."

> The street was filled with a crowd, among whom were many ladies and children, when Col. Sumner appeared with his forces, rapidly debouching into Kansas Avenue. With great rapidity and considerable military skill he threw his men forward, and by rapid orders, shouted in a stern, shrill voice, formed his companies into the strongest form they could occupy for

their service. . . . On the one hand, the armed and uniformed dragoons, with flashing sabres; on the other, only two Topeka companies, with their two banners. . . . While the dragoons approached, the band was playing, but the drummers continued to drum until the drumsticks nearly touched the noses of the advancing horses of the dragoons. . . . One little boy was beating the kettle-drum, and rattled it manfully, never turning to look at the dragoons. . . . The two pieces of artillery were planted about a hundred yards up the street. They were said to be loaded with grape. The slow-match was lighted.[78]

For the next several moments the two sides stared at one another—a rash move on the one hand or a foolish word on the other could precipitate a bloody clash between the rebels and the U.S. Government. When no aggressive acts were forthcoming from the free-soilers, Col. Sumner boldly dismounted and stalked into the legislative hall.

"Gentlemen," announced the antislavery officer to the assembly, "I am called upon this day to perform the most painful duty of my whole life. Under the authority of the President's proclamation, I am here to disperse this Legislature, and therefore inform you that you cannot meet. I therefore order you to disperse. . . . I shall use all the forces in my command to carry out my orders." [79]

As Sam Walker later revealed, however, Sumner's words echoed in a nearly empty chamber.

The legislature was . . . not there to hear the order. It was gone, all gone. . . . And the orators, where were they? Ask of the corn-fields and hazel brush that for miles around concealed their quivering forms. . . . The member who had been speaking when Sumner came up made his exit through a back window, jumping fifteen feet to the ground, and through the dust of his exodus could dimly be seen in the far distance a flying coat tail and a pair of heels punishing the ground forty-five strokes a second.[80]

"[T]hus the Topeka government was brought to an end . . . ," ran Sumner's report on the affair. "They had the good sense to yield at once. . . ." [81]

Though the colonel was naturally pleased with the outcome, others were outraged. "A few goddamned white-livered lawyers succeeded in getting through a resolution . . . not to molest or hinder the U. S. troops," fumed John Lawrie, a Hoosier who had come west solely to fight slavery. "[D]amn and curse lawyers and professional politicians. . . ." [82] And John Brown, lurking all day along the steaming banks of Shunganunga Creek, waiting for a chance to kill soldiers, also rode from Topeka in utter disgust. Indeed, as others drifted dejectedly from the town, there was a feeling that the fledgling free-state government had been crushed for all time.

"Her legislature was dispersed by federal troops; her leading men were languishing in prison," one dispirited Northerner lamented. "The Missouri River was closed to emigrants from the free states, and the tedious uncertain route through Iowa was menaced. . . ." To this writer, at least, the situation seemed hopeless.

One voice was yet to be heard from, however—a voice that could inspire others to action like no other Kansan. Whereas patience and politics and preaching and prayers had failed, he would now give war a try, serious war. Jim Lane was coming to Kansas . . . and a storm was coming with him.

## CHAPTER EIGHT

# THE DOGS OF WAR

AT THE CONCLUSION OF HIS FIERY, TORCHLIT TOUR OF THE NORTH, JAMES LANE left the cities where he spoke in a flame for "Free Soil, Free Men, Free Kansas, and Fremont." State and national Kansas committees sprang up overnight; thousands upon thousands of dollars were raised, and more importantly, hundreds of eager recruits poured into Chicago prior to embarking for the territory. When the boats of the initial parties were stopped on the Missouri River, most turned back to Illinois for another try.[1]

By early July 1856, Lane's "Army of the North," as it was called, came streaming across the overland route through Iowa and Nebraska. True to its name, the march resembled an invading army, with officers, uniforms, flags, cannons, and scores of baggage wagons. Although generally well equipped, the various companies received contributions of supplies and arms as they moved west. At Iowa City, while Governor James Grimes obligingly looked the other way, abolitionists raided the state arsenal and carted off several loads of weapons.[2]

"In three weeks," reported another company from Mt. Pleasant, Iowa, "we had thirty or forty wagons and teams loaded with powder, lead, provisions and arms, and 300 men had come into camp, mostly active young men wanting to go to Kansas to make it a free state."[3]

Though many—maybe most—of Lane's followers were indeed "active young men" aflush with idealism, a large number were mere mercenaries who came for pay and plunder.[4] "Seventy-five drunken rowdies from . . . Chicago, passed through our town, accompanied with a quota of *nymph du pave* on their way to Kansas," noted one Illinois editor in disgust. "This gang of bawdy-house bullies were uniformed like a crew of pirates. . . . A more ruffianly looking gang we have never seen before."[5]

143

After witnessing another company pass his own window, a Nebraska journalist agreed.

> Each man carried a bowie-knife, a revolver, a pair of breeches, a shirt and
> a very don't-care a damn expression. . . . The stews and brothels, the hospitals
> and poor-houses of the East can furnish thousands more of just such scaby,
> scurvy, scape-goats, who will rejoice in a fancy jaunt to Kansas.
>    We are in favor of Kansas becoming a Free State, we hope it will. But
> if freedom has so far fallen from her high estate, that she has to use such men,
> such means, and such measures as are now being employed . . . to disgrace
> the name of Freedom, then indeed, have the American people mistaken the
> character of their patron saint. . . . We believe that the very worst type of
> men from the North are in Kansas, and that they have the pleasure of
> meeting there the very worst rowdies of the South. The two armies in
> Kansas are composed of the dregs of the respective parties. . . . [6]

Although federal troops and Kansas militiamen tried to halt the invasion at the
Nebraska line, the forces deployed were either too far east or too far west, and the way
into the territory lay wide open.[7] By early August some of the first recruits in Lane's
army began spilling into the territory. One group that joined Lane in Nebraska was
the band led by John Brown. Sam Walker and his hard-pressed squad also made the
trip north. When he and his men finally spotted Lane, they "nearly went wild over
him." Leaving those who yet followed to open a road into Kansas, build bridges,
and fortify strategic points, Lane, Brown, and Walker set off south.[8] When the latter
revealed that Lawrence free-staters were boldly assailing Southern settlements near
Osawatomie almost as they spoke and a similar assault was planned for Franklin
in a few days, Lane put spurs to his mount. In Walker's words:

> [H]e said we must get down there by the next night. The streams were full
> and no fords. Lawrence was 150 miles away. . . . Our party now consisted
> of about thirty persons. . . . Accordingly we struck out for Lawrence,
> Lane leading. All that night he pushed on, halting a little just before
> morning to let the horses graze. The boys threw themselves upon the grass,
> and were soon fast asleep. Brown himself went some distance from the
> camp, sat down with his back to a tree and his rifle across his knees, and
> also went to sleep. When Lane got ready to go ahead he directed me to
> go and awaken Brown. I found the old man asleep . . . and not thinking
> of danger, I put my hand on his shoulder. Quick as lightning he was on
> his feet, with his rifle at my breast. I struck up the muzzle of his gun not

a second too soon, as the charge passed over my shoulder, burning the cloth of my coat. Thereafter I never approached Brown when he was sleeping, as that seemed to be his most wakeful time.[9]

With Lane setting a mad pace over the rain-soaked prairie, exhausted riders began dropping out one by one. Walker continued:

At about ten o'clock that night we reached the Kansas River, opposite Topeka, our party having been reduced to six. . . . We could not cross the river by ferry, as the ferryman lived up in Topeka. The only chance left was to ford. My horse was the only one able to swim across with its rider. The others refused to swim and one was mired in the quicksand. Lane and Charlie Stratton swam over. Going into town we three got something to eat, the first we had since leaving Nebraska City.[10]

After bolting down their food and jotting out a note to the Lecompton prisoners, offering to raid the camp and release them if they but said the word, the frenetic free-staters were back in the saddle.[11] Sam Walker:

Lane and Stratton got fresh horses and we started for Lawrence, though it was raining as hard as it could. Before I reached my home I fell off my horse three times from the effects of hunger and fatigue. Each of the three times Lane helped me to my saddle again. On reaching home I could go no further. Stratton continued two miles before he gave up; and Lane went into Lawrence alone, reaching there at three o'clock in the morning [August 11].[12]

After the aborted attack in June, the Lawrence militia was determined to clear nearby Franklin from the board once and for all. Not only was the hamlet a Border Ruffian rendezvous and a continual thorn in the side of its neighbors, but rumors hinted, and spies confirmed, that a desperately needed fieldpiece—one of those used to batter the Free State Hotel in May—was stored somewhere in the town.[13] Buoyed by the thought that reinforcements were pouring down from Nebraska, heartened that their old militia general had returned, the Northerners swung to the attack.

At eleven P.M. on August 12, roughly eighty free-staters took up positions around Franklin. Only fourteen Southerners were in town that night, and these quickly sought shelter in a log hotel. "They sent one of their men up to demand our arms," a proslavery defender declared. "Our Captain . . . replied that he would not give them up, and called his men . . . and they all said they would die before the abolitionists should have them. The abolitionists then surrounded the house and commenced to fire upon it, which our men returned."[14]

For several hours the sniping continued with little effect on either side, although one free-stater was killed and a handful of each party were badly wounded. Mysteriously, even though he and a few friends watched from a safe distance, Lane took no part in the fight.[15] "[H]e occasionally sent to know what we were doing, and told us to blaze away," recalled an increasingly frustrated Thomas Bickerton, who was hoping to make the rumored cannon the centerpiece in his militia battery.[16] Bickerton went on:

> Finally I got tired of lying there, especially as I had nothing but a pistol; so I went over to [Joseph] Cracklin, behind the stable, and told him something must be done, as it was useless to waste ammunition any longer. I proposed getting some hay and setting fire to them. Caleb and Fuller volunteered to go with me, each with a bundle of hay. So we went around to the end of the hotel, on the road, thinking there were no windows there, where they could see us. But just as we got within reach of their guns, they began to fire on us. . . . I found an empty wagon, which we loaded up with dry hay. Minister Fuller, a brave little man, volunteered [to] take hold one side of the tongue of the wagon, while I took the other side, giving him these directions: "Now, Fuller, if I am shot down, kick me out of the way and go on with the wagon; and if you are shot I will serve you the same way. . . ." [S]everal others volunteered to push it from behind. Just as we landed on the front doorsteps, down came a volley from the chamber, just over our heads, throwing the dirt into our faces and eyes. . . . We then went around behind the wagon, and found two of our men still there, one of whom had a wisp of hay already lighted, from which we set the load on fire on all sides.[17]

"[O]ur boys commenced singing out 'There she goes!' 'There goes the roof!' 'Stand off, boys, maybe there's powder in it!' " recounted another free-soiler, John Lawrie. "By and by it began to work on the garrison, and they screamed out 'Quarter! Quarter! Quarter!' I spoke out pretty loud, 'They are calling for water.' 'No,' said they, 'Quarters! Quarters! for God's sake, give us Quarters!'"[18] Returning to Thomas Bickerton:

> We entered the front door just in time to see our opponents leaving by the back one. We immediately drew away the wagon from the house, and turned it over, and saved both it and the house from destruction. Over

the floor of the house were strewn United States muskets in profusion, while in one corner of the room we found the object of our search. . . .[19]

"Some of the men fell upon the cannon and kissed it," laughed a witness.[20]

While the joyous free-soilers busied themselves looting the town and securing several prisoners who failed to escape, the wife of one captive, fearing he was about to be murdered, ran screaming to his side.

"Oh, don't shoot my husband—don't shoot him!" the woman sobbed.

"He deserves to die;" replied a free-stater; "he is a great villain!"

"I know it," answered the frantic wife; "that's just the reason I don't want him shot."[21]

Even the strain of the previous four hours could not contain the laughter that followed. After handing back the husband to his grateful spouse, the triumphant Northerners turned back to Lawrence with their prized cannon in tow.

Now a captain of artillery, Thomas Bickerton had a cannon but no cannonballs. It then dawned on Bickerton that some of the newspaper type that had been tossed into the river during the sack of Lawrence had been recovered.[22] Related the desperate officer:

G. W. Brown, publisher of the *Herald of Freedom* . . . was a prisoner in Lecompton. I went to Miss Gleason, his clerk, for the type. She said that Brown had left orders not to disturb anything till after his release. . . . I then . . . told her that the walls of the building must come down if I could not get the type without. She began to cry; I told her as much as I disliked to see women cry, I had rather see all the women in Kansas cry than not have the type for bullets. She then gave me the keys to the building. . . . We took the type to a blacksmith's shop . . . [and] soon had over 100 round balls, with canister to match, with match-rope, cartridges, and other implements, all complete.[23]

Two days following Franklin, the free-state force, now grown to five hundred men, struck for the southern stronghold on Washington Creek. Learning of the fight from survivors and realizing that their time was nigh, forty-five proslavery settlers hastily erected earthworks here around the log home of James Saunders.[24] Since their arrival on Washington Creek, the emigrants from Georgia and Alabama had lived with threats on a daily basis. "We were warned by the Abolitionists," one Southerner said, "that we must leave or they would kill us, and [they] notified the neighbors that if they helped us they would murder them. For some time we heard of companies and spies of Abolitionists being out in the neighborhood." One such spy had just been executed in the area.[25]

When Lane, John Brown, and the rest of the small army finally drew up at Washington Creek, they paused. Despite the disparity in numbers, the earthworks surrounding Saunders's cabin appeared formidable, and a direct assault seemed doomed to failure. At length, Lane ordered squads of men to scour the farms around the area. In the words of Sam Walker:

> Collecting all the wagons he could get, he had poles cut about as long as a man, and then tied hay to one end of them; placing them in the wagons, it produced the impression that they were filled with men. When we climbed the hills in sight of the fort . . . we made a big show in front with our mounted men behind the wagons, and, still further behind, the men on foot. At a distance it looked like an army of 1200 men. We could see the enemy standing on top of their blockhouse, looking at us.[26]

"[T]he column, as [it] appeared to us," admitted an awestruck defender, "extend[ed] for a mile in length, marching ten abreast."[27]

When he felt the enemy had been sufficiently impressed, Lane finally deployed his men and prepared to charge. "Before a shot was fired," John Lawrie later wrote, "we received the order . . . 'Double quick, forward march!' and the way we put in to it was a caution. We scaled their stockade, rushed across their embanked breastwork and entered the fort in less time than I have been writing. . . ."[28]

"Captain Brown, with his men, was among the first to reach the fort . . . ," noted one of those racing forward.[29] To Brown's surprise, however, he found the works empty and the cabin cleared. Prudently, the Southerners had fled for their lives at the first rush. "We followed on in the wake of the retreating Ruffians," recalled John Lawrie, "charged through two deep ravines, and made the discovery that the enemy knew the country better than we did. . . ."[30]

Meanwhile, those sifting through the cabin found dinner sitting on the table. They also uncovered a large cache of guns, powder, and lead nearby.[31] Sam Walker:

> After the plunder was all gathered up I noticed that something was happening at Mr. Campbell's house, just in sight of the fort. Mr. Campbell was a proslavery man, and owned slaves. Going over to the house, I found a young lady with an ax in her hands, brandishing it, and declaring that she would kill the first one that attempted to enter the house. A number of the men were disputing with her about entering, but they all knew that she would hurt the first one that offered to go in. Coming up, I told her our only object was to search for arms and Border Ruffians—nothing else would be disturbed. She said that I might take one man and search

the house. We found Mrs. Campbell fanning a beautiful young lady, a sister of the one at the door. She was in bed, and apparently had fainted. I asked what was the matter. Her mother said that she was frightened to death. I informed her that I was a good doctor, and could cure her. Reaching under the clothes, I drew out a fine silver-mounted rifle and a navy revolver. The young lady sprang out of bed, threw her arms around my neck, and begged me not to take them, as they belonged to her cousin in Missouri. I told her that she was better off without them, as they had evidently made her very sick.[32]

"In the evening," Walker continued, "Lane called us all together and turned the command over to me, and without another word of explanation or advice of any kind he turned, put spurs to his horse, and galloped away toward Topeka, followed by fifteen men. That was the last we saw or heard of him for a long time. . . . Lane never gave any reason for his strange conduct. . . ."[33] Some, dismayed by his poor showing at Franklin and Washington Creek, were not sad to see Lane and his "bogus military reputation" go. "Lane dresses in men's clothes, but he's far from being one," spit a contemptuous free-soiler.[34] All the same, and as Sam Walker and perceptive others agreed, Lane's ability to fire men into action was worth a regiment.

After torching Saunders's home and outbuildings, the victorious Northerners set off for Lecompton, determined to sweep all Southerners from the territory.[35]

When the white-eyed survivors of Washington Creek reached his spacious log cabin one mile south of the capital, Henry Titus knew what was coming. Since

*The Saunders Farm.* KANSAS STATE HISTORICAL SOCIETY, TOPEKA.

his advent in Kansas, the handsome, swashbuckling Floridian had become a symbol of southern resolve in the Lecompton area. As a consequence, Titus had also become one of the most loved and hated men in the territory. Described by the *New York Tribune* as "a two-legged specimen of savage tigerhood," the big, burly slaver was one of the more conspicuous leaders during the sack of Lawrence. Henry Titus was also—personally, as well as politically—a bitter foe of his neighbor Sam Walker. Regarding the fiery free-stater as little better than a "robber, incendiary and horse thief," Titus offered five hundred dollars to the man who would bring in Walker's head, "on or off his shoulders." [36] And thus, when the huge Southerner heard the news from Franklin and Washington Creek, he knew his wait would not be long.

On the same day as the Saunders affair, Titus led a patrol down the California Road in an effort to locate Walker and his army. Later that evening the two parties collided not far from Walker's home. The fight was short but sharp, and when Titus fled pell-mell, he left one man dead and one captured. Rather than pursue in the dark, Walker wisely went into camp on his claim.[37]

Henry Titus's hatred of Samuel Walker was reciprocated fourfold. The latter's loathing of slavery and anyone associated with it ran deep long before he and his family were kicked off the steamer by hooting Missourians in March 1855. After that event, however, and the humiliating trek to the territory, Sam Walker's fight for a free Kansas became fanatical.

Originally intent on attacking Lecompton first, then doubling back to deal with Titus, Walker changed course when contacts inside the U.S. Army camp three miles southwest of the capital—the same camp in which free-state prisoners were held—warned that the military would fight for the town. Henry Titus was another matter. With many officers, including camp commander Maj. John Sedgwick, in collusion with the free-soilers, Walker was promised a free hand.[38]

"In a conversation with the major some time before," revealed Walker, "he stated that if we could attack and capture Titus before the governor sent orders to him that he would not interfere, but that if he got the orders he would be compelled to stop us." [39] Walker continued:

> All that night I slept but little. . . . Daylight began to break . . . when the stage from Lecompton to Kansas City drove up to the door of my cabin. . . . The driver called me to one side and asked me whether I wanted to take Titus; that if I did now was the time. He said that in the skirmish of the night before Titus's men had become scattered, and that the greater part of them were in Lecompton, thinking that we were coming there. . . . Mounting my horse, I went to the camp and ordered every man that had a horse to follow me; the rest to stay and cook breakfast, and follow . . . us.[40]

After a short ride, Walker's force halted on a ridge overlooking the Titus cabin. In addition to the log home itself, as well as a stable and shed, a group of tents were clustered in a nearby grove. [41]

"I counted [my] men and found there were just fifty," Walker recalled. "I then . . . divided them into three squads. I gave ten men to Capt. Joel Grover, with instructions to get between Titus's Lecompton troops and those of the United States, and allow no messenger to go to the camp. . . . I gave ten men to Captain [Henry] Shombri [*sic*], with instructions to place his men along a fence that ran in front of Titus's house, and about 200 yards from it." [42]

With the balance of his force, Walker ordered a charge and went roaring down on the camp. Except for one man who was shot and killed, the startled Southerners raced from their tents to the cabin. [43] "[T]he moment that we charged the camp Titus was standing in his door," Walker said, "and he called to his men to come into the house. Shombri, seeing the move, mounted his men and dashed up to the door of the . . . house. There were a number of men already in the house taking aim through port-holes. When Shombri had advanced to within six feet of them they fired, and . . . wounded every man but one." [44] Shot through the stomach, Henry Shombre was one of the first hit.

"He fell forward but still stayed on his horse," remembered Luke Parsons. "I went to him and led his horse behind the stable and helped him off and set him up against the stable." [45]

"A steady fire was opened on us from the blockhouse . . . ," noted the hardpressed Walker, who suddenly found his force pinned down. "We sheltered ourselves as best we could behind trees, fences, and outhouses, and returned the fire, but in a short time we had eighteen out of the forty now comprising the attacking party wounded." [46]

After assisting the mortally wounded Shombre, Luke Parsons rejoined the fight from the cover of a small tree.

We had to watch for their smoke and then try to work a bullet in between the logs. While behind the tree, a man came to the upstairs gable window, struck it with his gun and knocked out all the glass and most of the sash. He stuck his gun out and fired at me, at the same time I was trying to get my gun in a line with him. But he was in too much of a hurry to get good aim. He then stepped away but another man immediately took his place and leveled his gun on me. I immediately recognized him as Col. Titus and as I had good aim on that very spot before he came I shot first. He dropped his gun, threw up his hands and fell over backward. I then ran to the shed and stood looking over the top of the spring wagon and fired where I saw smoke come out of the cracks of the logs. Here I caught a bullet in my

shin. . . . It was a small ball or it would have broken my leg. I went behind
the stable and pulled off my boot to see how badly I was hurt. The bullet
had flattened out on the bone as large as a dime. I had just got straightened
up when Capt. Walker came up . . . and said: "Parsons why dont you
shoot?" I said "I dont see anything to shoot at." He jumped off his horse
and squatted down behind the buggy and began to fire his revolver.

I could not see a thing to shoot at, except the logs. Finally he laid down
his pistol and said: "Hand me your gun if you are afraid to shoot." I gave
him my gun. He fired and handed it back. I put in another charge and
handed it to him. . . . [47]

According to Walker:

[J]ust as I got the rifle to my shoulder a musket was stuck out of [a] hole.
Both guns were discharged at once. I do not know what effect my shot
had, but I received three buckshot in my breast and a man behind me
got eleven. The shock was hard enough to knock us both down, but the
wounds were not dangerous. The men jumped and picked me up; then
springing up they poured such a hot fire into that hole that there was no
more firing out of it. [48]

In danger now of being overwhelmed himself, Walker sent a rider racing back
to the main column ordering the artillery and infantry forward at full speed. Thomas
Bickerton recalled:

When we were about one-half way there [to Titus's] we saw a horseman . . .
riding toward us in great haste, saying to us that our men were fighting
like devils, and many of them were wounded. We then hurried up as fast as
we could, and soon came in sight of Titus's house. I took my position on the
side of the hill overlooking the house. My men soon partook of the excitement around them, when I ordered them to stop and get cool, and work
the gun as though they were in Lawrence drilling in the presence of the
ladies. After getting the gun loaded, I gave the men these instructions:
"Now, men, if you fire too high you cannot see where the ball strikes;
but if you fire low you can see it strike, and aim her right next time."
Then I took a pretty low aim, and took my position at one side, so as to
be clear of the smoke; then I gave the order to "Let her off easy, men!"
Bang goes the gun, and I clapped my hands and said "Good!" The shot
strikes the ground just this side of the house, and bounds up to the third
log, thundering through it, and on beyond, cutting the limbs from the
trees a half-mile back of the house. [49]

"This is the second edition of the *Herald of Freedom*," the cannon crew yelled as they fired another round. When the balls struck the cabin, recounted an elated free-stater, they sent "plastering and chinking flying at every shot."[50] Inside the home itself, the severely wounded Titus and his men were desperately trying to dodge the deadly missiles. "[T]he balls," Titus later wrote, "[were] going through and through the house, shattering everything in their passage."[51]

Meanwhile, as rain began to fall, the sounds of battle and the booming of the big gun ignited a "universal stampede" in Lecompton, one mile to the north. "The stoutest and most noisy boasters in town rushed to the river," reported one man, "some on foot and others on horseback, and in their fright and hurry jumped into the water to swim across. Governor Shannon . . . was found concealed in the bushes on the river bank."[52]

At the army camp two miles west of Titus's house, there was no doubt about what was occurring just over the rise. "[F]iring was heard near our tents, and one of the cannon balls whizzed past us," recalled Sara Robinson. "Two or three horsemen were standing upon a high hill, a half a mile distant, apparently watching the troops in camp. . . . The bugle-call had sounded, and the troops were soon on their way to Lecompton. At the moment the troops started, the horsemen on the hill disappeared."[53] From another tent in the camp, John Brown Jr. had recovered his reason long enough to pen a letter to his father. "[I]t seems that heaven is

*Henry Titus.* KANSAS STATE HISTORICAL SOCIETY, TOPEKA.

smiling on our arms," he wrote. "[M]ore than two hundred shots have been fired within the past half hour."[54] While Brown and other prisoners were thrilled by the fighting, one man was concerned. "It is easy to commence operations," sagely warned Charles Robinson, "but difficult to stop at the right time & in the right way."[55]

As promised, although Major Sedgwick sent men to stand between the free-staters and the capital, he moved not a muscle to part the contesting foes. While a file of troopers watched on, the unequal fight continued.[56] Though the defenders continued to resist heroically, when a wagon loaded with hay was run up along the house, it proved too much. From the blasted cabin, a white flag appeared.[57] As the free-soilers held their fire, nearly a score of Southerners, including Henry Titus, marched out with their hands up. Sam Walker:

[Titus] was all covered with blood, having received several severe wounds. The moment he was seen a hundred rifles were leveled at his head and he shook like a leaf. Seeing me on my horse he cried, "For God's sake, Walker, save my life! You have a wife and children; so have I. Think of them and save me." He was a pitiable object and his appeal touched me. . . . I took Titus into the stable. The men were intent on his life, and I had to knock one fellow down to keep him from shooting the poor wretch on the spot.[58]

"Titus . . . begged so like a whipped puppy—so cringingly," John Lawrie scoffed, "that he was thought too goddamned mean, too despicable to notice sufficiently to kill him. One of his negroes, who was out at the stable during the fight, said, 'Massa Titus wanted six abolitionists for breakfast! Yah! Yah! Gorra Massy! guess he get his belly full dis monin'!'"[59]

"As soon as we surrendered," recorded Titus, who, in addition to a hideously mutilated hand, had a Sharps rifle ball in the shoulder, "several empty wagons which they brought with them were driven up and they commenced pillaging the premises; they took every movable article of any value . . . [and] even went so far as to take the clothing of my wife. . . . They also told my servants that they were free and advised them to go to Topeka, yet they took the clothing that belonged to them. . . ."[60]

When the looters began torching the home, Titus begged Walker to spare it. "God Damn you, and God Damn your house," the free-stater swore. "Men, bring on the hay."[61] Tossing Titus and his wounded companions into a wagon, the jubilant Northerners left for Lawrence with the cabin and sheds wrapped in flames.

"They came in by way of Mount Oread," gloated an angry witness in Lawrence, "then took a winding path into town, following precisely the trail of the posse, who invaded us on the 21st of last May, when Marshal Titus rode in the front column and seemed bloated with the pride of his position. . . . [Now] he came a wounded prisoner . . . his head resting in the lap of a friend."[62] Another man reminded the gathering crowd that during the sack of Lawrence, Titus had vowed "that if ever he came into the place again he would kill every damned abolitionist in it."[63]

"Our arrival . . . created intense excitement," said Sam Walker. "The citizens swarmed around us, clamoring for the blood of our prisoner." One of those in the snarling mob was John Brown. Another was a Unitarian clergyman. "When I looked on Titus and thought of his part in the proceedings last May . . . ," the minister admitted, "I came very near joining the cry 'Hang him on the spot. . . .' The wretch cowered and pleaded for his life promising to leave the territory."[64]

Sam Walker and cooler heads did prevail, however, and the following day Governor Shannon and Major Sedgwick journeyed to Lawrence and arranged for an exchange of prisoners. But once back in Lecompton, Shannon realized that events were beyond his control. "This place is in a most dangerous and critical situation at this moment," wrote the shaken governor to Maj. Gen. Persifer Smith at Fort Leavenworth.

> We are threatened with utter extermination. . . . I have just returned from Lawrence. . . . I saw in that place at least eight hundred men, who manifested a fixed purpose to demolish this town. I know that they intend an attack. . . . There can concentrate at this place, in a very short time, some fifteen hundred or two thousand men, well armed, with several pieces of artillery. It would seem that the business of "wiping out," as it is called, of the Proslavery party has been commenced. . . . The women and children have been mostly sent across the river, and there is a general panic among the people. The force here is small—say eighty or a hundred dragoons, and some hundred and twenty citizens poorly armed, and badly supplied with ammunition.[65]

The following day Shannon submitted his resignation. "I am unwilling to perform the duties of governor of this territory any longer," he informed President Pierce. "Govern Kansas . . . !" the Ohioan later snorted. "You might as well attempt to govern the devil in hell."[66] Wilson Shannon was not the only person sobered by the sudden turn of events.

> *Platte City Argus* . . . IMPORTANT FROM KANSAS—CIVIL WAR AND REBELLION—WOMEN AND CHILDREN FLYING FROM THEIR HOMES FOR THEIR LIVES! . . . unprovoked, inhuman, and unparelleled attack. . . .

> *Leavenworth Herald* . . . REBELLION! VIOLENCE! MURDER! HOUSEBURNING! BLOODSHED! . . . destroying settlements, destroying crops . . . murdering our citizens!

> *Leavenworth Journal* . . . EXTRA! WAR! WAR! WAR! THE "BLOODY ISSUE BEGUN!" "LET SLIP THE DOGS OF WAR"

With an urgency unlike any time in the past, outraged Missourians marshaled once more in the hope of heading off this latest threat to their way of life.

### Meet at Lexington on Wednesday

Bring your horses, your guns, and your clothing—all ready to go on to Kansas. Let every man who can possibly leave home, go now to save the lives of our friends. . . . We must go *immediately.* There is no time to spare, and no one must hold back. . . . [O]ur motto this time will be, "No quarter" . . . Let no one stay away.[67]

"For more than a week," reported the *Lexington American Citizen,* "our city has been in a state of the most feverish excitement. . . . The streets have been crowded with men, horses and wagons—men armed with bowie-knives, swords, revolvers, shotguns, Sharp's [*sic*] rifles—and the company which left this place for the scene of action, took with them two pieces of artillery—a six and a eight pounder."[68]

At Westport, a traveler watched as armorers busily repaired gun carriages at a wagon shop.

Men might be seen in every direction armed . . . and preparing for the intended rush into the Territory. . . . [A]t Kansas City . . . I perceived that the steam ferry boat was engaged night and day transporting armed men from Platte and Clay counties. I observed that not only the young men were going, but old men stooped with years and gray-haired. Every day some fugitives arrived at Westport, or Kansas [City], who had been driven out by the Abolitionists. These people told their tale of woe, and hourly increased the already excited fury of the "Border Ruffians." Wherever you meet a few men collected together you are sure to hear such expressions as the following—"Clean out the damned set of murderers," "no quarter to the assassins," "Blood for blood. . . ."[69]

"War to the knife and knife to the hilt . . . ," cried the rough and ready *Squatter Sovereign.* "Let the watchword be 'Extermination, total and complete.' " At least one Border Ruffian welcomed these words at their literal worst.

As he sat drinking with friends in Leavenworth, in a rage over recent events, Charles Fugett bet "$5 against a pair of boots" that within two hours he would "lift the hair" of an abolitionist. Encountering a free-stater a few miles from town, Fugett promptly shot the man dead, claimed his trophy, then "flapped the scalp around among comrades boastingly during the night."[70]

"I went out for the scalp of a damned Abolitionist," Fugett yelled, "and I have got one."[71]

While Missourians mustered for the showdown and free-soil forces under Walker, Lane, and others ravaged the countryside, smaller guerrilla bands scoured the land, meting out personal and political "justice." In Coffey and Anderson Counties to the south, the war for the first time was felt. "We have been forcibly ejected and driven from our homes," wrote one terrified group of citizens, "our houses burned, robbed and our crops destroyed and our lives threatened by organized bands of Abolitionists. . . ."[72]

*Free-State Cannon Crew.* KANSAS STATE HISTORICAL SOCIETY, TOPEKA.

Assuming an independent role once again, John Brown led his squad on raids south of Osawatomie, terrorizing southern settlers and collecting "taxes" in the form of horses and cattle.[73] On the morning of August 26, Northerners surprised a band of Border Ruffians and Texans on Middle Creek, eight miles southwest of Osawatomie. One of the free-state leaders, Samuel Anderson, described what happened.

> [B]efore I had my men fairly stationed, the firing commenced. After a few discharges, the enemy were heard with heavy tramp like distant thunder rushing through the timber toward where my men were stationed. When they had reached within about fifty yards of us, we cried loudly for them to halt and surrender. Some turned to the right and others to the left . . . while fourteen in number, of footmen, came forward and surrendered. Many of the horsemen dismounted and left their horses, and passed through the brush on foot and escaped. . . . [A]s they refused to halt, I ordered my men to fire. The effect produced by this fire wounded two men. . . . [74]

While the panic-stricken Southerners scattered over the prairie, "so frightened that they ran their horses almost to death," laughed Anderson, the free-soilers laid claim to the booty, which included dozens of horses, guns, three wagonloads of supplies, and a black flag emblazoned in blood-red letters: VICTORY OR DEATH.[75]

Although he missed the fight himself, John Brown rode down to the creek soon after. When the captives, already "very humble" and dubious of their fate, saw the dreaded terror of the Pottawatomie approaching, they were sure their time had come. On that score, however, they were gratefully deceived. Murderous as the old abolitionist could be, there was also a merciful side to John Brown. One of the prisoners, a Missourian mortally wounded, raised up from the wagon in which he had been placed and asked to see the old man before he died.

"You wish to see me; here I am," Brown announced as he stepped to the wagon. "Take a good look at me, and tell your friends when you get back to Missouri what sort of man you saw."

"I don't see as you are so bad;" whispered the Southerner; "you don't look or talk like it."

Clasping the dying man's hand, Brown's eyes began to moisten. "I thank you," he said softly. "God bless you!"[76]

By late August 1856, an army of perhaps fifteen hundred Missourians led by David Atchison had massed on the state line near Little Santa Fe. When all was ready, Atchison set the militia in motion. As before, the column was a motley assortment of men and boys of all ages and physical conditions, under "little or no discipline," wielding a wide array of weapons that ranged from cannons to corn knives.[77] Nevertheless, spirits were high. "I . . . felt that when we got into action we would soon settle the war," exclaimed an eighteen-year-old from Fayette, "for with our shot-guns and single barreled pistols we felt certain we were invincible."[78]

While Atchison continued west, several hundred men under John Reid forked from the column and headed for Osawatomie, home of the hated Browns. On the cold, drizzly night of August 29, a smaller band split in turn from Reid's group and moved up Ottawa Creek toward the farm of John Tecumseh Jones, a wealthy, educated Indian known as "Ottawa Jones." With their roomy log home a longtime rendezvous of abolitionists, Jones and his Vermont wife were also unabashed admirers of John Brown and his "work of benevolence and philanthropy."[79] Hence, the enmity Missourians reserved for Jones was well placed. Wrote Old Brown's son, Jason:

> A little after midnight [Jones] heard a great noise among his dogs, and sprang out of bed; as he did so, he heard the scabbards of the Missourians strike on the flag-stones in front of his house as they dismounted from their horses. They had let down his cornfield fences, and ridden on all sides, hoping to find a force of Free-State men there in his double log-house . . .

but there was nobody in it except Jones and his wife, an Indian boy, and a "neutral" named Parker from Missouri. The Ruffians shouted, "We've got you now,—come out, come out!" Nobody replying, and fearing an ambush, they cried, "Fire the house!" and began to do so, setting it on fire in several places. Jones had seized his gun and stood in his front hall, thinking what he could do. "I knew we must shoot," he told me; "we must fight, or make our escape the best way we could." He opened the door and cocked his gun; the enemy hearing it called out, "Don't shoot!" whereupon he sprang out in his night-clothes, and ran as far as he could into a thirty-acre cornfield close by, the enemy shooting at him, but missing. . . . Mrs. Jones, in the mean time, had put about four hundred dollars in gold and silver into a bag, and tried to conceal it and herself in the house. The captain of the Ruffians, looking through the door, saw her and said: "Come out! we won't hurt you. . . ." As she went out, she dropped the money in the grass, and it was picked up by . . . some of the band. They found Parker . . . in bed; as they approached him with their weapons, he said, "Don't kill me,—I'm sick." "We always find a good many sick men when we come round," was the reply,—and with that they dragged him out into the road, knocked him in the head and cut his throat, but did not sever the jugular vein; then dragged him to the bank of the Ottawa and threw him in among some brush.[80]

After ensuring that the home burned, the Missourians moved north and shot up nearby Prairie City.[81]

At dawn the following day, August 30, John Reid and the balance of his command approached Osawatomie from the west. Since the first raid earlier that summer, the settlement edging the Marais des Cygnes had lived in constant dread of an encore. The fact that John Brown used Osawatomie as his headquarters was cold comfort to those of the original two hundred residents who yet remained. Indeed, the fear that his presence would invite further attacks had forced most men to bury valuables and pack their families east. Additionally, because many of the Indians on the surrounding reservations favored slavery, there was little hope of advance warning from that quarter.[82]

As Reid's vanguard neared Osawatomie, it passed the cabin of Samuel Adair, brother-in-law of John Brown. Guiding the party into town was Martin White, a proslavery preacher who, along with his sons, had been run from the region by the Browns.[83] As fate would have it, the first person the minister met that morning was Brown's son Fred, who was walking up the road toward the Adair home.

"Why, I know you," White growled. Without a second thought he raised his rifle and shot young Brown through the heart, killing him instantly. "The ball passed clean through his body," bragged the murderer. Spotting two other free-staters nearby, the horsemen gave chase, catching and killing one and wounding the other.[84]

Fourteen-year-old Spencer Brown—one of the few Browns in Osawatomie not related to the old man—was getting breakfast when he heard the gunfire. "I immediately ran to the door," the boy remembered, "and seeing them I . . . started for town. . . . I ran as fast as I could. . . . The first house I came to . . . [t]hey were eating breakfast. Hearing the news [the] wife began to cry." [85] In a matter of minutes, the entire population had cleared their homes, flying for cover. "All was confusion," acknowledged one of those racing for safety.[86]

At his camp a mile east of Osawatomie, John Brown and fifteen followers were just beginning to stir. Wrote Luke Parsons:

> While we were cooking breakfast . . . a man dashed into camp, saying the Border Ruffians were coming from the west, and had just killed Fred Brown. . . . Brown started right off, and said, "Men, come on . . . !" I started with him, and it was some minutes before any overtook us. While we were hurrying on by ourselves, Brown said, "Parsons, were you ever under fire?" I replied, "No; but I will obey orders. Tell me what you want me to do." He said, "Take more care to end life well than to live long."
>
> When we reached the blockhouse in the village he motioned to several to go in, myself with the rest. He then said to me, "Hold your position as long as possible, and hurt them all you can; while we will go into the timber and annoy them from that side." I fastened the door with a large bar. . . . There was a second floor in the blockhouse, and part of the boys had gone up there. [87]

With the few followers remaining, Brown raced through the village. "I then gathered some fifteen more men . . . and we started in the direction of the enemy," said the old man. "After going a few rods we could see them approaching the town in line of battle, about half a mile off. . . . I then gave up all idea of doing more than to annoy, from the timber near the town . . . which was filled with a thick growth of underbrush. . . ." [88] Discovering a group of citizens already in the woods, Brown took control.

"Here," he noted, "the men, numbering not more than thirty in all, were directed to scatter and secrete themselves as well as they could, and await the approach of the enemy." [89]

Anxious to learn the size and situation of the Missourians, Brown sent a volunteer, James Holmes, to reconnoiter. Encountering Reid's men abruptly on the ridge west of town, Holmes fired once, striking a Southerner in the face, then turned and fled. While some of his men pursued Holmes, Reid swung his column into long battlelines and moved forward. "[T]he sight was truly appalling," Luke Parsons recalled as he and his comrades stared from the portholes of the blockhouse. "They were slowly advancing in two long lines, all mounted, with two brass cannon in the center. Their swords and guns glittered in the morning sun and, as nearly as I could estimate, there were four hundred." [90]

When the rows of men stopped, Reid charged his cannons with grapeshot, then cut loose on the woods. Frightened amid the shower of leaves and limbs, and despite Brown's orders, the excited free-staters opened with their Sharps at long range. Unaccustomed to the tumult, Reid's men likewise had trouble controlling their "green horses," and for the next fifteen minutes the Southerners struggled to re-form their line. [91]

At the blockhouse in town, Luke Parsons and his companions were quickly unnerved by the sounds of war.

[S]ome one on the second floor called out: "They have cannon, and will blow us all to pieces in here. I am going to get out of this." I said: "No, you must stay." Old man Austin said, "Stay here, and let them blow us to hell and back again!" I went upstairs to get a better view of the enemy, and before I knew it the door was opened and most of the men gone. . . . [We] then went up the Marais des Cygnes River, in the timber, and joined Brown at the fight. . . . [92]

While he and the others dodged and ducked behind stumps and bushes, trying to avoid the rain of grape, Parsons was stunned to see Old Brown standing calmly in the smoke, watching the battle. "He showed no fear whatever . . . ," averred the young abolitionist. "Brown kept walking back and forth along the line, speaking to each man as he came to him, assuring him that all was going well. He would say: 'Keep cool, take good aim, aim low, be sure to see both sides of your gun'. . . . " [93] Suddenly, Brown felt a sharp pain as a spent ball struck his back. Luke Parsons:

[H]e came to me [and] said: "Do you see anything on my back? Any blood? Are my clothes torn? Something hit me an awful rap on that shoulder.["] Upon being told that I saw nothing, he said: "Well, I declare, I don't intend to be shot in the back if [I] can help it." [94]

Though the roar of artillery was frightening, it did little damage, and the stream of fire from the woods did not diminish. "Our men were armed with double barreled shot guns that were of no use at that distance," one frustrated Missourian later wrote. "During this long distance firing we had three men . . . wounded but none fatally." [95] At length, Reid ordered his eager troops to charge. Galloping toward the woods, the Southerners finally found the range and let fly "a hail of buckshot." [96]

"They pressed us back slowly," recalled Luke Parsons, "but when they gained the timber, they dismounted and made a steady advance. We fell back one at a time as it got too hot for us. . . ." There, the strain of the past hour became too great, and the free-staters, Old Brown included, "fled in all directions." [97] While he himself was dashing for dear life to escape the screaming Border Ruffians, George Grant stamped in his memory the "queer figure" John Brown cut as he waded the river "in a broad straw hat and a white linen duster, his old coattails floating outspread upon the water and a revolver held high in each hand, over his head." [98]

Others, like Luke Parsons, were escaping in any way they could.

> [The Missourians] rushed up to the bank and did a good deal of shooting. It was here that most of our men were killed. I jumped down the bank and ran along the water's edge, followed by Austin, and he called to me, saying: ["]Hold on, Parsons, don't leave me. . . . ["] Austin dropped down behind a pile of logs, saying: "I wont run another step. . . ." After I had crossed and was clambering to get up the other bank, I heard voices saying: "Halt! Halt! Halt!" and several shots were fired that tore up the dirt right by me. As soon as I could gain a footing, I turned to fire, and saw two horsemen making off at full speed and one horse with an empty saddle following and a man kicking on the ground. Austin jumped up from the logs and came over to me. [99]

While Brown and his breathless band scattered through the woods, Reid turned back to deal with Osawatomie. With the exception of three houses sheltering women and children, every building in town was soon set ablaze. After loading a dozen wagons with plunder, the Missourians quickly retraced their steps, carrying with them six prisoners, a number of wounded, but, miraculously, none dead. [100]

Passing the body of Fred Brown—one of five free-staters killed that morning—the Southerners again approached the Adair cabin where John Brown's pregnant sister, Florella, stood trembling inside.

> Fifteen or twenty came dashing down to our house and up to the door yelling out who lives here, and where is the man. A sick woman and three little children having fled to us for protection commenced screaming and crying don't kill us, don't burn the house down over us while I stood in the door and begged they would spare our lives and they might have all they could find in the house or on the place. Seeing us frightened almost to death, the Captain said hold on boys there is nobody here but women and children and we are Gentlemen we never abuse women and children, don't be frightened Ladies we won't hurt you, "but if we get the men we will put the rope over their heads mighty quick." [101]

When the last raider finally disappeared over the hill, those in hiding began to come out. According to John Everett:

> We were almost the first in town after the burning. The first house we came to was a farm house. . . . They had moved their goods nearly all out. The mob came there but providentially did not burn up their shelter. The next house we came to was smoking but standing. We went in and found the floor had been fired from underneath, but was then only half burnt. We put out the fire with some wet wash clothes standing in a tub and saved that house. Others came in, and we went down to the timber to the field of conflict, to look for wounded or dead. We found one body on the bank of the river shot through the breast. He appeared to have died instantly. . . . We got a couple of poles, laid shingle boards across them, and four of us mournfully carried him to an empty house. . . .[102]

Another who reappeared from the brush was John Brown. As the fierce old fighter stood gazing at the burning town, his face smeared with powder and dirt, tears began to well in his hard, gray eyes. "God sees it," he muttered to his son Jason nearby. "I have only a short time to live—only one death to die, and I will die fighting for this cause. There will be no more peace in this land until slavery is done for. I will give them something else to do than extend slave territory. I will carry this war into Africa."[103] Already, the next step in John Brown's crusade was being planned.

*Florella Adair.* KANSAS STATE HISTORICAL SOCIETY, TOPEKA.

After murdering one of their prisoners just outside town and killing another the following day, Reid's force marched north, laying waste as it went.[104] While Atchison and Reid swept clean the region south of the Kaw, the proslavery party of Leavenworth decided that the time had come to sweep clean their own streets as well. Soon after Charles Fugett shot and scalped the hapless stranger, a "Dutchman" slipped quietly into Leavenworth and relayed messages from James Lane to free-staters still ensconced in the town. The courier was quickly caught and killed. This event, coupled with the rumor that

Lane was coming, proved more than enough to hurl Leavenworth into a "flame of excitement."

Cried the frenzied editor of the *Leavenworth Journal:*

> Now that the issue . . . is forced upon us, let us be up and doing. Let no quarter be given, but war to the extermination of the miscreants be the motto. Let us begin at home! Let Leavenworth be cleansed of these traitorous lepers! Let not one traitor remain to "give aid" to the enemy!! Let no quarter be given!!! [105]

While men blowing horns and others "shouting at the tops of their lungs" raced through the streets, summoning citizens and warning all free-soilers to clear out, wild, snarling speakers urged torchlit audiences to "butcher by the board." [106] The following morning, September 1, a vast, angry mob met outside the mayor's office. According to one observer:

> I . . . found the street crowded to a jam with armed citizens and Missourians, and a Col. Moore harangueing them. . . . When his speech ended [Capt. Frederick] Emory's horse company rode off to search free State houses, and disarm the men; they first went to the house of Jerrold Phillips where a number of free State men boarded. [107]

Also in the home was Phillips's brother, William, who had the year before been tarred, feathered, and ridden on a rail by many of the men in this very same mob. Because of the incident and her husband's refusal to leave, Phillips's wife had become "a raving maniac." [108] Understandably, when he saw the crowd coming, William Phillips was in no mood to play wait-and-see yet a second time. An eyewitness continued:

> Phillips, supposing he was to be driven out of house and home, resolved not to submit to the indignity, and bravely took the initiative himself. Standing boldly out upon the veranda of his house, when the ruffians drew up in front of it, he fired upon them, killing two of their number. They instantly directed a volley of bullets at him and the house, and Phillips fell pierced in a dozen places, the door casing being literally riddled with the leaden storm. He expired almost instantly in the presence of his wife and another lady. His brother, who was with him, had his arm so badly broken with bullets, that he was compelled to submit to an amputation. [109]

Now mad with excitement, the mob encompassed Leavenworth, driving scores of free-soilers from their coverts and forcing them onto steamboats. The victims, one bystander noted, were driven "like so many cattle." While guns were discharged and crowds cheered their approval, a number of suspected homes swiftly went up in smoke. Over the next two days the rioters ran amok, combing the city for hidden free-staters.[110] Those who escaped the net fled either to the woods, where they were "hunted like wild beasts," or they raced north three miles to the sanctuary of Fort Leavenworth. "[T]here are 50 or 60 families of us here in the same fix," wailed a refugee from the fort, "without house, or home, or shelter, or means—some *enceinte* women under a tent on the bare ground, expecting every hour to be confined—others with babes, one, two and three weeks old, and several sick women and children, all exposed to a terrible fate." [111]

Horrid as the riot at Leavenworth, the burning of Osawatomie, and the bloody mayhem elsewhere were, ever-ready propagandists throughout the territory mangled and magnified events until they bore small resemblance to reality. EIGHTY FREE STATE MEN, WOMEN AND CHILDREN MURDERED, blared the Eastern headlines. HORRIBLE BUTCHERY! BRUTAL MASSACRE!!

"Think of this, my sisters in New Hampshire," wrote a breathless Julia Lovejoy from Lawrence, "pure-minded, intelligent ladies fleeing from fiends in human form whose brutal lust is infinitely more to be dreaded than death itself." [112] "Even children, 'over six months *must be murdered*,' " she added with a straight face.[113]

Not to be outdone by anyone, the prolific Sara Robinson penned reams of hair-raising reports based on little or no fact.

[A] young free-state lady, of Bloomington, was carried from her home a mile and a half, by four ruffians, her tongue drawn out of her mouth as far as possible, and cords tied tightly around it. Her arms were pinioned, and she was otherwise so wantonly abused, that for days her life was despaired of.[114]

Revealed another creative writer:

[A Border Ruffian] came into camp, holding upon the point of a Bowie knife, a *human heart!* "Boys," said he, "see here; here is the heart of a damned Abolitionist; he told me he was an Abolitionist and I up with my rifle and dropped him! I cut his heart out and it ain't cold yet; now I'll cut it open and see how it looks inside; then I'll fry it and see how the damned thing tastes!" [115]

"What voracious and blood-thirsty barbarians these reporters must be," exclaimed one stunned border editor after tales of wholesale murder, rape, and torture appeared in a Chicago paper. "Still, we suppose, they are not so much to be blamed, after all. The Chicago folks want lies and nothing but the most trancendent mendacity will satisfy them. A respectable, reasonable hoax would be no more to them than a slice of meat to a hungry hyena." [116]

"A reward of one thousand dollars will be paid for the best cold-blooded murder by the 'border ruffians,' than can be got up in Kansas," mocked another incensed individual. "It is suggested that if a few families could be burned at the stake, it would add greatly to the horror of the scene." [117] As this skeptic implied, in their all-consuming hatred of slavery and zeal to win Kansas, many were ready, willing, and able to invent almost any story that would help them win it. Unfortunately, and as the man also made note, too many in the East were ready, willing, and able to accept almost any tale issuing from Kansas. Meanwhile, with each apocryphal report, the gulf splitting the nation yawned wider and wider, making compromise increasingly more difficult and national civil war increasingly more likely.

Curiously, some of the most gory and gruesome atrocities in the territory went unreported. John Brown and his bloody band continued to lurk along the footpaths and trails of the territory, waiting to waylay lonely travelers. If the answer to a very simple question was wrong, a lead ball or steel blade cut short the conversation. [118] Farther south, Brown henchman John Cook made a sweep along the Neosho River, robbing and running proslavery settlers from the valley. Near Emporia, the gang stopped late one night at the cabin of Christian Carver. While the men beat and kicked at the door, Carver and his pregnant wife, seventeen-year-old Sarah, huddled in terror. Sarah's brother described what happened:

> [Sarah] had raised up and was sitting on the bed close by an opening between the logs, used as a window. A man outside, poked a gun through this opening nearly against her and fired. She cried out at once "I am shot! I am killed!" [W]ith loud profanity, several men crowded into the house, boasting, "We are Jim Lane's front guard! We are the boys!" One man dipped his hand into a pan of honey that set on the table and exclaimed, "Boys, here is some honey, let's eat it." At this instant one raised a gun at Carver and said, "Damn him and his honey too," but another stopped him and said, "Let him alone now, we will be back in three days and if he is not out of the country then, we will hang him." [119]

Her unborn child already dead, the young mother succumbed several days later. [120]

Another group, a secret death squad called the "Danites," prowled the land as well, dealing out free-soil justice from the muzzle of a gun. Organized by James Lane, but led in fact by Charles Leonhardt, the Danites succeeded one night in trailing over a score of Missourians, known as the "Shannon Guards," to a ravine along

Appanoose Creek.[121] One of the Danites, Richard Hinton, revealed what occurred on that cool, misty night.

> We marched in silence until we came within a mile of the ravine. Then the captain ordered us to halt. There were thirty men of us. He divided us into two companies or platoons in order to get the highwaymen between a cross fire. We could see their camp lights twinkling in the distance. We then made an extended detour and slowly approached the ravine. Not a word was spoken. Every man stepped slowly and cautiously and held his breath as we drew near to the camp of the enemy. We knelt down until we heard a crackling noise among the brush on the opposite side, which announced the presence and approach of our other platoon. The Shannon Guards heard it also, and sprang to their feet. . . . Our captain, then, in a deep, resounding voice, gave the order: "Attention! Company!"
>
> The Shannon Guards, hitherto huddled together around the fires, tried to form in line and seize their arms. But it was too late.
>
> "Take aim!"
>
> Every man of us took a steady aim at the marauders, whose bodies the camp fires fatally exposed.
>
> "Fire!"
>
> Hardly had the terrible word been uttered ere the roar of thirty rifles, simultaneously discharged, was succeeded by the wildest, most unearthly shriek that ever rose from mortals since the earth was peopled. I saw two of them leap fearfully into the air. I saw no more. I heard no more. That shriek unmanned me. I reeled backward until I found a tree to lean against.[122]

Firing their weapons furiously, the Danites poured round after round into the begging, screaming mass. Finally, all sound and movement ceased. Learning from companions that he had fainted, Hinton revived just in time to hear the order "March" given.

> I obeyed the command mechanically. We marched back in truly solemn silence. I had walked a mile or two before I noticed that the other platoon was not with us. I asked where it was.
>
> "Burying them," was the brief and significant response.
>
> "Were they all killed, then?"
>
> "Every one of them."
>
> I shuddered then; I can't think of it yet without shuddering. . . . That scene haunts me. It was a terrible thing to do.[123]

*Charles Leonhardt.* KANSAS STATE
HISTORICAL SOCIETY, TOPEKA.

The region nearest Missouri remained, for the most part, under proslavery control; farther inland it was another matter. As an ever-increasing flood of free-state fighters flowed down from the north, the southern tide began to recede. The surge of newcomers turned Topeka into an armed camp. As a consequence, from the beleaguered capital, Lecompton, acting governor Daniel Woodson gave Lt. Col. Phillip St. George Cooke his orders to march. "Your command . . . ," Woodson wrote to the U.S. officer, "will . . . proceed at the earliest practicable moment to invest the town of Topeka, and disarm all the insurrectionists or aggressive invaders against the organized government of the Territory. . . . All their breastworks, forts, or fortifications should be levelled to the ground." [124] Much to the governor's chagrin, Cooke curtly refused.

The next day, September 3, a band of fifty free-soilers from Topeka dashed into the pretty proslavery town of Tecumseh. After terrorizing the inhabitants and committing numerous robberies, the marauders soon left. The following day, however, two hundred more raiders returned, hauling a train of empty wagons. In a short time, the village was utterly gutted, "even down to the brooms," complained one incredulous citizen. [125]

On the same day as the Tecumseh foray, Jim Lane in Lawrence drew up an even more audacious plan. Dividing his force, Lane sent over one hundred men under James Harvey marching up the north bank of the Kaw to cut off escape from Lecompton. With his remaining eight hundred troops, Lane set out along the south shore, aiming to assail the capital from that quarter. [126] If the expedition succeeded, the southern defenders would be surrounded and snared, and the free-state prisoners released.

Since the attack on Titus two weeks before, the Lecompton region had been devastated by roving guerrilla bands. Columns of black smoke rolled skyward on a daily basis, and the few homes still standing were mostly deserted. While some proslavery settlers had fled to Missouri, more sought safety at the capital, where they huddled two, three, even four families to a dwelling. Several hundred fighting men and two cannons defended the village, but it was not enough to prevent panic when Harvey and his free-staters were spotted across the river on the morning of September 5. To the town's great relief, however, Harvey soon decamped. Having spent a miserable night enduring a terrible storm, the Chicagoan promptly returned to Lawrence when Lane and the main force failed to appear at dawn as expected.[127] It was not until later that afternoon that Lane finally reached Lecompton. Planting his artillery and deploying his men on a high ridge just east of town, the free-state leader then sent Sam Walker and a company of cavalry to the heights southwest of the capital to cut off retreat in that direction.

"The town was thoroughly frightened," said Walker, "and we could see them running here and there and some swimming the river to escape." [128]

Not everyone in Lecompton was running or swimming. While a number of Southerners took cover in the foundation of the partially completed capitol, an even larger force, which included Axalla Hoole, marched forth to fight.

> We came in gunshot of each other. . . . We had strict orders . . . not to fire until they made the attack, but some of our boys would not be restrained. I was a rifleman and one of the skirmishers, but did all that I could to restrain our men though I itched all over to shoot. . . . I did not see a pale face in our whole army, every man seemed keen to fight. I for one, did not feel as nervous as I am when I go to shoot a beef or a turkey.[129]

While the sniping among the rocks and trees continued, couriers were sent galloping from the capital to the army camp three miles southwest of town.[130] Still with her husband at the prison was Sara Robinson.

> Three messengers from Lecompton, to Col. Cook [*sic*], followed each other in quick succession. They reported one thousand men about to attack Lecompton. There was soon an unusual stir in the camp. The different bugles sounded, and, in just thirty-five minutes after, the troops began to move towards Lecompton; not in a body, but at the earliest moment each company was ready. The artillery went out, mingling its deafening sound of heavy metal with that of iron hoofs, and the clanking of the sabres of their riders.[131]

From his lookout southwest of town, Sam Walker saw a large force of dragoons approaching.

When [Cooke] came in sight of my men he formed four quadrants in line and charged us, sword in hand. I said to my men: "Sit still and don't make a move; we have done nothing, and they dare not ride over us." The colonel, seeing that we were not frightened, called a halt when he got within 100 yards of us, and riding up, he called out to me: "Walker, what in ——— are you doing here?"

"We are after our prisoners," I replied.

"How many men have you," [asked Cooke].

"About 400 foot and 200 horseback."

"Well, I have 600 men and six cannon, and you can't fight here except with me."

"I don't care a damn how many men you have; we are going to have our prisoners, or a big fight!"

"Don't make a fool of youself, Walker; you can't fight here. Show me to General Lane." [132]

Fearing arrest, Lane quickly ducked into the ranks when he spied Colonel Cooke approaching, and Walker took command. As the angry free-soiler had insisted moments earlier, however, only the release of the prisoners could avoid a clash. After speaking briefly with the besieged proslavery leaders, Cooke announced to Walker that the prisoners would indeed be released and escorted to Lawrence posthaste. Happy that his demands had been met and a fight—not only with the determined defenders of Lecompton but with the U.S. Army—had been avoided, Walker gladly turned about and marched his men to Lawrence. [133] Phillip St. George Cooke was also quietly pleased.

Lecompton and its defenders were outnumbered and apparently in the power of a determined force. Americans thus stood face to face in hostile array and most earnest of purpose. As I marched back over these beautiful hills, all crowned with moving troops and marching men, I rejoiced that I had stayed the madness of the hour and prevented, on almost any terms, the fratricidal onslaught of countrymen and fellow citizens. [134]

Well-intentioned as Cooke's efforts were, the colonel had merely parted the wave, not calmed it. Although the "madness of the hour" had indeed been stayed, when the time was up each side was more than ready to have another go at the other.

## CHAPTER NINE

# DELIVER ME FROM HONOR

THE INTERVENTION OF COLONEL COOKE AT LECOMPTON WAS FORTUITOUS AND prevented much bloodshed, but the taxed U.S. Army could not be everywhere at once. On the Santa Fe Road near Palmyra, a band of free-staters swooped down on a large wagon train in early September and completely stripped the traders of animals and goods. "They were just up from Santa Fe," snapped the *Atchison Squatter Sovereign,* "and having escaped the Cheyennes and Arapahoes, had thought themselves free from Savages." [1]

As risky as the roads were, life in the sundry proslavery settlements scattered throughout the territory had become untenable. Easton, Allen, Council Grove, Summerville, Indianola, and other communities were captured one after another and their citizens cast to the wind.

Meanwhile, as Kansas "went to smash," new territorial governor John Geary was on his way west to reoccupy that much-occupied seat. Long before the tall, handsome Pennsylvanian reached the battleground, he saw signs that the job ahead would be difficult, if not impossible. Wrote Geary's fiercely free-soil private secretary, John Gihon, as their boat, the *Keystone,* hove to at Glasgow, Missouri:

> On approaching this town, a most stirring scene was presented. The entire population of the city and surrounding neighborhood was assembled upon the high bank overlooking the river, and all appeared to be laboring under a state of extraordinary excitement. Whites and blacks,—men, women, and children, of all ages, were crowded together in one confused mass, or hurrying hither and yon, as though some terrible event was about to transpire. A large brass field-piece was mounted in a prominent position,

and . . . belched forth a fiery flame and deafened the ear with its thundering warlike sounds. When the Keystone touched the landing a party of about sixty . . . Missouri volunteers for the Kansas militia, descended the hill, dragging their cannon with them, and ranged themselves along the shore. . . . Each one carried some description of fire-arm, not two of which were alike. There were muskets, carbines, rifles, shot-guns, and pistols of every size, quality, shape and style. Some of them were in good condition, but others were . . . unfit to shoot robins or tomtits. . . .

While these parting ceremonies were being performed, a steamboat, bound down the river, and directly from Kansas, came alongside the Keystone. Ex-governor Shannon was a passenger, who, upon learning the close proximity of Governor Geary, sought an immediate interview with him. The ex-governor was greatly agitated. He had fled in haste and terror from the territory, and seemed still to be laboring under an apprehension for his personal safety. His description of Kansas was suggestive of everything that is frightful and horrible. Its condition was deplorable in the extreme. The whole territory was in a state of insurrection, and a destructive civil war was devastating the country. Murder ran rampant, and the roads were everywhere strewn with the bodies of slaughtered men.[2]

Shaken by Shannon's lurid description, though certain it was highly seasoned, Geary and Gihon resumed their journey up the Missouri. The further they went, however, the more credible became the ex-governor's words. John Gihon:

Active preparations for war were discernible at all the river towns. At Lexington, a large crowd was assembled on the levee, many of the persons composing it loaded with arms. But at Kansas City, the warlike demonstrations were still greater. . . . The Keystone no sooner touched the shore at Kansas City, than she was boarded by a half dozen or more of the leading ruffians, who dashed through the cabins and over the decks, inspecting the passengers and the state-rooms to satisfy themselves that no abolitionists were on board.[3]

Reaching Leavenworth a short time later, the governor found the largest city in Kansas enduring a virtual state of siege. Fearful that Lane and his northern horde would soon attack, hundreds of militiamen anxiously watched and waited from behind a barricade of freight wagons looped around the town.[4] Receiving a wagon of his own filled with soldiers to act as escort from the nearby fort, Geary soon stepped into a carriage and set off for Lecompton. It was not many miles before the governor witnessed for himself the effects of war.

"Along the road," noted Gihon, "were exhibited fearful evidences of ruffian violence. Almost every house had been destroyed, and the sites they had occupied were marked only by solitary chimneys standing in the midst of heaps of ashes."[5]

Arriving at Alexandria, thirteen miles from Leavenworth, Geary and his entourage saw debris in the streets and learned that the hamlet had been raided but moments before.[6] Soon after leaving the place, the new governor discovered firsthand the pitfalls of travel in Kansas. Wrote Gihon:

[U]pon reaching an elevated piece of ground, [we] saw six horsemen crossing the prairie at a distance of about half a mile. Upon observing the carriage, they turned toward it, putting their horses to a gallop, with the evident intention to attack and rob it. As they came within a few hundred yards . . . the covered wagon ascended the hill, thus exhibiting the character and strength of the governor's party, when the intended assailants instantly turned and fled in the opposite direction. They were pursued by the sergeant, the only mounted man in the company, and a more interesting chase was never witnessed. The horses were put to their utmost speed, their tails standing straight out, and making time rarely equalled on a race-course.[7]

Reaching the Kaw, the governor ferried to his capital and found Lecompton "in a great state of excitement," still suffering from Lane's scare of the week before.[8] Geary also realized for the first time that the task facing him was vastly more serious than he had thought. Penned the official to Washington:

It is no exaggeration to say that the existing difficulties are of a far more complicated character that I had anticipated. . . . The actual proslavery settlers of the territory are generally as well-disposed persons as are to be found in most communities. But there are among them a few troublesome agitators . . . who labor assiduously to keep alive the prevailing sentiment. It is also true that among the free-soil residents are many peaceable and useful citizens; and if uninfluenced by aspiring demagogues, would commit no unlawful act. But many of these, too, have been rendered turbulent by officious meddlers from abroad. The chief of these is Lane. . . . [N]o man's life is safe. The roads are filled with armed robbers, and murders for mere plunder are of daily occurrence. Almost every farm-house is deserted, and no traveller has the temerity to venture upon the highway without an escort. Such is the condition of Kansas faintly pictured. It can be no worse.[9]

But it did get worse—and very soon. On September 12, only days after Geary's arrival in the territory, a company of South Carolinians and Kickapoo

Rangers under John Robertson stormed into Grasshopper Falls.[10] Reported Robert Kelley of the *Squatter Sovereign:*

> They rode in a trot until within about a mile of town, when they charged with a yell that struck a panic in the ranks of the white-livered Yankees.— Not a shot was fired at them, though one man snapped at Capt. R., and was shot on the spot. . . . At the time of the attack, Capt. [William] Crosby's company, numbering about thirty, were on parade, but scattered like a flock of startled sheep without firing a gun. So terror-stricken were they that numbers of them lay in corn-fields and permitted our troops to pass within a short distance of them without firing a gun. Crosby's store, with all its contents—consisting chiefly of provisions and supplies for this band of thieves whose rendezvous was at that point—was burned to the ground. Some arms and horses, stolen during the depredations of Crosby's gang, were brought away, but everything else that could be used to sustain the midnight assassins was destroyed.[11]

At the same time that Robertson was looting Grasshopper Falls, James Lane and his Northerners were plundering nearby Osawkie. On the following morning, the two forces finally faced off at Hickory Point. While Lane paused on the prairie above to survey the situation, Robertson and his thirty men, along with a like number of locals led by Percival Lowe, quickly sought shelter behind the log walls of the store, hotel, and blacksmith shop that constituted the village.[12]

"From where we stood we had a magnificent view of the surrounding country," remarked free-stater, Samuel Reeder.

> General Lane soon made his dispostions for attack. The cavalry were formed to the south of the road. They crossed the stream and occupied an elevation about four hundred yards southeast of Hickory Point. . . . As my steed seemed hardly in fighting trim I tied him to one of the wagons and fell in with the infantry. . . . Our formation was one rank and we had at least fifty men. . . . We had all sorts of guns; perhaps not more than one-third of our force had Sharp's [*sic*] rifles . . . [and] there were a good many condemned United States rifles and muskets. The rest of us were armed with sporting rifles and shotguns.
>
> We were now all ready for the work before us. . . . General Lane was in the saddle less than thirty yards from where I stood, and by his side was . . . other officers. There was a short consultation, then a horseman

left the group carrying a white handkerchief tied to a ramrod. He galloped down the hill waving his flag as he went. We saw two or three men on foot coming to meet him from the direction of the shop. They walked deliberately, and met our messenger near the rising ground.[13]

Once they were eye to eye, each side queried the other under the white flag. "They said they were abolitionists to the backbone," recounted one of the Southerners. "They asked who we were; I answered pro-slavery." [14]

"[He said] that he had on the ground 200 well armed men, and two thousand within one and [a] half miles of the place," a proslavery comrade added, "and in addition five pieces of artillery. He demanded an immediate surrender of the place, with all the munitions of war within five minutes; if not . . . no quarter should be given." [15]

Returning to Samuel Reeder:

The conference was very brief, and when . . . [our messenger] returned I heard him say to the general: "The leader of the gang read your summons and returned it with these words, 'Take this dirty paper back . . . and tell him we will fight him and all the hireling cutthroats and assassins he can bring against us.'" [16]

His bluff called, Lane prepared for battle. It was at this point that young men like Samuel Reeder and tall, soft-spoken James Butler Hickok abruptly came face-to-face with themselves for the first time in their lives. Sam Reeder noted:

The sensations and emotions of soldiers waiting for the signal that may possibly mean death, are as various, perhaps, as the temperaments of the men themselves. For myself I felt almost as if it were a dream, and this feeling of unreality benumbed a latent dread of possible wounds and death. While a sense of duty and a natural curiosity to participate in actual battle, pride and the fear of ridicule and disgrace, all contributed in keeping me at my post.[17]

Suddenly, the focus of friend and foe alike shifted elsewhere. Sam Reeder snapped from his reverie.

"Look!" cried some one, "there goes one of their men now." Some five hundred yards to our left we saw a man on foot with a gun on his shoulder, walking briskly in the direction of Hickory Point. A young man named

Shepherd left [our] cavalry line and dashed past out front to engage the Ranger in single combat. The attention of the entire command was enlisted. With silent, thrilling interest we watched every movement of the actors in this possible tragedy. We could almost imagine ourselves back in the days of chivalry, as Shepherd, like a gallant knight, urged his horse to its utmost speed across the slope, and rapidly neared his man. The footman saw his pursuer, and changing the direction of his course a little to the north, ran with great swiftness toward the trees and bushes on the creek. He had too much of a start to be cut off, but Shepherd succeeded in getting within less than one hundred yards of the Ranger. He then suddenly reined up his horse, quickly dismounted and took deliberate aim at the fugitive. As the man saw Shepherd about to fire, he stooped as he ran, so as to almost resemble a four-footed beast. I could not help mentally wishing he would not be hit—it looked cold-blooded and cruel. The white puff of smoke came, the report of the rifle followed— but the human target ran on! If hurt the man was not disabled, and in a few moments he disappeared from view.

"Well!" exclaimed one of the men, "that's the first time I ever saw a man chased and shot at, like a wolf."

But the spectacle was not ended. We saw Shepherd insert a fresh cartridge in his breech-loader, swing himself into the saddle, and ride rapidly in the direction of the rising ground near the shop. When he reached it and was in full view of the enemy, he suddenly checked his horse, took a rapid aim and fired. As he wheeled around and put spurs to his horse, a scattering volley came from the buildings. Shepherd swayed in his saddle from side to side, while his horse galloped zigzag back and forth across the road as he ran in our direction.

"There—he's shot!" cried one.

"Yes, he's falling from his horse," said another. "He'll keep his seat!" "He'll come out alright!" was heard from all sides, as the rider straightened himself up and urged his horse up the hill. As he neared us . . . [a friend] rode forward and met him. They were both laughing when they reached our position. Shepherd was unhurt; his pretense of being wounded was a ruse to induce the Rangers to cease firing. There was a reckless daring in the whole performance that was captivating, and the praise of Shepherd's gallantry was heard on all sides.[18]

At last the long line of free-state infantry moved forward and let fly volley after volley toward Hickory Point. Terrified by the rain of lead, Lowe's farmers dived for cover in the store. "[H]is men were not all they should have been . . . ," one Southerner spit, "and cries of 'surrender' were often heard. . . . [I]t was only when Capt. Robertson placed some of his company at a post to shoot all who attempted to run that this cowardly spirit was checked." Nevertheless, it was soon noted that "there were but few shots fired by Capt. Lowe's party." [19] Robertson's tough Carolinians, however, went to work with a will.

"I could hear the sound of shots from the direction of Hickory Point, accompanied at intervals by fierce yells," remembered Sam Reeder. "A young fellow near me remarked: 'Our men must be hitting them the way they holler.' It was not that; it was the . . . Southern war cry. . . . Our line fought in silence so far as cheering was concerned." [20] Reeder continued:

> I was looking at the shop when I saw a tiny, circular cloud of white smoke appear; then in the road some thirty paces in front of our line a sudden dash of dust was seen, followed by a fearfully wicked whiz, that came buzzing over our heads like a monster hornet. Our line recoiled a few paces for ten or fifteen feet on either side of the diabolical sound. I was not in the slightest danger, as the glancing bullet sped some dozen feet to my right, but I must acknowledge taking several backward steps. At the stern command of our captain we all dressed up into line again, and there was no more dodging. The enemy's fire was very deliberate. . . . Their bullets generally passed over our heads with a clean-cut "zip," that was far less unpleasant than the nerve-shaking whiz of the introductory one. We were learning to "face the music." [21]

Although the spectacle of battle was, as Reeder later wrote, "in the highest degree inspiring," it became apparent after several hours that there was little either side could do to hurt the other. Sam Reeder:

> The rangers had now ceased firing altogether. . . . On our side we were wasting good powder and lead against the log walls that concealed our foe. Our own fire soon slackened and then died out completely. It was a regular deadlock; what next? A small group of men were collected about General Lane. "We can drive them out, but we should lose too many men," he said. "We must wait another day and get artillery." [22]

As a consequence, Lane pulled back to Osawkie and a secure source of water, there to await the arrival of artillery and men from Topeka. Unbeknownst to the commander, James Harvey and several hundred free-state reinforcements were indeed marching north, but by a different route. Upon reaching Hickory Point the following day, Harvey, in a situation similar to Lecompton, now found it was not he, but

Jim Lane, who was nowhere in sight. Undismayed, the captain deployed his men, and for a second straight day the beleaguered Southerners prepared for battle.

While the northern infantry let fly a fusillade from a neighboring cornfield, Thomas Bickerton carefully sighted his cannon, then loosed a round at the blacksmith shop, above which a black flag defiantly floated. Related one of those inside:

> The first fire was the only one that was productive of material injury. It struck a musket in the hands of [S.P.] Peace, wounding him in the calf of the leg, and breaking the gun in two, the butt striking Mr. John Ashby in the breast, laying him level with the earth. After this shot, the men watched the cannon, and whenever it was about to be fired they would lay flat on the ground.[23]

"Knowing that they would lay close to the floor at every discharge," Bickerton revealed, "I put every shot below the fourth log of the house."[24]

"The cannon balls danced over the heads of our men, cutting all manner of capers," said one defender. "Westbrook and another person had the skin scraped off their backs by balls as they passed over them, and numerous slight wounds were inflicted by splinters and fragments of rock from the forge."[25]

Added a comrade, Albert Morrall:

> I was flat on my back, right beside the work bench, the iron vise above me, just about the middle of my body. One of the cannon balls struck the legs of the bench, and the whole bench and all of the old iron, nuts and bolts, nails and chains covered me all over, as it fell, with dirt and dust. For a while the shop was foggy, but it soon cleared away. After the cannon was fired, we would all jump up and poke our rifles through the chinks in the logs and keep up a continuous fire until warned by the watch at each corner to look out for the cannon, when we would drop flat on the ground again, then get up and fire as fast as we could load.[26]

Terrifying as the cannonade was, Sharps rifle balls caused more casualties by far. One Southerner was mortally wounded by a bullet in the back, and several others received dangerous wounds, including Captain Robertson, who was shot in the buttocks.[27]

After five hours of indecisive fighting, Harvey called for volunteers. Albert Morrall recorded:

> [W]e noticed a wagon loaded with hay coming towards the shop, and no horses were attached. We at once concluded that they intended to burn us out, and we arranged, by placing two of our best marksmen at each corner

of the shop, to watch for the legs of the men rolling the wagon, and we kept up a constant fire. The wagon came up about seventy-five yards, when all at once it stopped. . . . We knew then that it was all right for us—for they got sick of it, and some of the men who were pushing the wagon had their legs broken. The wagon was set on fire and abandoned. In the shop we gave three cheers and kept up the firing.[28]

Utterly exasperated and fully aware that the day had ended in a draw, Harvey sent forward a flag of truce. When the terms were complete, it was agreed that each side would allow the other to part in peace. Surprisingly, both southern and northern fighters, only moments before mortal enemies, now "mixed freely," with some going so far as to share rounds of whiskey from the store.[29]

Even while the fight at Hickory Point was in progress, events were taking shape twenty-five miles to the south that had the potential for vastly greater consequences. As Lane, Harvey, Charles Leonhardt, and other free-soilers were raking the land, the proslavery army of David Atchison was also on the move. Gathering men and momentum as he moved west, the Missourian finally drew up near Lawrence with as many as three thousand soldiers in his ranks. For most Southerners, Atchison included, there was a feeling in the air that their hold on Kansas had slipped badly; among all was the hope that one bold stroke might regain the grip.

On Sunday morning, September 14, Julia Lovejoy and others in Lawrence were attending church. Because most men were off with Lane and Harvey plundering proslavery settlements, the streets in town were abnormally quiet. Thus, when the startling news arrived that a horde of Border Ruffians were at the gates, only a smattering of defenders were on hand. Julia Lovejoy:

[M]essengers came in telling us that the ruffian army, 3,000 strong, was at Franklin, and soon the smoke of burning houses at Franklin told us their whereabouts. Our men set to work at once to prepare for defense. . . . [They] were short of ammunition . . . [and] were told to divide their cartridges with their neighbor till ALL WAS GONE, then take to their

*The battle at Hickory Point.* KANSAS STATE HISTORICAL SOCIETY, TOPEKA.

bayonets, and those who had none, to use their pitchforks, as they were liberally distributed from the stores. . . .[30]

As the excited free-staters assumed their positions, the southern column arrayed on the broad Wakarusa plain, just east of town. Wrote a witness, Thomas Wentworth Higginson:

This force was in sight . . . and though Governor Geary's aid was invoked, it was known that it could not arrive till evening; thus allowing time for the destruction of everything. Against this force, the number at first counted upon was one hundred. . . . To the surprise of all, however, more than two hundred rallied to the fort. The lame came on crutches, and the sick in blankets. Two hundred men against fourteen times their number. . . . And yet . . . among this devoted handful the highest spirits prevailed; they were laughing and joking as usual, and only intent on selling their lives as dearly as possible.[31]

One of those not laughing or joking was John Brown. Buckling on his sword, the sturdy old man girded for battle.

Gentlemen. . . . Now is probably the last opportunity you will have of seeing a fight, so that you had better do your best. If they should come up and attack us, don't yell and make a great noise, but remain perfectly silent and still. Wait till they get within twenty-five yards of you; get a good object; be sure you see the hind sight of your gun,—then fire. A great deal of powder and lead and very precious time is wasted by shooting too high. You had better aim at their legs than at their heads. In either case, be sure of the hind sights of your guns. It is from the neglect of this that I myself have so many times escaped; for if all the bullets that have ever been aimed at me had hit, I should have been as full of holes as a riddle.[32]

"[A]bout 4 o'clock in the afternoon," noted a nervous Julia Lovejoy, "the advanced guard of the enemy, 100 strong, headed by Sheriff Jones, galloped boldly toward the town, followed by the main body with their bloody flag floating in the breeze."[33]

'T'was a sight sublime to see our boys, only eighty strong, headed by the gallant Capt. Walker, gallop out to meet them, and then wheel and turn toward town, as though running from such overwhelming numbers, to decoy them as near as possible, and they in full chase, when our boys turned, spread out to cover as much space as possible, and then poured a volley of balls into them—the Missourians returned the fire and then retreated into a ravine behind a cornfield to screen themselves as much as possible—our men then returned to town, and about . . . fifty foot-men marched out on to a high rolling prairie, and drew themselves up in line of battle. . . . [34]

Infantry captain Joseph Cracklin continued:

In a few minutes they made their appearance, coming out of the timber and heading towards us. As soon as they got in range I ordered the boys to open fire. We had not fired more than a dozen shots, when, looking towards town, I saw quite a number of men on the run to our assistance. In the meantime the enemy had disappeared in a hollow or ravine.

As fast as my friends arrived I placed them in line, deployed as skirmishers at six paces intervals, until my force amounted to fifty-eight. Not seeing anything of the enemy, I sent Ed. Bond, who was mounted, to see what they were doing. We watched him until he arrived at the entrance of the ravine, where the enemy were concealed, when he stopped, levelled his rifle, and fired; he then put spurs to his pony and galloped back. . . . I then ordered a forward movement, with my line extended as skirmishers. We had a space of half or three-quarters of a mile to cross before we would reach the ridge that separated us from the enemy. On reaching it, we discovered them just going out of the upper end of the ravine. . . . I ordered the boys to open fire, to load and fire at will; our whole line immediately commenced blazing away. They fired several shots in return, but they fell short. One of their men was seen to fall. . . . They put spurs to their horses and galloped away towards Franklin. [35]

"[T]hey wheeled and fled like frightened sheep . . . ," Julia Lovejoy hurrahed as she and others cheered the victory. "[O]ur men followed hard at their heels, firing as they went . . . and thus on and on they flew as in a race for life. . . ." [36]

Despite the euphoria, there was no question in anyone's mind that once the proslavery mass moved in earnest, Lawrence would swiftly go down. Surprisingly, the southern host hesitated, wary no doubt of the earthworks and forts as well as the long-range rifles and cannon. While the Border Ruffians bivouacked for the night along the Wakarusa, besieged Lawrence looked west for succor.

"For the first time in our free-state campaign," one man admitted, "we hoped for help from the direction of Lecompton." [37]

"We kept scouts out to keep watch all night," added Edward Fitch, who anxiously eyed the twinkling campfires east of Lawrence. "I was in the saddle almost all night myself." [38] To the great relief of Fitch and his fellow townsmen, Lt. Col. Joseph Johnston and a large force of U.S. cavalry rode in later that evening and debouched between the contending foe. [39] At ten o'clock the following morning John Geary, John Gihon, and Colonel Cooke also arrived.

"About three hundred persons were found in arms . . . ," Gihon surmised as he surveyed Lawrence. "Among these were many women, and children of both sexes, armed with guns and otherwise accoutered for battle." Almost immediately, the three set off for the Wakarusa flats, where the southern army, "with cannon-matches lighted [and] banners flying," was once again spreading for battle. [40] After a brief ride Geary's carriage encountered an advance guard of three hundred Border Ruffians.

"Who are you?" the new governor angrily demanded.

"We are the territorial militia," replied a spokesman, "called into service by His Excellency, the Governor of Kansas. . . ."

"I am Governor of Kansas. . . ." raged Geary.

"You're not Woodson."

"I'm Geary, and I am Governor." [41]

Ordered to turn back, the three hundred horsemen, clad in "red shirts and odd-shaped hats," escorted the carriage through Franklin and down onto the plain. [42] "There, in battle array, were ranged at least three thousand armed and desperate men," wrote John Gihon.

> In the background stood at least three hundred army tents and as many wagons, while here and there a cannon was planted ready to aid in the anticipated destruction. Among the banners floated black flags. . . . The arms and cannon also bore the black indices of extermination. In passing along the lines, murmurs of discontent and savage threats of assassination fell upon the governor's ears. . . . [43]

When Atchison, John Reid, L. A. Maclean, George Clarke, Henry Titus, Sam Jones, and other leaders were finally tracked down, the governor asked for a parley. Remembered Gihon:

> Governor Geary . . . addressed them at length and with great feeling. He depicted in a forcible manner the improper position they occupied, and the untold horrors that would result from the consummation of their cruel designs; that if they persisted in their mad career, the entire Union would be involved in a civil war, and thousands and tens of thousands of innocent lives be sacrificed. To Atchison, he especially addressed himself,

telling him that when he last saw him, he was acting as vice-president of the nation and president of the most dignified body of men in the world, the senate of the United States; but now with sorrow and pain he saw him leading on to a civil and disastrous war an army of men, with uncontrollable passions, and determined upon wholesale slaughter and destruction. He concluded his remarks . . . and ordered the army to be disbanded and dispersed.[44]

Surprisingly, Atchison and Reid quickly acquiesced. Several of their compatriots, however, were outraged. According to John Gihon:

General Clarke said he was for pitching into the United States troops, if necessary, rather than abandon the objects of the expedition. General Maclean didn't see any use of going back until they had whipped the damned abolitionists. Sheriff Jones was in favor, now they had a sufficient force, of "wiping out" Lawrence and all the free-state towns. And these and others, cursed Governor Geary in not very gentle expressions, for his untimely interference with their well laid plans.[45]

"They, however," concluded Gihon with supreme satisfaction, "obeyed the order, and retired. . . ."[46]

Thus, except for the torching of several buildings in the area and the theft of random livestock, the dispirited proslavery army once more marched from the Wakarusa without a parting shot. John Geary, of course, was elated. Equally pleased were many sane leaders on both sides who were grateful some guiding hand had stepped in and stopped a situation seemingly beyond control. In less than a week, the new governor had saved Lawrence from immense bloodshed, parted warring armies, sent U.S. troops to arrest James Harvey and his band for their attack on Hickory Point, and witnessed a marked decrease in guerrilla activity. To John Gihon, at least, when one month later Geary's horse trod on a rattlesnake coiled in the road, crushing the serpent's head, the event was a portent of better times to come.[47] Gihon apparently saw no omen in another incident, one that followed on the heels of the affair at Lawrence.

Returning to the capital via the river road, the governor's party trailed a company of Kickapoo Rangers heading for the Lecompton ferry and their homes near Leavenworth. "They still carried the black flag," Gihon recalled, "and their cannon, guns, swords and carriages were yet decorated with the black emblems of their murderous intentions."

Six men of this detachment, when within a few miles of Lecompton, halted by a field where a . . . lame man, named David C. Buffum, was at work. They entered the field, and after robbing him of his horses, one of them shot him in the abdomen. . . . Almost immediately after . . . Governor Geary . . . arrived upon the spot, and found the wounded man weltering in his blood. Although suffering the most intense agony, he was sensible of his condition. . . . Writhing in agony, the cold sweat drops standing upon his forehead, with his expiring breath he exclaimed . . . "They asked me for my horses, and I plead with them not to take them. I told them that I was a cripple—a poor lame man—that I had an aged father, a deaf-and-dumb brother, and two sisters, all depending upon me for a living, and my horses were all I had with which to procure it. One of them said I was a God damned abolitionist, and seizing me by the shoulder with one hand, he shot me with a pistol that he held in the other. . . ." The governor was affected to tears. He had been on many a battle-field, and been familiar with suffering and death; but, says he, "I never witnessed a scene that filled my mind with so much horror. There was a peculiar significance in the looks and words of that poor dying man that I never can forget. . . ." [48]

While Geary could indeed take pride in his accomplishments, he also discovered firsthand, as had his predecessors, that in the boiling cauldron called Kansas, it was one thing to reach the territory—quite another to stay.

One reason for the relative calm that settled over Kansas in late September was that the "Grim Chieftain," Jim Lane, had made his hasty territorial exit. Few, it seemed, mourned his loss. While admirers insisted that he and his Army of the North were responsible for the present peace, others argued just as hotly that when Lane turned his horde loose on Kansas "like a cloud of devouring locusts," it lost forever the moral high ground Charles Robinson had worked so hard to attain. Additionally, others feared that northern aggression might even cost John Frémont the November election. [49] When Lane turned logic on its head and lamely argued that his army had been "fighting for peace," George Washington Brown simply sneered.

"[T]he kind of peace which followed in their train," snapped the editor, "we hope never to witness again in Kansas. The peace . . . was the *peace* seen in burning towns, desolated hearthstones and a depopulated country." [50]

Another reason for the rare quiet in Kansas was the departure of John Brown. Tired of inaction following Geary's arrival, the abolitionist rushed east to raise funds for future operations. The early onset of winter was an event that no doubt had a settling influence as well. But perhaps the greatest single reason for the mutual termination of the slavery struggle in September 1856 was simple war weariness. Though not Napoleonic by any means, either in breadth or degree, the civil war that swept Kansas was nevertheless sharp, vicious, and pervasive.

The continual stress of the guerrilla war, the day-in, day-out uncertainty of life and property, quite simply exhausted the meager resources of the territory not only physically and financially, but emotionally as well. And for many a young free-soil and proslavery fighter, the summer in Kansas had at long last allowed them to gain a glimpse of that much-discussed and much-coveted creature, "the elephant." Many, like Richard Foster, had no desire to ever see the animal again.

> [W]ar is a terrible thing. I have before heard of it; I have now seen it.
> I have heard the balls whistling about my ears. I have stood where men
> were shot down as you would shoot wild beasts. I have heard the groans
> of the wounded and dying. I have seen the bloody corpses of the dead
> and truly war is a terribly cruel thing.[51]

"I have seen since I have been here sites that would make the wickedest hearts sick . . . ," echoed young James Butler Hickok.[52]

And even a son of old John Brown, Jason, while gazing into the face of a wounded enemy, found he, too, had no stomach for his father's grim and gory profession.

> As he lay there, pale and exhausted from loss of blood and suffering, he
> spoke of his home and friends in Mississippi, and how he wished he had
> never come to Kansas. He said he would soon be at rest. He asked me if
> I would not take care of him for the few hours he had to live. I told him
> I would. As I was sitting by his bed and saw the tears flowing from
> a heart full of sorrow and trouble, alone among strangers, and far from
> home, I thought this: If these are some of the things which make war
> glorious and honorable, deliver me from the honors of war.[53]

To many astute Southerners, David Atchison included, it was all too apparent that the summer of 1856 had not gone as the proslavery party of Kansas had hoped. Despite much work and much money, the incredible swarm of angry Northerners had clearly turned the tide. But while the military initiative had obviously been lost, there yet remained the political option. In the November election, the abolitionist candidate for president, John Frémont, had indeed failed, and a man sympathetic to the South, James Buchanan, would soon enter the White House; a friendly U.S. Congress still ruled the land, and in Kansas itself, the Territorial Legislature—backed by federal bayonets—yet held the reins of government. While slavery had received a bloody reverse in '56, the coming year might yet witness an event that many insisted was fundamental to holding the South in the Union: statehood for Kansas—*with* slavery!

## CHAPTER TEN

# THROUGH THE LIFTING SMOKE

IN THE SUMMER OF 1855, WHEN THE TERRITORIAL LEGISLATURE WAS SEARCHING for a home, Tecumseh and Lecompton were two of the top contenders. After the former offered thirty acres of land and 300,000 bricks if the vote went its way, the latter bid fifty acres of land and raised the ante to a half-million bricks if the decision tilted in its direction.[1] Thus, rather than situate at what many considered the most beautiful and promising site in Kansas, the government moved to what some regarded as the "most inaccessible and remote" spot on the map. Lecompton, sniffed Sara Robinson, was "a little town down in the ravines." Sara was also quick to add—as were other spiteful free-soilers—that the new capital was one of the most "unsavory sinkholes" in America.[2]

Wrote John Gihon soon after his arrival in the village:

> Lecompton was . . . and now is, a sort of moral plague spot in Kansas, and as such is shunned by all good people coming into the territory. . . .
>
> [T]here were, perhaps, two hundred men in the town . . . at least one-half of whom were out of employment, though they were evidently supplied with funds from some invisible source to supply their immediate wants and support them in idleness. Laboring men and mechanics were greatly needed, but the idlers could not be induced to work. It was much easier to lounge about the groggeries and denounce abolitionists, than make a livelihood by honest industry.[3]

"The only business places besides one or two stores are lawyer's shops and grogshops," a visitor added. With little to do in the capital but play cards and tipple,

187

it is not surprising that many soldiers in the nearby camp became "almost unfitted for duty." [4] Nor is it surprising that in a territory already noted for its wild and wicked towns, Lecompton was perhaps the wildest and wickedest of the lot. Continued John Gihon:

> [A]n altercation took place . . . between two South Carolinians. They were personal friends, but had been drinking too freely. One of them, incensed at some remark of the other, drew his pistol and fired, and was about to repeat the shot, when his companion, after warning him, discharged into his body the contents of a gun loaded with buckshot. The wounded man lingered three or four days, in great agony. . . . Two or three days later, another serious shooting affair occurred. . . . A free-state man living in the vicinity, brought in a load of beef for sale. He proceeded to one of the stores, where . . . he got into conversation, during which he denounced the institution of slavery. . . . A quarrel and fight ensued, when the free-state man ran for his life. He was pursued to a cluster of woods on the edge of the town, his pursuers firing at him a number of times, he turning to fire back. He at length dodged behind a tree, whence he fired a few more shots. Some of his assailants had run for guns, and succeeded in shooting him three times, as he attempted to make his escape, the balls having entered his back, abdomen, and side. He was laid, dangerously, though not mortally wounded, upon the beef on his wagon, and brought into town with his ox-team. . . . These occurrences had become so common that they attracted but little attention. Whilst this man was writhing apparently in the agonies of death on one side of the street, the groggeries opposite were filled with loungers too unconcerned to take any special notice of the circumstance.[5]

Unfortunately for the one hundred free-staters captured by federal troops following the fight at Hickory Point, Lecompton was the site of their imprisonment. Although several were acquitted, the rest languished for weeks on end under terrible conditions. As one prisoner revealed:

> A few of our guards will ever be remembered by us with emotions of the deepest gratitude for their kindness; but the greatest portion of them are drunken, brawling demons, too vile and wicked for portrayal. Times without number have they threatened to either shoot or stab us, and not unfrequently have they attempted to carry out their base and hellish threats. Several nights have the guard amused themselves throughout

their different watches, by cursing us, throwing stones at the house, breaking in glass, sash, &c. Two large cannon stand planted but a few yards from our prison . . . heavily loaded with shot and slugs. . . . These, however, are only slight, compared with other insults and sufferings heaped upon us daily. Most of us are poorly clad—few have any bedding. Our prison is open and airy, yet small; without, surrounded with unearthly filth; within, all is crawling with vermin, all, everything, mixed with misery. . . . Last night all the physicians in town were sent for, and each refused to come. . . . Dr. Brooks was sent for five times; but as he was at a card-table playing poker, he swore he "would not leave the game to save every ——— abolitionist in the territory."[6]

Into this drunken bedlam dropped John Geary. Though leaders on both sides were heartily pleased when the governor stepped in to stop the war in September, Geary discovered as winter passed that this did not necessarily mean either was willing to let him govern. Recorded John Gihon on the governor's first encounter with free-staters at Topeka:

They were disposed to be refractory and some of them quite insolent. . . . Some endeavored to annoy him with what they considered smart and perplexing questions; others proposed entering into a treaty, the terms of which they were to establish; whilst still others averred that they had a governor of their own choice, to whom and to whom only, they owed and would yield allegiance.[7]

Replied Geary:

Gentlemen . . . I come not to treat with, but to govern you. There is now in the territory no other governor than myself. I will protect the lives and property of every peace-loving and law-abiding citizen, with all the power I possess. I will punish every law-breaker. . . . Don't talk to me about slavery or freedom—free-state men or proslavery men—until we have restored the benign influence of peace to the country; until we have punished the murderer, and driven out the bandit and rabble. . . . Do not, I pray you, attempt to embarrass me with your political disputations. . . . This is no time to talk about party, when men, women and children are hourly being murdered at their own firesides, or whilst sleeping in their beds, or are being driven by merciless bands of marauders from their homes without money, food, or clothing.[8]

Although hopeful that the governor was secretly backing their side, the proslavery party soon perceived correctly that Geary and Gihon surreptitiously favored the free-soil cause. Hence, by January 1857, John Geary discovered to his disgust that neither camp was willing to follow his lead. The daily proceedings of the legislature were increasingly devoted to diatribes directed at the governor. Reflected John Gihon:

> Never again will a similar amount of that peculiar style of eloquence emanate from any legislative body. So determined were some of these gentlemen to denounce the governor . . . that they entered upon their work with a most commendable spirit and energy whenever they could obtain the floor, or stand upon their feet, which was not always the case. . . . Nothing could have been more amusing than to witness the efforts of some of these orators to preserve their equilibrium whilst delivering themselves to their wisdom. The desperate struggle to stand erect—the hiccups which interspersed the most eloquent sentences—the rocking to and fro, and grasping at the backs of chairs or tops of tables, and most of all, the palpable desire to appear sober, all conspired to furnish a most admirable study. . . . [9]

The growing antipathy among Southerners erupted in fury when, upon the resignation of Sam Jones as Douglas County Sheriff, Geary refused to commission his chosen successor, William Sherrard.[10] Because of the reverses of the summer before, many slavers saw Sherrard as the only man capable of regaining lost ground.

"Sherrard had boasted," one free-soiler remarked, "that, as Sheriff, within a week he would restore the border rule as it was before the advent of Geary." [11]

Hence, when the governor refused to validate the selection, the situation in Lecompton became explosive. Characterized by Alfred Jones, editor of the *Lecompton Union,* as "a lion, well educated and . . . the perfect gentleman," Sherrard was depicted by others as "an untamed hyena," drunken, brutal, and vicious. "Mr. Sherrard had been engaged in several drunken broils, fighting and shooting at persons with pistols, and threatening others . . . ," wrote Geary, citing his reasons for denying the position to Sherrard. "[H]is habits and passions rendered him entirely unfit for the proper performance of the duties of that office." [12]

On February 9, Geary, Gihon, and an aide visited the legislative hall to attend a session. Still seething at his rejection, William Sherrard was also there. "[They] had taken their seats in the house," a witness remembered, "when Sherrard, observing them, suddenly arose and left the hall. His appearance and manner were so peculiar as to elicit special notice. . . . " [13] John Gihon continued:

The governor remained a half-hour or more, and then took his leave. As he was about to step from the main hall into the adjoining ante-room, Sherrard stood in the door, having gone off and procured an extra pistol to the one he usually wore, both of which . . . he had placed conveniently in a belt . . . [H]e also carried a huge bowie-knife. Before the governor had closed the door, Sherrard accosted him with "You have treated me, sir, like a damned scoundrel." The governor passed on without noticing the man. . . . [I] was the last to leave the hall and enter the ante-room, when [I] saw Sherrard spitting after the governor, at the same time uttering oaths and threats of defiance, his right hand firmly grasping one of the pistols in his belt. . . . Had he halted to speak to Sherrard, or turned upon him, or in any possible way given an excuse for the deed, he would have been shot down like a dog, and himself and companions riddled with balls. . . . The ante-room is in the second story of the building, the stairs leading to the ground being on the outside, and as the governor descended, Sherrard stood upon the platform above, with pistol in hand, hesitating whether even yet to fire or not. He followed on, and did not abandon his purpose until the length of the building was traversed, when pronouncing an audible oath, he turned off and took a different direction.[14]

Certain that Sherrard was "but the tool of others" and that a plan was afoot to assassinate him, Geary returned to his office and immediately requested two companies of dragoons to act as body-guards. Much to his dismay, Persifer Smith at Fort Leavenworth refused. "Insults or probable breaches of the peace do not authorize the employment of the troops," the general cooly informed the governor.[15]

With federal support denied, free-state friends of Geary agreed to stage a mass "indignation" meeting at Lecompton on February 18 to denounce the affront. Proslavery men in the area, including Sherrard, Sam Jones, and Robert Bennett of the *Lecompton Union,* threatened to disrupt the gathering. John Gihon recorded:

*Legislative Hall, Lecompton.* KANSAS STATE HISTORICAL SOCIETY, TOPEKA.

Before the hour specified, numbers of persons came pouring in from the surrounding country; and it was soon discovered that Brooke's Hotel, where the assembly was to have met, was too small to accommodate half the persons present, and it was therefore adjourned to Capitol Hill. . . . The meeting assembled at two o'clock. Nearly four hundred persons were in attendance, composed of all classes. . . . A committee of five was then appointed to draft resolutions expressive of the sense of the meeting, who having retired, Captain L. J. Hampton . . . made a very mild and sensible address, which was received with universal approbation. Having concluded, R. P. Bennett, junior editor of the *Union,* obtained the stand. He had, in order to screw up his courage to the sticking point, poured down such liberal quantities of Thompson's vitriolic whiskey, that it required some considerable effort to keep his feet. . . . Bennett's speech was a gem. It was well known by all present that his object was to create a disturbance. . . .

"I tell you," said Bennett, "this meetin' is not a meetin' of gen'lmen—(hic). It aint the law'd order party—(hic)—that's sure."

His tongue was as thick as his brain was addled, and his words were chopped off very often in the middle.

"I say—I tell yer—(hic)—this meetin's the rag—(hic)—the rag-tail and the bob-tail—(hic)—of the ab'lishonists—tha't what I—(hic)—what I tell yer, and by God, I know it!"

As Bennett halted for breath, the boys cried out, "Go it, Bennett; that's the way to talk!" "You're one of the orators—you are!" "Have a little more whiskey, Bennett!" "Why don't you pitch into the governor?"

"I tell yer," continued the speaker, "Sherrard is—(hic)—so he is, by God, the soul of—(hic)—chiv'l'ry, and it's a pity he did'nt—(hic)—yes it is—for damn Governor Geary—(hic)—. Them's my sentiments, and I don't kere a damn who knows it!" [16]

At length, and as expected, when the committee returned and read the resolutions to the heavily free-soil crowd, Sherrard was condemned and Geary was praised.

"No sooner were these resolutions read," Gihon continued, "than Sherrard sprang upon a pile of boards, and in a loud voice exclaimed:

"Any man who will dare to endorse these resolutions, is a liar, a scoundrel, and a coward!" His manner was highly excited. He wore a large bowie-knife and two six-shooters in his belt. . . . A Mr. [Joseph] Sheppard, living near Lecompton, and who stood in the midst of the crowd, quietly remarked: "I endorse them, and am neither a liar, a scoundrel, nor a coward . . . !"

Sherrard drew a revolver, and fired all the loads as rapidly as he could pull the trigger, aiming at Sheppard, though endangering the lives of others. Three balls took effect on Sheppard, and a fourth slightly wounded another person. As soon as Sherrard commenced firing, Sheppard pulled off his gloves, and attempted to return the shots; but his caps being wet, burst without discharging the loads; and seeing that Sherrard was about to draw his other pistol, he clubbed his revolver, rushed toward Sherrard and struck at him with the butt, Sherrard not having an opportunity to fire, returning his blows in a similar manner. They were separated, and Sheppard was removed, severely . . . wounded. Whilst Sherrard was firing, some dozen or more shots were fired by other parties. . . . An old man, over seventy years of age, named Thomas W. Porterfield, was among the crowd. . . . Seeing Sheriff Jones with a pistol in his hand, old Porterfield deliberately took off his spectacles, and pulling out his pocket handkerchief, wiped them carefully and again adjusted them. He then drew a navy revolver, and having examined the caps, placed the barrel upon his left arm, and took precise aim at Sheriff Jones, waiting for him to give the first shot. As the sheriff moved about, the old man steadily eyed him, keeping his pistol all the time properly aimed. . . .

No sooner was Sheppard taken off than Sherrard seized his other pistol and advanced, with finger on the trigger, toward . . . [John] Jones, the young man whom he had assaulted a few days before, when Jones, perceiving his danger, also drew. Several shots were then simultaneously fired, and Sherrard fell, mortally wounded. One ball had struck him in the forehead, penetrating the brain, and another had grazed his side. . . .[17]

Sherrard was carried away by friends, but it was obvious little could be done to save him. As Sam Jones noted:

[T]he shot fired at Sherrard took effect in the head, fracturing the skull bone as large as ten cent pieces or larger, which were taken from his head by the physician. I also put my finger up to the joint in the wound, or hole made by the ball. I saw a portion of the brain, that had come from the wound.[18]

With Sherrard's death the following day, "the defiant spirit of Border Ruffianism was snuffed out," proclaimed an elated free-stater. Border Ruffianism was not the only thing "snuffed out." Shaken by the Sherrard incident, stunned by lack of federal support, disgusted by the treachery of free-soilers, beset by legislators and lobbyists bearing bribes, his mail opened on a regular basis, John Geary had seen quite enough of Kansas. For reasons of "gradually sinking" health, the governor slipped from Lecompton one dark night in March 1857, and with a pair of revolvers strapped to his side, he fled the territory, never to return.[19]

Though most violence had ceased with the arrival of autumn 1856 and John Geary, it did not end entirely. After such a fearsome head of steam, the momentum of the late civil war carried into early 1857, as a number of wrathful Northerners attempted to even the score with the proslavery remnant.

Despite the murder of his brother by John Brown in May of 1856 and the stampede of southern settlers from the valley, "Dutch Henry" Sherman stead-fastly held to his hard-won claim along the Pottawatomie. One night in November, men with blackened faces raided the German's home and burned it to the ground. When Sherman still refused to leave as ordered, he was ambushed and murdered four months later.[20] At the former southern stronghold of Tecumseh, when Judge Rush Elmore spotted John Kagi, author of a defaming article in a Lawrence newspaper, the wealthy slave owner prepared to administer a thrashing with his cane. Before the blows could be struck, however, Kagi drew a revolver and shot his attacker in the leg. Pulling a pistol of his own, Elmore fired at the fleeing man, wounding him slightly before he escaped.[21]

Proslavery holdouts were not the only targets of vindictive free-soilers. Gangs of midnight "regulators" raked the land, wreaking revenge on those in their own ranks inclined to collaborate or compromise with the enemy. Near Lecompton, the speaker of the Free-State Legislature, because of his moderate stance, was dragged from bed one night and stripped, then given fifty lashes on the back "until it ran with blood." Like other men in the area, the victim was allowed ten days to clear out of Kansas . . . or face the consequences.[22]

For the most part, though, the winter of 1856–1857 was a season of "masterly inactivity" as the victorious free-state party awaited what they hoped would be a heavy flow of Northerners in the spring. Their prayers were more than answered. Indeed, by late March, with the violence curtailed and the situation seemingly stable, the "tide of immigration became a flood."[23]

"[T]he roads are white with the long lines of covered wagons," gleefully reported the revived *Herald of Freedom*.[24]

"Emigration came pouring in by the hundreds and thousands," added another spectator. "[I]t came, like an avalanche, it seemed more like a fiction than a fact":

> I was at Westport, a short time after two boats had discharged their pas-
> sengers at Kansas City. The . . . town turned out to witness the influx of
> immigration; a menagerie of wild beasts could not have attracted greater

interest. Desirous to hear the opinion of its citizens I mingled with the by-standers . . . [where] some of the leaders of the border ruffian clan had assembled. One of them with true depth of feeling, remarked: "My God! The cause is lost." The reply was: "I'll be damned if it don't look like it." [25]

At Leavenworth, free-soilers arrived in such overwhelming numbers that almost overnight the proslavery party became an insignificant minority. Upriver, nothing illustrated the sudden shift more than the sale of the radical *Atchison Squatter Sovereign* to free-staters. "In the future," laughed new owner Samuel Pomeroy with heavy understatement, "the course of the paper will be slightly different from what it has been." [26] Even David Atchison, once so confident, now knew full well that the cause in Kansas was lost and advised southern friends to direct efforts else-where. "At one time we had high hopes that in Kansas we should soon have another outpost protecting the institutions of the South," the dispirited Missourian wrote. "But we are no longer laboring under any such flattering illusion." [27]

While there was gloom and despair in Dixie, there was joy and hope in the North. Perhaps the happiest people in America were a quiet group of individuals who had never set foot in Kansas. Viewing the spectacle of free-soil emigration from afar, Eli Thayer and Amos Lawrence of the New England Emigrant Aid Society realized that all the time, energy, and money spent by their organization had at last been molded into victory. "We look on the great question as now settled," sighed Lawrence, "and all political movements in Kansas as having chiefly a local interest. . . . Now we must be magnanimous to the South." [28]

Though territorial leaders generally agreed with Lawrence that the struggle was indeed over, few so near the fire were in any mood to be "magnanimous" until the reins of power were firmly and forever in their hands. So long as the territorial government remained under proslavery control, victory would never be complete. As the summer passed and the October vote for members to the legis-lature approached, Northerners once again formed militia companies "for pro-tection of the ballot-box." [29] On election eve, wary Kansans along the Missouri cut ferry cables and set skiffs adrift to prevent a Border Ruffian crossover. When the polls closed the following day, however, the anticipated invasion had failed to materialize. Although flagrant ballot-box stuffing had occurred at isolated polls adjacent to the Missouri border, and although a considerable number of illegal votes from Iowa and Nebraska had been cast, the elections passed peacefully. And, as expected, when the final tally was in, the free-state party had swept the field. [30]

With power finally in the hands of Charles Robinson and his joyous adherents, the only hurdle to complete and total triumph lay with the proslavery constitu-tional convention. If free-soilers remained firm and forceful, however, there was little or no chance that a state constitution other than free could ever be foisted on Kansas. And with Charles Robinson once again in the driver's seat, it was a certainty that Northerners would never stray far from their course. Ironically, it was not the constitutional convention, the dwindling proslavery presence in the territory, or even the Missouri Border Ruffians that posed the greatest threat to Free Kansas and peace. It was James Lane.

"Do what I will, I can not like that man . . . ," confessed one free-soil fighter in his journal. "[T]here is not, to my thinking, honesty in his face. . . . Let a man speak to him no matter whom it may be, he passes his arm around his waist or leans fimiliarly [*sic*] on his shoulder. . . . [T]here is something to much about him, of the seeker after popularity and the political demogogue." [31]

Always stormiest when times were most calm, acutely aware that his power rested squarely among the more turbulent and violent free-staters, Lane tried with might and main to sabotage Robinson's patient policy. Shortly after the October election, Lane summoned his murderous Danites to Lawrence and proposed the assassination of constitutional convention members. While the tranquil times hardly seemed to warrant such a bloodthirsty scheme, and more moderate members were aghast at the notion, a majority of those assembled followed their leader implicitly and "cheered him to the echo." [32] Listening quietly to the harangue, one of Lane's best men, Joel Goodin, finally arose.

> Gen. Lane tells us that further peaceful measures are out of the question; that our only remedy for this new trouble is by shedding blood. I fully agree with him! (Boisterous cheers.) Nothing but blood will quiet this agitation, and restore tranquility to Kansas. Nothing but blood will make Kansas a Free State. (Cheers.) I came here expressly to spill blood, and I propose to do it before I return home. (Protracted cheering.). . . . [A] little waste of worthless blood will restore order and tranquility again. (Cheers on cheers.) But I may differ with some of you as to the proper place to begin this blood-spilling business. (Hear! Hear!) No person has occasioned more strife, or been the more fruitful cause of our disturbances than—James H. Lane! He demands blood! We all want it; but it is his blood that is demanded at this time; and if he presses on his assassination project, I propose he shall be the first person to contribute in that direction. [33]

"Gen. Lane seemed perfectly confounded," a witness later wrote. "The whole throng were taken by surprise; and . . . were delighted beyond expression, that some person had the ability and sufficient force of character to meet a bold, bad man, and throttle his murderous plans at their inception." [34]

Although Lane tried to provoke a bloody confrontation in Lecompton a few days later, then proposed yet another scheme of wholesale slaughter throughout the territory, his reckless plots came to naught.[35] Clearly, the days of violence—for the northern half of Kansas, at least—were over. Military victory had been won. Political conquest was in sight. Despite the agitators and demagogues, most settlers were more than ready to lay down their arms and at long last enjoy the fruits of peace.

For the first time in its short history, Kansas now faced the pleasant prospect of sowing seeds in the spring and actually being on hand to harvest the result in autumn. Because contending armies and guerrilla bands had ravaged the land time and time again—burning barns and crops, destroying miles of fence, stealing hundreds of horses and cattle—there had never been an opportunity to engage in serious agriculture. When Kansas farmers finally sampled the soil of their new home, they were stunned by its richness.

"Sweet potatoes grow to an immense size and . . . [b]eets and the other tubers are gigantic," raved John J. Ingalls from Sumner. "I saw a pair of beets the other day nearly four feet long and eight inches in major diameter."[36]

"This is one of the greatest countries for melons I ever saw . . . ," echoed another man from Tuscarora. "One of the sixteen that we bought was so large that we were forced to cut it outside our cabin. And if the rind was of such a material to stand frost we should trouble ourselves no longer about a protection from winters blast."[37]

While such tall tales to homefolk were customary, others who planted corn and wheat or experimented with tobacco, cotton, peanuts, and even sugar cane could attest that the soil in Kansas was more fertile than anything previously known.

The progress of territorial towns and villages had also been sharply stymied by the late war. While proslavery and free-soil soldiers had marched off to fight, improvements in the settlements had ground to a halt. Stumps, rocks, and gulleys remained in the streets, and with no appreciable grading for runoff, the result was a bottomless swamp in wet weather and rock-hard ruts in dry. Except for Leavenworth, whose raw and rowdy population of nearly ten thousand seemed impervious to the vicissitudes of war, few communities in Kansas could qualify for the title of "town" much less "city." Many places, like the village of Sumner, were little better than pig sties—low, muddy, foul, "reeking with filth and heavy with malaria."[38] Even Lawrence, for all its notoriety and vaunted "New England tidiness," was hardly more than a squalid collection of cabins, shacks, and "hencoops."

"[I]f you ask a man why he doesn't repair his uncomfortable house," revealed a visitor to Lawrence in 1855, "he tells you he would but for the war; and the same reply will be tendered you if a cow elope in search of better shelter than her owner's pen affords, or a pig breaks out of his dilapidated stye; it is ever 'the war, the war' . . . past, present and prospective. . . ." [39]

With almost no construction in Kansas during the early years, lodging lagged far behind. Hotels remained small and primitive, with several men to a dozen sleeping in a room. An English guest at one hostel found that in territorial Kansas, "boarding" meant every man for himself.

> "Step in, stranger; the crowd's going to eat," was my summons. . . . I entered the dining-room, saw the table covered with breakfast fare, including the usual small dishes of meat and cakes and apple preserve. The "crowd" was standing around the table, each man with a hand upon the back of his chair. The female portion of the company having been seated, a signal was given, and a simultaneous action ensued. The movement of the chair with one hand, the seizure of the nearest small dish with the other, the sudden sitting down, and the commencement of a vigorous eating, were the work of a moment. In five minutes the company had left the table for the gallery on the street front. . . . At dinner it was the same—fat bacon, corn-bread, and tea or coffee. At supper, the same; and at each meal in about equal quantity. The next day the same, and so every day. [40]

Because of the disruption in trade and commerce, as well as the very real fear that shelves would be cleared in a raid or riot, many stores and shops remained poorly stocked. And even in the best of times, some merchants in remote regions were sorely pressed to maintain a viable inventory.

"[T]he merchandise in this establishment *might* fill a waggon . . . ," grumbled one trader at Iola. "[T]he opposition store appeared pretty well used up,—for I could discern no other articles of commerce than six bags of coarse salt,—half a barrel of the vilest whiskey,—six boxes of sardines, and a chunk of tobacco!" [41]

Shamed by the primitive conditions that existed throughout the territory, Kansas quickly turned its energies inward with war's end. At surging Leavenworth and upriver at Atchison, new and costly works were raised to receive the flood of immigrants arriving on the levees. The first bridge spanning the Kaw was opened for traffic at Topeka in May 1858, and others, including a rival at nearby Tecumseh, were planned. At Marysville, Mound City, Garnett, Olathe, Burlington, LeRoy, White Cloud, and Manhattan, miserable, muddy villages soon began to resemble respectable towns. Of all the settlements in Kansas, however, none went to work with a greater will than Lawrence. With an energy unmatched in the territory, the thrifty, industrious citizens in that much-assailed town raced to make good on lost time. Soon the daily stir along Massachusetts Street became so great that strangers often guessed the town's population at five, ten, even twelve times its actual size of one thousand. [42]

"Business of all kinds very brisk," noted one surprised visitor as he strolled through the city, "and a great many strangers in town inquiring and prying into everything. One Jewelry & Drug store looked as well as anything of the kind I have saw in the States. Ladies appear on the streets in full dress. . . . Hoops[,] flounces and nun bonnets appear to be the rage." [43]

"There was as much style and fashion . . . as would be seen in an eastern city," added another traveler. [44]

Few projects in Kansas demonstrated more faith in the future than did the Eldridge House of Lawrence. Built defiantly on the ruins of the old Free State Hotel, the four-story edifice was by far the most costly and lavishly furnished structure in Kansas. "The best hotel west of the Ohio," as one enthusiastic guest perhaps overstated it. [45] To the people of Lawrence, the Eldridge was more than a beautiful building; it was a stone and satin monument to their victory over slavery.

"One of the wonders of the age is Lawrence . . . ," penned a proud George Washington Brown in his *Herald of Freedom*. "Whatever else may be said of Lawrence, it may be truthfully asserted she has *backbone.*"

While the boom in building and soaring optimism were sorely needed in a land that had never known either, there were the drawbacks. Rampant in all new territories, speculation was especially reckless in Kansas. With the sudden rush of settlers following the war, demand for land rose astronomically. "Prices were fast rising, money plentiful, and everybody speculating," a stranger in Leavenworth recorded. "One lot, which cost eight dollars six months before, had just sold for twenty-two hundred dollars. . . . Shares often doubled in two or three weeks. Servant girls speculated in town lots." [46]

Rapacious town promoters, eager to cash in, sent east wildly exaggerated prospectuses of choice lots for sale in model cities with churches, schools, parks, railroads, and factories already in place. What the unwary sojourner often found upon reaching Kansas was similar to what John J. Ingalls found.

> No respectable residences; no society; no women except a few woebegone, desolate-looking old creatures; no mechanical activity . . . no schools, no children; nothing but the total reverse of the picture which was presented to me. . . . [O]nly [one] street in the place which has any pretension to a grade, the others being merely footpaths leading up and down the wild ravines to the few log huts and miserable cabins which compose the city. None of the premises are fenced, the whole being open to the incursions of dogs and pigs, which exist in large numbers, and seem, in fact, to constitute the greater amount of the population. [47]

Just off the boat, Richard Cordley had a like experience at another "paper city," Quindaro.

There were no sidewalks . . . and the streets were nearly torn up where they were marked at all. The houses were scattered "helter-skelter" about the place wherever a break in the hill or an opening in the bluffs gave room for one. They were all hastily built wooden structures, standing on stilts, and seeming ready to walk off at a moment's notice. . . . It had been raining three days when we arrived. The mud surged from one side of the street to the other, and it was not easy to tell where the river ended and the street began. The water in the river and the mud in the street were about the same color, and not very far from the same depth. The next morning when I arose, I heard a familiar voice. Opening the window and looking out, I saw one of our traveling companions of the day before making his way down the street in high boots. At every step he was crying: "Three feet; three and a half; four feet." Just as he came opposite the hotel he plunged into a hole and cried out, "No bottom." [48]

"[I]f Quindaro can succeed," added another arrival, "it will only serve to show that capital *may* make a town where nature *never* intended any." As many a gullible greenhorn soon learned, in Kansas anything could be a flourishing "city," from "a board-pile upwards." [49]

"Land sharks, speculators, userers and politicians . . . swarm over the West thicker than frogs in Egypt," spit one disgusted newcomer. [50]

The frenzy for land speculation often had an adverse and graphic impact on those with visions of instant wealth, as another traveler through the territory, Horace Greeley, soon discovered.

As to the infernal spirit of land speculation . . . I think no state [*sic*] ever suffered from it more severely than this. . . . There are too many idle, shiftless people in Kansas. I speak not here of lawyers, gentlemen speculators, and other non-producers, who are in excess here as elsewhere; I allude directly to those who call themselves settlers. . . . To see a man squatted on a quarter-section in a cabin which would make a fair hog-pen, but is unfit for a human habitation, and there living from hand to mouth by a little of this and a little of that, with hardly an acre of prairie broken . . . with no garden, no fruit-trees, "no nothing"—waiting for some one to come along and buy out his "claim" and let him move on to repeat the operation somewhere else—this is enough to give a cheerful man the horrors. Ask the squatter what he means, and he can give you a hundred good excuses for his miserable condition: he has no breaking-team; he has little or no good rail-timber; he has had the "shakes"; his family have been sick; he lost two years and some stock by the Border Ruffians, etc., etc. . . . [51]

Although some shrewd speculators did indeed strike it rich, many, like the man above, found Kansas a "hard road to travel." Among the human flotsam littering the territory was a middle-aged ne'er-do-well seemingly at the end of his rope. Down and out, "adrift seeking employment," the redheaded Ohioan soon reached rock-bottom on Indian Creek. "I am doomed to be a vagabond, and shall no longer struggle against my fate . . . ," William Tecumseh Sherman wrote from his cheerless cabin near Topeka. "I look on myself as a dead cock in the pit, not worthy of future notice. . . ."[52]

In addition to land speculation, another facet of Kansas life that seemed more pronounced than elsewhere was the almost total lack of religion. While the uncertainties of the late war no doubt played a role, much irreverent conduct could be attributed to a phenomenon typical to all frontiers in which young immigrants, for the first time in their lives, were free from the conventions and constraints of their more civilized homeland. "[W]hen once outside the restraints of eastern society, they act out the native depravity of the human heart," groused one angry and unemployed Kansas preacher.[53]

Although some settlers gave a grudging nod to Sunday as a day of devotion, most Kansans did not. "There is very little regard paid here to the Sabbath," a devout resident of Douglas admitted. "Now, while I am writing, the hammers of the carpenters are going just as if it were not Sunday. . . ."[54] Echoed John J. Ingalls from Sumner:

> [M]ost of the citizens employ the day in hunting prairie chickens or ducks and geese over in the Missouri bottoms. I went up to Atchison . . . last Sunday, on a boat . . . in hopes of finding an Episcopal church. . . . I was unsuccessful in my search, and was surprised to find the shops all open, whisky shops full of cursing Democrats, and the click of billiard balls and the dull thunder of tenpin alleys mingling with the nasal notes of a Hardshell Baptist preacher, who was holding forth in a small upper room directly over the same.[55]

Unlike Ingalls, some who sought the scarce churches did so for reasons other than spiritual. "Spent sunday in a pious way, cost me only 25 cents," Daniel R. Anthony of Leavenworth confessed to his sister, Susan B. "[C]hurch is cheaper than the Theatre, although the acting is not near as good."[56]

Even Lawrence, reviled so long and often by Border Ruffians as a haven to "tract-peddlers and Psalm-singers," seemed supremely indifferent to matters religious. "I had formed a very poor opinion of the morality of the Territory when I was at Lawrence . . . ," said a shocked visitor to the town. "[A]lmost everyone I met was profane."[57]

*John J. Ingalls.* KANSAS STATE HISTORICAL SOCIETY, TOPEKA.

Christian backsliding was not the only transgression Kansas men and women fell prey to. Penned one traveler in his journal:

> The habit of smoking is here supreme male and female addicting themselves to it alike, in nearly every house I have visited the women smoked, indeed I have watched them making the biscuits and frying the meat, at the same time filling up a dirty smoke blackened pipe, —lighting it,— pushing down the coarse tobacco with their fingers,—and then sucking away at the short stem with all their might. . . .[58]

Though this picture perhaps was overdrawn in the case of females, the use of tobacco was almost universal among Kansas menfolk. Of all the numerous ways to enjoy the plant, however, one form was loathed by women, and many men, above all others. According to the Lawrence *Herald of Freedom:*

> One of the greatest nuisances that a decent man can be guilty of, is to chew tobacco. He is forever spitting the nasty stuff somewhere—it makes but little difference with him where. If he would but swallow his favorite dish, it would make it some better; but tobacco chewers seem to

have an idea that they are a privileged class to spit when and where they please. . . .

The truth is, there can be no such thing as neatness where there is a squirter of tobacco juice about. We have seen too much of the dirty habit to know there can be. . . . The private mastication of tobacco, in one's own home, bed-room, or kitchen, as the case may be, is an affair to be settled with one's self. We do not intend to interfere with the police regulations of the home—they are in abler hands than ours. If indulgent wives choose to have their door-steps and balcony floor discolored, their carpets ruined, and their parlors and bed-rooms irrevocably defiled with tobacco juice—if they relish the contact with their own mouths, of lips that have been all day saturated with yellow saliva—if they like the smell of tobacco-scented breaths, coming from between dirty and disgusting teeth—we have nothing to say. But we have a right to protest, and we do protest, against the outrageous public nuisance of tobacco chewing. No man has a right to go to a . . . public gathering, and seating himself in the midst of cleanly Christians, squirt out random streams of tobacco juice around him.—To do this . . . is little short of blackguardism.[59]

Whiskey was another staple the struggling territory could seemingly not survive without. Because of the heavy emigration of young, unattached adventurers and fighters, from both North and South, the consumption of liquor was as great as or greater than in rough-and-tumble territories elsewhere. At Leavenworth, Atchison, Lecompton, and other river ports, countless dark and dingy "doggeries" catered to the insatiable demand. "There are but five habitable houses in the town," remarked a visitor to Pawnee. "Three of these are used for vending intoxicating drinks."[60]

Even once-staid Lawrence, whose original population prided itself on temperance and derided Missourians as "drunkards" and "pukes," did not escape the blight of "demon rum."

"[T]here are grog-shops on every hand," one Lawrence minister complained, "and the majority of young men are frequenters of such places."[61]

"[W]hiskey—poor whiskey, too—is poured down on every hand," agreed an Eastern correspondent in the town. "It is dealt out in almost every building.—Drinking is the principle business. . . ."[62]

Among the resident Indians, "crazy water" had long since become a cherished fact of tribal life. As Peter Bryant from Topeka observed:

They lounge around town a good deal, and most of them are willing to drink all the whiskey they can get. The Squaws are just as fierce as any of them for it. I met a drove of Squaws the other day. Three of them

were girls and tolerable good looking, and they hailed me with "How."
I said "how," then "Where goin?" "Up creek." "Where from?" "Topeka.
Any tobac?" "No." "Any Whisk?" "No." "Ugh, ugh," and they went on.
I suppose if I had had the "whisk" I could have lit on their fections like
a hot pancake, but as it was I was "no good," and they didn't care any-
thing about me.[63]

Caught in a violent rainstorm far from home, Sam Walker was compelled to
spend the night in an Indian cabin.

About nine o'clock I was aroused by a series of the most unearthly yells it
was ever my privilege to enjoy. . . . About thirty men and women rode
up to the house and dismounted. They had a ten-gallon keg of whisky
with them. They all entered the house, arranged themselves around the
keg, and proceeded to arrange themselves around its contents. They
dipped it out and handed it around, all the time singing, laughing, and
yelling. . . . They kept it up all night, and in the morning those who were
still able to kick got on their ponies and rode off. When I got up I counted
six squaws and nine bucks lying promiscuously in a heap, all dead drunk.[64]

Going hand in glove with drinking, of course, was violence. Brawls, beatings,
and fistfights on the streets of the territory became almost too common for notice.
"[Y]ou dont no what a Country this is for drinking and fighting . . . ," wrote James
Butler Hickok, who, after a short stint in Kansas, was well on his way toward
earning the nickname "Wild Bill." "[T]hare has been two awful fights in town this
week you dont no anything about sutch fighting at home as I speak of. . . ."[65]

Gambling was another curse associated with drinking. "I am appalled at the
amount of drinking and gambling that has existed in Kansas, especially in the
Missouri River towns . . . ," grumbled the now safe and fully recovered Pardee
Butler. "Under the shade of every green tree, on the streets, in every shop, store,
grocery and hotel, it has seemed as if the chief business of the people was to gamble
and drink."[66] While all Kansas towns wagered a little or a lot, it was Leavenworth
that again led the way. "Cards could have been picked up in the streets by the score,"
said a stunned stranger, "and in a town where the very first demands of civilization were wanting in the furnishing of the house, there was no lack of such costly
indulgences as gaming-tables. . . ."[67] Added another arrival to the city:

Their "boss sportsman" was a certain A. B. Miller, who had run up
a shanty with a showily fitted-out bar and rooms. . . . There roulette,
pharo, and poker were going on from midday all through the night, and

large sums changed hands. Now and then some unlucky gambler would end his miseries in the mighty Missouri, and many another was shot in the saloon itself during the constant night rows.[68]

Almost anywhere drinking men met was a fit field for professional "sharpers." During a land sale at Paola, Julia Lovejoy paused for a moment to watch them at work.

The gamblers are very shrewd in decoying their victims into their meshes. One man advanced in years, whom they had singled out to fleece, as they probably supposed him a green-horn at the business, they persuaded to try his luck at the gaming table, and so sure were they of their anticipated money they purposely let him win. When the game was concluded, the old man scooped up his money and was off for himself, and all their honeyed words had no effect on him afterwards; they found they had caught a Tartar instead of a green-horn![69]

Unbeknownst to Julia, it was she and other laughing spectators who were the dupes, for the victorious old "Tartar" was undoubtedly a decoy, or "shill," who acted out his role of winner day in and day out.

While vice and prostitution were not unknown in the territory, few towns in Kansas had a clientele capable of supporting "dens of infamy." As always, booming,

*Leavenworth, Kansas.* KANSAS STATE HISTORICAL SOCIETY, TOPEKA.

brawling Leavenworth was the exception. "No element of vice or crime seemed to be absent," a foreign visitor grimaced. "Every species of shameless wickedness and unchecked outrage met one's gaze at every turn." [70]

"We have in our city," protested one of the rare preachers in Leavenworth, "some of the most abandoned & degraded men in the whole world. . . . There is an Irishman . . . who keeps the lowest brothel & drinking house I have ever known," the clergyman concluded, apparently unaware of the irony in his words. [71]

Though wholesale theft and violence had almost disappeared by the spring of 1858, it did not end altogether. The precedent set in the preceding years was simply too strong to stop at once. With hundreds of mercenaries from Lane's army lingering in Kansas following the war, it was only natural that when there was suddenly no enemy to prey upon, the more unscrupulous would swiftly turn on their benefactors. "Here," hissed Julia Lovejoy, "nothing of value is safe for a moment, if exposed." [72]

While pilfering from stores and businesses was troublesome, theft of livestock was much more serious. During the war, gangs on both sides had "pressed" horses and mules out of what was termed "military necessity." Facing such numbers and weaponry, a hapless farmer could do little. What was "pressing" in war, however, became simple stealing in peace and, as a laborious letter from the newly elected constable of Montecello makes clear, such activity would not be tolerated. James Butler Hickok:

> There has been 25 horses stolen here Within the last ten days by to men by the name of Scroggins and Black Bob They have narry one been taken yet but I think they will ketch it soon. if they are caught About here they Will be run upawfull soon to the top of Some hill . . . where they wont steel Any more horses. [73]

What was frowned upon and put down with an iron hand in Kansas, however, was winked at when it occurred "over the way." With an army of unemployed free-state fighters milling about the territory, many Missourians were quick to perceive the peril—and perhaps divine the future. "Think you," one Missourian warned, "that desperate men, with arms in their hands, will permit themselves to starve whilst herds of fat cattle, grain, flour, bacon and stores of other necessaries superabound in the border counties of Missouri—an enemy's country?" [74] The answer, of course, was no.

Late in 1856, James Holmes, a minion of John Brown, led a band of men on a raid through Bates County, Missouri. The expedition was a complete success. "This is the first foray into Missouri," James Redpath gloated, "and having led the way it will not probably be the last." It was not. A short time later more raids occurred, and Missouri livestock soon began "emigrating" to Kansas.[75] Revealed George Washington Brown:

> [H]orses are brought into our principal towns every few days and sold at auction for from one-fifth to one-half their real value. Purchasers buy them with the understanding that they do so at their own risk. These things are common occurrences. . . . [H]orses . . . [are] almost a drug in the market.[76]

While killings in Kansas for political motives had been rife, murders for pelf were surprisingly rare. Nevertheless, several gruesome homicides did occur. When the stabbed and hacked remains of two strangers were found floating in the river at Leavenworth in August 1857, suspicion immediately fell on a gang of cutthroats operating about the city. Three men were quickly arrested, their hands literally "covered with blood." While one of the accused was being questioned at a hotel, an angry mob assembled. "Influenced by threats, and promises of protection from the infuriated crowd which was fast gathering around the place of trial, he confessed the deed," reported a newsman, "and told where the money was concealed, which they had taken from their victims."[77]

Keeping their promise, the officials hustled their prisoner to the safety of the nearby fort. The two accomplices, however, remained trapped in the jail. The journalist continued:

> By this time, the mob had increased to about two thousand persons, demanding the prisoners from the authorities, and insisting upon taking the law in their own hands. Judge [Samuel] LeCompte made a speech, exhorting them to quiet, and assuring them that justice should be meted out to the culprits. The crowd hissed him down . . . and moved off to the jail where Baize and Squarles were confined. . . . The mob, arriving at the jail, took out the prisoners, and dragged them to a large elm tree, at the mouth of Three Mile Creek, about 1/4 mile below the city. The noose was placed round their necks, the rope passed over a limb of the tree and the crowd pulling at the other end. Squarles was first strung up. Not expiring so readily as the mob could wish, several took hold of his legs pulling him down in such a manner as to break his neck.
>
> Meanwhile, Baize stood in the crowd talking with an officer from the fort, who, unperceived, slipped the noose from his neck, whereupon Baize ran for the jail. He was placed in jail, and the authorities, and some few citizens, again, without success, endeavored to protect him. The mob broke open the jail, took him out and he was soon hanging on the fatal tree.[78]

While sheriffs, regulators, and mobs worked manfully to keep the underworld down, higher society struggled to rise. Clubs and lyceums were organized, debates and "moral" lectures were held, and even professional entertainment occasionally ventured into the western backwater, as when "Washburn's Great American Colossal Circus" gave a one-day performance at Leavenworth.[79] Predictably, as clubs and churches took root and people shared idle hours, gossip flourished. "Kansas is *almost* too new for scandal," winked one wry observer.[80]

"Mrs. Clark . . . [w]ants to be a little too popular for a poor Methodist preacher's wife, on a missionary station," an envious Mary Sly of Richmond whispered to her sister. "She wears *only* 7 hoops all the time and does not see how she could do without. . . . I despise them on a minister's wife."[81]

Then too, there was the brow-raising rumor circulating through Kansas of the bride who wed in hoops only to give birth a fortnight later.[82]

While new rivalries and jealousies developed following the war, old animosities occasionally matured. One in particular had tragic consequences, not only for those involved but for all of Kansas.

As was the case in any new country, property lines were often vague or ill defined. Although land disputes among neighbors were usually settled peacefully, if not always satisfactorily, the contestants occasionally came to blows. Such was the case involving Gaius Jenkins and James Lane. Recognized as leaders within their own free-soil factions—Jenkins among the easterners, Lane among the westerners—both men laid claim to a large and loyal following. Unfortunately, both men also laid claim to the same bit of land in Lawrence. During one of Lane's lengthy trips north to raise men and money for the war, Jenkins used the hiatus to seize his neighbor's cabin and lot. Described by friends as "generous" and "whole-souled," Jenkins was also labeled "impulsive" and "violent," especially when he drank, a habit in which he frequently indulged.[83]

Not content with merely tearing down the paling, or picket fence, that enclosed the grave of Lane's little daughter, Jenkins also effaced the plot when he plowed the surrounding lot. In the summer of 1856, while many free-state leaders were being hunted down and jailed at Lecompton, Jenkins was captured by an alert slave and also imprisoned. In the meantime, Lane returned to Kansas and reclaimed his home and property. When he discovered the "beastly and inhuman act" committed by Jenkins, he could barely believe his eyes. According to James Christian:

> Lane and myself spent several days hunting and digging, about where we supposed the grave was located, and both came to the conclusion that the body had been dug up, as no trace of the coffin could be found. . . . I shall never forget the expression of his face, as with compressed lips, he exclaimed: "Such a———ghoul is not fit to live. If I was only certain that

he dug up my child out of revenge upon me, I would kill him at first sight." The tears started in his eyes; I tried to calm him by telling him we might be mistaken. . . . "Yes," said he, "but why did the—brute tear the paling away and plow over the grave, so that it could never be found?"[84]

"I will have the blood out of his God damned black heart," vowed Lane.[85]

Following the war, the land office finally agreed to settle the dispute, and in 1858 both men appeared at Lecompton to deliver testimony. James Christian continued:

Some one foolishly remarked, in the presence of Lane and Jenkins, that "the best way for them to settle the difficulty was to go out and fight it out." Jenkins instantly remarked, in a loud voice, that that would suit him . . . ; that if Lane would go out, the case would be decided in a few minutes. Lane instantly jumped to his feet, folded his arms across his breast, and with a most terribly bitter sneer upon his face, remarked: "Any man that would let a——nigger take him prisoner need not talk to me about fighting!" Jenkins . . . [was] red with passion.[86]

Only the timely arrival of the register and his loud summons for "Silence!" prevented bloodshed then and there. When the claim decision favored Jenkins, the land office agreed on Lane's request to rehear more evidence at a later date. Meanwhile, the hatred mounted, with both men thirsting for the blood of the other.

At 1 P.M. on June 3, Jenkins, his two nephews, and a hired hand approached the gate separating his land from Lane's.[87] Because the spring he normally used had become "oily" and undrinkable, Jenkins began the habit of boldly crossing to the well near Lane's house and drawing water that he felt was rightfully his. Earlier that day, Jenkins's employee, Ray Green, had done the same thing but was hailed upon leaving.

"If you come in this yard again," Lane warned, "I'll shoot you, you damned scoundrel."

"The hell you will," countered Green.

When Lane repeated his threat, the hired man grabbed his pails and walked away.

"[S]hoot and be damned," Green laughed.[88]

Later, after lunch, when Jenkins's wife wanted more water, the four men, fully armed, returned. "Lane was in the yard walking to and fro when we arrived at the gate," Ray Green recalled. "He said: 'Jenkins, if you come into this yard I'll shoot you.' Jenkins replied: 'Enough of that talk.'"[89]

Grabbing an ax, Jenkins began chopping at the gate, which Lane had nailed shut. Henry Jenkins was by his uncle's side.

Lane said: "I'll shoot you Jenkins, if you come in the yard. . . . " While he was in the act of knocking down the gate, Lane repeated: "I'll shoot you if you come in the yard. . . ." Just as he got it about knocked down, Lane started for the house after the gun. Uncle was about through when Lane came out with the gun. . . . Lane said again, "I'll shoot you. . . ." After [my uncle] had advanced thirty feet or more, Lane drew his gun and fired. A second after, perhaps more. . . . Uncle fell on his side forward, dead in his tracks. I rushed up and put my hand on his breast.[90]

Pulling a pistol, Ray Green fired several rounds, striking Lane and forcing him into the home. His uncle riddled with buckshot, Henry Jenkins quickly saw that there was little he could do. "I rolled him over on his back," said the boy. "His wife I think was the second person who came up to him. . . . I saw her coming, and crying, 'Is he killed . . . ?' I tore open Uncle's shirt. . . . The blood was gushing out of his mouth."[91]

A visitor to Lawrence, Albert Richardson, was in the office of the *Herald of Freedom* at the time.

[S]uddenly a voice was heard from the street: "Jim Lane has killed Gaius Jenkins, and a mob has gathered around his house to hang him. . . ." [W]e all hastened to Lane's house half a mile away. Around it were two or three hundred excited men, a few proposing to lynch Lane, but the majority declaring that he should be tried by due course of law. . . . I found General Lane upon a bed in his house, crippled by a pistol shot in the knee, and surrounded by his wife and children, all in tears.

At the residence of Jenkins only a few yards away, lay the bloody corpse of the husband and father, while the air rung with shrieks from the widow and the fatherless.[92]

Jenkins's body was packed in ice and preserved until Sunday, when hundreds of Kansans attended the funeral. Though Lane was acquitted of murder, most felt he was guilty and treated him thus. Because of his role in the fight for Free Kansas and his growing national renown, Jim Lane had considered himself a viable candidate for president in 1860, some backers even going so far as to print a large number of lithographs with an inscription below his portrait: THE SIXTEENTH PRESIDENT OF THE UNITED STATES. Following the death of Gaius Jenkins, however, Lane became all but an outcast.[93]

"I consider this the greatest misfortune of my life," moaned the fallen former hero.[94]

As the Jenkins case illustrated, death in Kansas did not take a holiday simply because armies had stopped marching. Although the incident at Lawrence was a sensational story that drew headlines nationally, disease and sickness methodically worked their will and unceremoniously carried away hundreds of nameless victims.

"I averaged four funerals a week," revealed one minister in 1858.

Terrible tragedy could also strike swiftly and without warning. On the weekend of July the Fourth, citizens of Burlingame and Superior assembled for a community picnic along the cool, shady banks of nearby Dragoon Creek. One of those on his way to join the jubilee was John Drew, whose family included a pretty and popular sixteen-year-old, Naomi. A local newspaper continued:

> An ox team [and wagon], containing most of the family . . . was crossing the creek at the usual ford, when the oxen, without any apparent cause, suddenly turned and ran into deep water. Every possible assistance was promptly rendered by the numerous bystanders, and with some difficulty all were rescued, except Miss Drew. She sank immediately, and all efforts to find and rescue her seemed baffled as if by fatality. Her body was recovered at the end of perhaps fifteen minutes, but the most patient and persevering efforts failed to recall any signs of life. All further thought of a celebration was at an end, and the multitude assembled sadly followed the remains to the home of the bereaved family.[95]

One of those who witnessed the drama was a close friend, James Stewart. Penned the sad young man in his journal:

> The remainder of the day I read some,—and thought much on the uncertainty of life—the transition of all things. Naomi you no longer need our sympathies—but we feel that we have sustained a very great loss in your misfortune. Torn from our midts—in the bloom of youth, when hopes are high. . . . [W]e feel your loss, and mourn your fate. . . . farewell Dear friend.[96]

By far, however, the thoughts and energies of most Kansans following the war was spent not on sadness or drinking or gossip or theft, but on building their homes and farms and the everyday labor of life.

Recorded a young Kansas farmer:

> **Saturday 12** Dug 106 post holes 3 of us and thought we were doing very well. . . . The weather has been very fine all week. . . .
> **Sunday 13** I walked out over my farm and was pleased with [it] more than ever
> **Monday 14** dug 120 post holes to day with Conner
> **Tuesday 15** dug 100 holes to day

**Wednesday 16** finished digging the holes and set over one hundred posts

**Thursday 17** set some posts and nailed on a few rails

**Friday 18** set all the posts he had and carried the rails around

**Saturday 19** nailed on the rails on one side and quit for the week

**Sunday 20** Went over to Gardner to day 3 miles from here to church for the first time in Kansas. Heard a young man try to preach on the resurrection and an old man exhorted in a manner which pleased the outsider very much

**Monday 21** Washed one pair of my drawers a woolen overshirt and a check shirt and some collars

**Tuesday 22** Worked at the fence

**Wednesday 23** Worked at the fence

**Thursday 24** Worked at the fence

**Friday 25** Went into the timber and hauled a load of posts

**Saturday 26** Hauled a load of poles for Conners cabin [97]

And toil though they did, many Kansans, after so many years of strife, finally had time to enjoy the simple side of life.

A young Kansas father:

Oh, the sweet little creature. You may think I am only bragging, but I tell you she is the smartest child I ever saw, has the most sense, is the prettiest, and the best everything else. She can crawl, stand up and hold to a chair, has cut six teeth and will soon have two more . . . but she has precious little hair on her head.[98]

Meanwhile, as the welcome winds of peace mercifully fanned the once-inflamed north, to the south, beyond the Marais des Cygnes, dark clouds were building, and the first rumble of a distant thunder was beginning to echo over the land. It was here, in a region that had for the most part escaped the violence of "Bleeding Kansas," that a name was rising that would resound for years and years to come—Jayhawkers!

# CHAPTER ELEVEN

# MINISTER OF
# THE DEVIL

BY THE TIME THE SMOKE OF '56 HAD FINALLY CLEARED IN NORTHERN KANSAS, only a small number of diehard Southerners remained. Many of their defeated and dismayed comrades returned whence they came, either to Alabama, South Carolina, and other southern states, or simply back across the line to Missouri.[1] A large number of proslavery families merely loaded their wagons and set off on a four- or five-day trek to what they hoped was the warmer, as well as politically sunny, climate of southern Kansas. Although a handful of agitators no doubt drifted down with them, most emigrants came not to rekindle old embers or make of Kansas a slave state, but simply to till in peace the rich, virgin soil. Many of their new northern neighbors had other ideas, however.

Led by former minister James Montgomery, a gang of nominally free-soil regulators, soon to be known as "Jayhawkers," began robbing, flogging, and sometimes killing southern settlers almost as fast as they arrived. By the winter of 1857–1858, the pattern of violence that had so stamped the north was being repeated in the south. When, on February 11, 1858, the Jayhawkers brazenly raided the proslavery stronghold of Fort Scott, U.S. troops finally moved in.[2] Thumbing their noses at the federal government, Montgomery's marauders continued their attacks apace.

On April 21, almost within sight of the army cantonment at Fort Scott, the Jayhawkers swept up the Marmaton River valley, plundering proslavery and free-soil settler alike. When word of the raid reached town, a deputy marshal asked for and received a file of twenty dragoons to act as posse. Surprising the gang eight miles west of Fort Scott, the soldiers, armed with sabers and revolvers, quickly pressed the bandits toward a belt of timber along Yellow Paint Creek. Without warning, the raiders wheeled and fired their weapons, striking several horses and severely wounding one of the soldiers. Though the dragoons returned fire and held their ground, when reinforcements eventually arrived, the Jayhawkers had vanished without a trace.[3]

Returning with their wounded comrade to Fort Scott, the soldiers were stunned when the trooper took a turn for the worse and suddenly died. "His death threw a gloom over officers, soldiers and citizens . . . ," the *Fort Scott Democrat* acknowledged. "He was a favorite in the company, a young man of studious habits, liberal education, the son of a respectable Philadelphian. . . . It is right that those who shot him should know that he came from the North. . . ."[4]

Not everyone was shocked or saddened by the news that a federal soldier had, for the first time, been killed in the Kansas violence. "[T]he prestige of U.S. soldiers as posses for border ruffians to harrass the people with, is destroyed," gloated John Speer of the *Lawrence Republican.* "It has been satisfactorily demonstrated, that a Sharpe's [*sic*] rifle ball, well and carefully directed, will have the same effect on a dragoon, as upon any common man."[5] Encouraged by sentiment such as this, Montgomery embarked on a campaign that spring of 1858 to drive all proslavery settlers from southern Kansas. To further this plan and draw troops from the region, a band of Jayhawkers dashed north, pillaging farms and hamlets along the Santa Fe Road.[6] As was the case wherever they struck, an increasing number of raiders cared less for a man's politics than they did his property.

*James Montgomery.* KANSAS STATE HISTORICAL SOCIETY, TOPEKA.

"[I]f free-state he was cursed for [being a] Black Republican," noted a *New York Tribune* correspondent, "if pro-slavery, he was cursed for being a Border Ruffian; and thus both sides were plundered. This conduct indicates that the band was nothing more or less than bandits. . . ."[7]

Scrawled one victim on May 14 to a friend in Indiana:

[L]ast tuesday night . . . Sixteen men cum . . . and robed us of vary near of [every] thing that we had taken horses money clothing even to razor hardly left us a Second Suit to our back and gave us our orders to leave in two days or they would take our lives and we done so I went back after the second load . . . they followed me ten miles to kill me I got to the brush and give theme [the] dodg I feel like I was broakup. . . . I am cuming in as soon as I can sell my land and the territory may go to thunder.[8]

Wailed the editor of the *Fort Scott Democrat:*

It is a soul-sickening sight to see family after family . . . flying from their homes, dragging after them the few effects which robbery may have left them. . . . For days the roads have been lined with good, honest citizens, leaving the country of their choice for opinions sake—thus fathers, brothers and sons, have been obliged to leave mothers, sisters and wives, to flee the country from these merciless scamps.—Farms are abandoned with crops planted and everything wears a cheerless prospect.[9]

"It is impossible to give you an idea of affairs as they exist," reported a citizen of Butler, Missouri, as he viewed the stream of Kansas refugees. "Their numbers are increasing every hour." [10] Added another from neighboring Cass County:

[E]very vacant house and shed is filled with these unfortunate people— three and four families in a single hut—who are in a destitute condition, and for food to sustain life solely rely upon the charity of Missourians, who . . . are only restrained by Federal bayonets from entering the Territory, taking the law in their own hands, and executing justice upon these fellows by shooting them down like wolves, whenever and wherever they may be found.[11]

At least one man was not inhibited by bayonets, nor did he have any compunction whatsoever about shooting down Jayhawkers "like wolves." A hot-blooded scion of a rich and powerful Georgia clan, Charles Hamilton, like many another southern idealist, had marched off in 1856 to make Kansas a Slave State. Bitter over the reverses of that year, Hamilton nonetheless held to his home on the banks of the Marais des Cygnes River. In the spring of 1858, when James Montgomery and the Jayhawkers ran him and his neighbors from the territory, Hamilton made up his mind that he would not go down easy.[12]

"[C]ome out of the Territory at once . . . ," he warned his friends still clinging to Kansas; "we are coming up there to kill snakes, and will treat all we find there as snakes." [13]

As promised, on the morning of May 19, Hamilton and a band of fellow refugees reentered Kansas and moved up the Marais des Cygnes. On the outskirts of Trading

Post, the Southerners seized Patrick Ross. In the village itself, storekeeper John Campbell was also captured.[14] With his prisoners in tow, Hamilton pushed northeast. A mile or so from Trading Post, the Reverend Benjamin Reed was at a neighbor's farm, discussing school matters.

> While there conversing . . . Hamilton, with about 30 men, came up—all armed. He ordered me . . . to fall into line. I said "No." He drew a large pistol, cocked it and presented it, saying, "You won't, will you . . . ?" He then ordered me to . . . fall into line; I did so. He then with a number of his men went into Mr. Nichol's yard, and said they were going to search his house. Soon after, they returned with a number of guns. . . . Presently a man driving a two-horse team drove along side. He was ordered to stop. Some of the party said "Where do you live?" He replied, "Sugar Mound." Then the order was given to get out of the wagon and fall into line. He did so. . . . We were at this time heading nearly east, directly towards the Mo. line.[15]

Charles Snyder and Michael Robinson were in a field planting corn when they looked up to see horsemen approaching. In Snyder's words:

> We saw them galloping across the prairie, and, suspecting they were Missourians, and that something bad was at hand, we started for the house. . . . We reached the house about the time they rode up. Hamilton said to Robinson, he wanted him to go with them. Robinson, who was then standing in the door, replied, that he was not in the habit of going with men that he did not know. Hamilton said he was going to have him, dead or alive. . . . Robinson look[ed] around towards me in the room, and asked me, in a low voice, if it was not best to fight as long as we could. I answered, No! that I thought we had better give up, as I knew we were innocent of any and all charges. . . . We soon gave up, and went with them without resistance.[16]

Although a dozen captives—too young, too old, or members of the Masonic order—were soon released, and although a blacksmith Hamilton hoped to snare heroically fought off the gang, eleven others remained. The Reverend Mr. Reed was one.

> [W]e were then ordered to march. After marching 3/4 of a mile or there-abouts, we were conducted into a deep, narrow ravine, and ordered to halt and form a line. Hamilton gave the command to "Face front;" he then ordered his own men to form a line and "present arms" in front of us, the

horses' feet being nearly as high as our heads, and about ten feet from us. Some one said "The men don't obey the order." Capt. Hamilton gave the order again. They not all obeying, he gave it a third time, swearing terribly.[17]

"God damn you, why don't you wheel into line?" shouted Hamilton to W. B. Brockett.

"I'll be damned if I'll have anything to do with such a God damned piece of business as this," replied Brockett angrily. "If it was in a fight I'd fire."[18]

Terrified and trembling, the eleven men in the ravine now knew what was coming as the horsemen finally formed into line. "Hamilton drew out a large revolver," Rev. Reed remembered, "[then] presented it towards the prisoners . . . and gave the word, 'Fire.' "[19]

In a cloud of smoke and dust, Reed and the others dropped down in a heap. When the shooting finally ceased several riders dismounted. As the murderers moved along the ravine, the bodies were kicked over, and when any showed signs of life, they were shot again.[20] Miraculously—though lying absolutely still—six victims remained alive by the time the horsemen remounted.

"Soon I heard no more only the tramp of horses' feet . . . ," recalled Reed as he lay bleeding from his wound. "[S]ome began to groan. I spoke very low and said, 'Don't make a noise.' "[21]

When Reed's frantic wife reached the scene a short time later, the men begged her to bring help as quickly as possible. One of the victims had four bullets in his chest. A shotgun blast had ripped a hole through the stomach of another "from which his bowels protruded." Amos Hall rose from the ground and spit out the slug that had severed his tongue.[22] Although these men survived their wounds, the slaughter of the other five sent new waves of shock throughout Kansas and the North. Even Southerners, mindful of John Brown's butchery on the Pottawatomie and other northern atrocities, were quick to condemn the massacre on the Marais des Cygnes as well as the "fiends and monsters" who committed it. Raged one slavery journal, the *Leavenworth Herald:*

> The details are horrible in the extreme, and revolting to any one who has not the heart of a savage. . . . Such cowardly proceedings as these are a disgrace to a civilized country, and. . . . [n]o excuse can be offered in justification. We believe that the Proslavery men in that quarter have been harrassed and persecuted by their enemies, but no principle of retaliation can justify them in such acts of cowardly murder.[23]

"We were poor, but we were living very happily together on our claim," sobbed the heartbroken wife of one victim. "When I felt lonely, I used to take my work

*Marais des Cygnes Massacre.* KANSAS STATE HISTORICAL SOCIETY, TOPEKA.

out and remain with my husband in the field. Now the world is all dark, and I have nobody to go to for sympathy or advice."[24]

In the wake of the bloody tragedy near Trading Post, scores of fearful families fled either to Osawatomie, if free-soil, or to Missouri, if proslave. Many of the latter found small solace across the line, for James Montgomery was soon leading his wrathful Jayhawkers, complete with artillery, into the state to threaten and terrorize the population. "The border, both in Missouri and in the territory, had been vacated by the settlers for six or eight miles on either side," wrote a witness. It was "like driving through a grave yard," agreed another viewer.[25]

Meanwhile, beyond the wasteland, the bold exploits of Montgomery, the "original Jay-hawker," made him a hero among many free-soilers. "The people greeted him with cheers," said one stunned reporter, Albert Richardson. Standing nearby, a citizen nudged the journalist.

> Now you can judge of the estimation in which we hold Montgomery. Even the conservative Free State men, who censured him before the massacre, now regard him as their protector and champion. Were any attempt made to arrest him, the entire population of the county would resist it.[26]

Swept by emotion for her idol, one woman, when asked by Richardson what she thought of the Jayhawker, enthusiastically replied that she was "a Montgomery man." Another admirer felt the former clergyman was "almost a prophet." [27]

"[A] guerrilla company, to be effective, must be self-sustaining—must subsist on the enemy," lectured Montgomery during an interview with Albert Richardson. "Therefore we feed ourselves at Pro-slavery larders and our horses at Pro-slavery corn-cribs. . . . I live with my wife and five children, in a very good log house. I didn't erect it myself; a gentleman from Missouri built it; but soon after, he was unexpectedly compelled to leave the country, and so I have taken possession until he returns." [28]

"He was that most formidable of characters; a praying fighter," summarized Richardson after the talk. "He held daily religious worship in his family and was reported very amiable and just in private life. Quiet, modest and silver-tongued. . . . But his eye had the uneasy glare peculiar to hunted men, and his hollow laugh aroused the constant and unpleasant suggestion of a mind diseased." [29]

Following an audacious attempt to burn Fort Scott in early June 1858, and with Kansas and Missouri seemingly on the verge of war, new territorial governor James Denver, along with Charles Robinson, Judge John Wright, and many others seeking peace journeyed south in hopes of ending the trouble once and for all. On June 14, several hundred well-intentioned men of both parties assembled in front of a Fort Scott hotel to hear words of wisdom and peace delivered by their leaders. When Denver, Robinson, and Wright had finished their appeals, "tall, Herculean" Epaphroditus Ransom rose to speak. Despite being a former governor of Michigan, Ransom was a staunch slavery man, and soon after taking the stand, the gray-haired giant left no doubt as to which side was at the root of all evil in Kansas.

"Judge Wright . . . ," said a startled Albert Richardson, "as old as Ransom and quite as hot-blooded, instantly sprang up in front of the speaker and exclaimed:"

"It is false, sir, totally false!"

Ransom retorted by giving him the lie; and for a few seconds the two aged men faced each other defiantly. From the speakers' stand, I glanced down upon the assemblage. Instinctively, as by the law of gravitation, the auditors fell apart into two bodies, separated only by the space of eight or ten feet. For an instant, there was breathless silence, then the air was rent with the shouts:

"It's true!" "It's false!" "It's a damned lie!"

A few raised their rifles, and shot guns. The rest drew revolvers from their belts, and on every side was heard the sharp click, click, click of the cocking weapons. The speakers' platform, containing thirty or forty persons of both parties, presented a similar scene. Revolvers were drawn, threats exchanged, and Governor Robinson . . . stood close behind Ransom with clinched fists ready to hurl him down the steps the moment hostilities should begin. All this occurred almost in the twinkling of an eye; and a bloody fight seemed inevitable. But just at this moment Governor Denver who was in the hotel parlor conversing with a party of ladies, heard the tumult, rushed out, sprang between Ransom and Wright and commanded the peace.[30]

Order was indeed restored, and the following day both sides, "thoroughly weary of the reign of disorder," signed an accord to "avoid intemperate language, obey the laws and discountenance violence." Two days later, even James Montgomery promised to give peace a go and "devote himself to his cattle and cornfields."[31]

"I have accepted the olive branch," the Jayhawker announced.[32]

Although the shaky political truce held throughout the summer, when crops were harvested in the autumn, the raiders resumed operations. "Confound the place," an exasperated Governor Denver wrote his wife earlier, "it seems to have been cursed of God and man. . . . [I]t requires all the powers conferred on me by the President to prevent them from cutting each others throats. . . . They are ready to cheat, to swindle, to violate their word of honor given in the most solemn manner,—in fact they are in good part a most rascally set."[33]

While James Montgomery remained the most notorious Jayhawker in southern Kansas, other outlaws, acting largely under his direction, also raked the land. With his gang of horse thieves, the Reverend John R. Stewart swept livestock clean from the Marmaton and Drywood Creek areas. Called by friends the "Fighting Parson"—unlucky victims dubbed him the "thieving parson"—Stewart cut the manes and tails of stolen horses to prevent identification, then painted spots on their hide with "Bachelor's Hair Dye" to disguise them further.[34] Stewart's band also made brutal raids on isolated homesteads. At one farm near Fort Scott, the gang gutted a man's house of everything, "even bedclothes from over and under the sick, and the children's shoes and stockings." A little farther on the raiders plucked an absent farmer's cabin clean, then passed their time "choking and abusing his wife."[35]

Charles Jennison and Marshall Cleveland were two more Jayhawkers gaining in ill repute along the border. Soon, both would surpass even Montgomery himself in banditry, brutality, and cold-blooded murder.

Emboldened by his string of successes, outraged that a gang member was confined at Fort Scott on murder charges, Montgomery once more determined to attack the town and set his minion free. On the evening of December 15, 1858,

Sam Wood and a squad of men from the Kaw, Preston Plumb with a band from the Neosho, and a group of freebooters from the Little Osage—known as the "Osages"—rendezvoused with Montgomery several miles west of Fort Scott. Also making the trip down was John Brown and a handful of henchmen. When Montgomery was elected captain of the operation and quickly stipulated that there was to be no undue burning or killing, Old Brown retired in disgust.[36] Shortly before dawn, seventy-five Jayhawkers and one piece of artillery moved down the Marmaton.

Lulled by rumors of a raid the evening past, Fort Scott was caught completely by surprise.[37] Within minutes of entering, the marauders had the town entirely at their mercy. After overpowering the guards and freeing their comrade, the Jayhawkers next began the roundup of townsmen.

"They were hustled out into the square and a Sharp's [*sic*] rifle pen was formed around them," reminisced one of the raiders, twenty-two-year-old A. H. Tanner.

[A]s it was frosty . . . a fire was built for the comfort of the prisoners. The furniture of Judge Williams' office and all his books were used for fuel. Judge Ransom and Marshal Campbell complained bitterly and protested that it would go hard with us for handling United States officers in such a manner, but the boys ridiculed them and one little insignificant fellow, Avia Flint, ordered them to keep still and pushed them around with his little old squirrel rifle. He was a very small, cadaverous-looking fellow, weighing not over one hundred pounds, and ex-Governor Ransom was far above six feet and portly and he made a ludicrous spectacle marching at the command of such a very inferior guard. Judge Williams was jolly and good-natured and asked the boys to spare his fiddle and ward-robe, which they did; but his court and all the belongings were literally destroyed and he was compelled to witness it.[38]

Not everyone in Fort Scott surrendered meekly. A number of men tried to escape, and, despite Montgomery's orders, a hail of bullets followed their flight.[39] Another man who refused to go quietly was Deputy Marshal John Little. Cut off from friends, Little, George Crawford, and several others decided to hold out in a store until help arrived. James Jones of the *Fort Scott Democrat* described what happened.

As soon as they could dress, John stepped to the door with his gun to see the position of friend and invader. The guard appointed for that door advanced and was told not to come further. He did so, and in an instant

John fired, closing the door and remarking that he had shot one of them. The guard lodged a ball in the side of the door about an inch above his head.—The shots were simultaneous. . . . Soon after, a Sharpe's [*sic*] rifle ball was sent through the window, the stove pipe and the partition wall. . . . Mr. C[rawford] took his friend's gun to load, and L[ittle] disappeared into the store room by an inside door. He mounted a box and was looking to the hotel out of a window over the door when a Sharpe's rifle ball penetrated his forehead. . . . He fell instantly, his blood and brains pouring out upon the floor.[40]

For the next two hours those inside refused to give up. When the cannon was at last trained on the building, the standoff came to an end. The Jayhawkers broke through doors and windows, rushing past the mortally wounded Little in an effort to be first at looting the store.

"Some of them, fiend-like, seemed to exult over his dying struggles," reported the *Democrat*.[41]

At length, after a "splendid & bountiful breakfast," Montgomery mounted up, his raid on the last southern outpost in Kansas a complete success.[42] Though destruction was light and casualties few, at least one young woman had been shattered for the rest of her life, as a letter to James Montgomery made clear.

I heard you said in a speech a few days since, that you were not sorry you had killed John Little, that he was not killed to soon. . . . O, the anguish you have cause[d]. He was one of the noblest men ever created, brave and true to his country and word. You can't [say] he ever injured an innocent person. A few days more and we were to [be] married then go south to trouble you no more. But through you[r] influence he was killed, sent to another world without even time to pray or say good bye to his friends. But thanks to God if you did kill his body you can't touch his soul, no, no it is in the spirit land now, the cry of "the Osages are coming" can awake him no more, for he now quietly sleeps in our little grave yard.

But remember this, I am a girl but I can fire a pistol and if ever the time comes I will send some of you to the place where ther's "weeping and knashing of teeth;" you a minister of God, you mean a *minister of the devil.* . . .[43]

Though surprisingly little was looted while the Jayhawkers held Fort Scott, several raiders did attempt to lure a local slave from his master. The effort failed, however, and when the bondsman opted to remain put, the men politely left him in peace.[44] It was just such "milk and water" abolitionism that John Brown despised. In his war to end slavery, neither master *nor* slave had a say in the matter. As an enforcer of God's will, Brown knew the true course and would act accordingly.

Four days after the raid on Fort Scott, Brown took the first step of his long-awaited "war into Africa." On the night of December 20, 1858, the old man and two dozen abolitionists passed quietly along the snow-covered valley of the Little Osage and entered Missouri. Because the river was high and unfordable farther down, the party split to cover both banks.[45]

Like his nervous neighbors abutting the line, Harvey Hicklin was anxious lest Jayhawkers came calling. Because of Montgomery, James Holmes, and other freebooters from Kansas, horses, mules, and cattle were no longer secure. Slaves were another matter. Thus far, and despite the dire threats of abolitionists, slavery in Missouri had hardly been scratched. Although agitation in the territory persisted and attempts to coax chattel west onto the underground railroad continued, most efforts had proven notoriously unsuccessful.

"If the negroes had been abused, and were tired of their condition," a Vernon County chronicler explained, "they were but a few miles from Kansas, had abundant opportunities for escape, and in two hours could have been in the territory and free from their masters." [46]

Hence, when Harvey Hicklin was awakened at midnight on December 20 by a cry from without—"Hello! Damn you, get up and make a light!"—the Missourian thought not of abolitionists, but Jayhawkers.

I jumped out of bed, and as the moon was shining bright, I saw the yard was full of armed men. . . . The men were now battering in the east door of the room. Our two small children were sleeping in an old-fashioned trundle-bed in the middle of the room. I raised the feather tick of the trundle-bed and slipped the pocket-book with the money into the straw tick under the children. All this was done in double-quick time, and just as I stepped away from the bed the east door flew open. I had not put on my pantaloons nor had I struck a light, but there was some light from the . . . fire-place.

The men entered the room, covered me with their Sharp's [*sic*] rifles and ordered me to surrender. . . . They then went through all four rooms of the house. They took all the beds and bed clothing off of the bedsteads, made my wife get up out of her bed, and examined even the straw ticks very carefully in their search for money. I was afraid they would search the children's bed next, but they did not disturb it at all. Then one of them said, "Where is your money? We know you have it somewhere . . . Now, where is it?" I replied that I had loaned the money . . . but they would not believe me until I showed them the note. . . . By this time John Brown himself came into the room. He said to me, "Well, you seem to be in a pretty tight place. But you shan't be hurt if you behave yourself. . . ." He said he . . . was going to take off all of the negroes and free them. . . . He talked with me rather pleasantly for thirty minutes or more. He said he was doing the Lord's will and was not ashamed. . . . At last a man came to the door and said, "Captain, the wagons are loaded and all is ready." Then Brown rose and left, as did all of his men but two, who were left as guards over me with orders to stay with me for two hours, and to shoot me if I attempted to escape during that time.[47]

With Hicklin's five slaves, Brown's band continued down the Little Osage until they reached the farm of John Larue. After pillaging the house and rounding up an additional five slaves, the abolitionists turned back toward Kansas with Larue and a friend as hostages. Confused, uncertain of the future, several slaves wept as they were driven from their home.[48]

Meanwhile, on the opposite bank of the river, Brown's second column was also at work. Reaching the claim of sixty-year-old David Cruise, a "plain, unoffending farmer," the gang quickly surrounded the home.[49] A chronicler continued:

The raiders found the door of the house fastened and demanded that it be opened immediately, or they would demolish it. Mr. Cruise had feared trouble of some sort and had procured a revolver, which he then had in the house. His son Ralph had carried this weapon and had tied a loop of ribbon about the handle, partly for ornament and partly to suspend it by. The old man sprang out of bed, seized his revolver and attempted to shoot through the door at the robbers, but the ribbon caught in the cylinder and became entangled about it in such a way that it would not revolve and the weapon could not be discharged. The robbers broke in the door, and one of them . . . fired and shot down Mr. Cruise, who fell near the fireplace and died almost instantly, his blood flowing out upon the hearthstone.[50]

Terrified by the attack, one of Cruise's younger children ran screaming into the night, as did a frightened negro. After looting the house and seizing a slave, the abolitionists plundered a neighboring farm before they, too, turned back toward Kansas.[51]

By dawn of December 21, both parties were in the territory again and reunited. After releasing the white captives, Brown soon settled in along the Pottawatomie with his eleven blacks.[52] The following month, with nervous Missourians selling their slaves south or moving them back from the suddenly insecure border, and with many Kansans now fearful of a bloody retaliation similar to that on the Marais des Cygnes in May, Brown gathered his fugitives and started toward Canada.

"I shall now leave Kansas; probably you will never see me again," the fierce old fighter confided to a friend. "I consider it my duty to draw the scene of the excitement to some other part of the country." [53]

His career in the West ended, John Brown now turned his attention eastward, determined to transform the Kansas war into a national war.

## CHAPTER TWELVE

# *BRIGHT MORNING, GLORIOUS DAY*

IN THE EARLY HOURS OF MONDAY, OCTOBER 17, 1859, LEWIS WASHINGTON LAY fast asleep in the bedroom of his spacious country manor. One of the most respected and revered men in northern Virginia, the gentle descendant of America's first president had few, if any, enemies. Such was the colonel's indifference to crime or intruders or trouble of any sort that, although he owned several firearms, all were neatly stored away in the dining room, and even these were not loaded. Hence, when he was awakened at 1:30 by noises in his darkened home, Washington knew he was totally helpless.

> I was aroused from my bed by having my name called at my chamber door. Thinking some friend arrived . . . in the night train and had walked up to my house, I at once arose and opened the door, when in front of me stood . . . four armed men—three with Sharp's [*sic*] rifles, presented at my person, and the fourth holding in his left hand a burning torch and in his right a revolver. I was asked if my name was Washington; whereupon I said it was, and was then informed I was a prisoner, and they desired me to accompany them. . . . I said "probably you will extend to me the courtesy to explain this movement." When one of them said "our intention is to free all the slaves in the South, and we are fully prepared to do it." [1]

Confused by the words, stunned by the sight, the old Virginian began to mechanically put on his clothes.

After I had dressed myself we proceeded to my dining room, where my arms were demanded. I opened a gun-closet and handed them a rifle, double barrel shot gun, and a large horse pistol . . . when one of the party whispered to another, and I was asked if I had not some arms in my parlor. I then preceded to the parlor and opened a cabinet which contained a sword and pistol. Finding that they were aware of this sword and pistol being in the cabinet, I unlocked it to prevent its being broken open, as it had a plate glass door.[2]

Grabbing the weapons, including a ceremonial sword presented to General Washington by Frederick the Great, the abolitionists rounded up the slaves, and with their master seated in his own carriage, all struck north.[3] Pausing briefly to seize John Allstadt and his slaves along the way, the column at last halted on a high, rocky ridge. Below, the streetlights of Harpers Ferry had been extinguished, and the town and its famous arsenal were as dark as a tomb. In the blackness below, an idling railroad engine was heard hissing near the long covered bridge that crossed to Maryland. Among the unseen boulders and rocks nearby, two mighty rivers, the Shenandoah and Potomac, merged to flow as one eastward.

When the party at last moved down the hill, Lewis Washington was still confused.

After entering the Ferry I supposed they would halt at some house where they might, by some device, have obtained a room or rooms; but to my astonishment we drove directly to the Armory gate, where [the driver] said "All's well!" and was answered from the guard "All's well!" The gates were opened, and in he drove, when I was accosted by an elderly man, who said, "you will find a warm fire in there, sir," pointing to the watch-house.[4]

It was only when Washington entered the building and found friends already imprisoned that he began to understand what was taking place. The "elderly man" who had greeted the colonel so cordially at the gate was none other than the notorious John Brown of Kansas, already known throughout the land as "Old Osawatomie." With barely a score of men—seventeen white and five black—Brown had slipped quietly into Harpers Ferry the evening before, cut the telegraph wires, overpowered the arsenal guards, and, with thousands of weapons at his disposal, settled down to await the anticipated arrival of runaway slaves. Because of his raid the year before and the panic it had stirred among Missourians, Brown believed that a bolder stroke might bring the entire edifice of American bondage tumbling down. Except for a scattering of shots and a negro porter killed when he failed to halt, the plan was moving so swiftly and silently that only a handful in the sleeping town were aware of trouble.

*Harpers Ferry, Virginia.* KANSAS STATE HISTORICAL SOCIETY, TOPEKA.

Though Brown had assured all the hostages of their safety and treated them kindly, their perilous position was made abundantly clear when Aaron Stevens, a big, mean Kansan, made his appearance. Lewis Washington:

> A little before light Stevens and one of the prisoners . . . were holding a conversation at the door, when Stevens asked, "what are your opinions on slavery?" The reply was, "I am no slave holder, but, being born South, I sustain the cause. . . ." Stevens replied, "then as you sustain the cause as a non-slaveholder, you are the first man I would hang; you deserve it more than a man who is a slaveholder and sustains his interests."[5]

At dawn, Brown finally allowed the idle train with its terrified passengers to proceed on its way. Also with morning light, the abolitionists began arresting citizens as they unwittingly left their homes for work. While much of the town was now aware that something strange was occurring, many at first thought the disturbance was a labor dispute among the federal armorers or even a row with railroad workers.

"[O]ne of my servants came to my room door and told me 'there was war in the street,'" remembered John Daingerfield, paymaster at the arsenal. "I, of course, got up at once and dressed, and went out. . . . Upon looking around I saw nothing exciting."

I walked towards my office . . . just within the armory inclosure, and not more than a hundred yards from my dwelling. As I proceeded I saw a man come out of an alley near me, then another, and another, all coming towards me. When they came up to me I inquired what all this meant; they said, ["N]othing, only they had taken possession of the Government works.["] I told them they talked like crazy men. They answered, "Not so crazy as you think, as you will soon see." Up to this time I had not seen any arms; presently, however, the men threw back the short cloaks they wore, and displayed Sharpe's [*sic*] rifles, pistols, and knives. Seeing these, and fearing something serious was going on, I told the men I believed I would return to my quarters. They at once cocked their guns, and told me I was a prisoner. . . . I talked with them some little time longer, and again essayed to return to my house; but one of the men stepped before me, presented his gun, and told me if I moved I would be shot down. . . .

Upon reaching the gate I saw what, indeed, looked like war—negroes armed with pikes, and sentinels with muskets all around.[6]

Much like Daingerfield, others now came to the sudden realization that the situation was more serious than previously thought. Wrote a witness:

One of the citizens by the name of Boerley,—a well-to-do grocer, and an Irishman by birth,—when walking quietly along not far from his residence, happened to get within range of a picket,—a black fellow who called himself Dangerfield Newby,—whereupon the negro raised his rifle and without a word of warning shot him dead, with as little compunction as if he had been a mad dog.[7]

Paradoxically, although thousands of the most modern arms in America were crated in the arsenal below, only a smattering of squirrel guns and fowling pieces were available in the town. Nevertheless, the few citizens who had them began firing at the abolitionists with a will. The raiders responded, and a "brisk little skirmish" ensued. As the fight continued and the scant supply of lead ran low, desperate townsmen were forced to melt pewter plates and spoons and mold them into bullets.[8]

Crazed by anger and hatred, George Turner, a close friend of Lewis Washington, moved boldly toward the arsenal, shotgun in hand. "When he had approached within some fifty yards . . . ," said a spectator, "the same negro . . . who had killed Boerley, saw him coming, and, taking deliberate aim, shot him dead."[9] Revenge came swiftly; in moments an armorer sniping from a nearby house silenced the deadly marksman.

"I saw [Newby's] body while it was yet warm as it lay on the pavement . . . ,"
continues the witness, "and I never saw, on any battlefield, a more hideous musket-
wound than his. For his throat was cut literally from ear to ear, which was . . .
accounted for by the fact that the armorer, having no bullets, had charged his
musket with a six-inch iron spike." [10]

On the highlands west of Harpers Ferry, many were still unaware of the raid.
Schoolgirl Jennie Chambers was on her way to the Young Ladies' Seminary in the
valley below.

[C]oming in sight of town, my heart stopped beating and I dropped my
books. As I looked over the edge of the hill, I saw . . . shouting and brandish-
ing their guns, a crowd of men. It seemed to me they were all yelling; and
some of them were firing in the air. . . . I wanted to cry out, and . . . to
warn those I loved of the horrible, strange peril in the air. . . . Just then
I thought of a schoolmate who lived near by on the road-side, and that
gave me courage.

"It's the abolitionists," she said, running out as I came up to her door-
way; "they're down there arresting all our people." I didn't wait to hear
more, but my strength had come back to me, and I ran along through
the woods like a deer. I didn't know what minute an abolitionist might
jump out at me from behind a tree and eat me. They were cannibals, for
all I knew, from some far-off country. [11]

Just as Jennie reached home and screamed the news to her mother, a wagon
came crashing down the Charles Town Turnpike. "They've got Colonel Washington
and John Allstadt," the driver yelled as he passed, "and they've got their niggers,
and. . . ." Before Jennie heard more, the excited man was gone, spreading the word. [12]

Near Shepherdstown, ten miles northwest of Harpers Ferry, U.S. Congressman
Alexander Boteler had just arisen and was beginning his daily routine.

I . . . had hardly finished breakfast when a carriage came to the door
with one of my daughters, who told me that a messenger had arrived at
Shepherdstown, a few minutes before, with the startling intelligence of
a negro insurrection at Harpers Ferry . . . ! Ordering my horse, I started
at once for Harpers Ferry. . . . I observed, in passing the farms along my
route, that the negroes were at work as usual. When near Bolivar,—
a suburb of Harpers Ferry,—I saw a little old "darky" coming across
a field toward me as fast as a pair of bandy legs, aided by a crooked stick,
could carry him. From the frequent glances he cast over his shoulder and
his urgent pace, it was evident that the old fellow was fleeing from some

apprehended danger, and was fearfully demoralized. I hailed him with the inquiry:

"Well, uncle, which way?"

"Sarvint, marster! I'se only gwine a piece in de country for ter git away from de Ferry."

"You seem to be in a hurry," said I.

"Yes, sah, I is dat, an' it's 'bout time ter be in a hurry when dey gits ter shootin' sho 'nuff bullets at yer."

"Why, has any one been shooting at you?"

"No, not exactly at me, bless de Lord! kase I didn't give 'em a chance ter. But dey's been a-shootin' at pleanty folks down dar in de Ferry, an' a-killen of 'em, too."

"Who's doing the killing?"

"De Lord above knows, marster! But I hearn tell dis mornin' dat some of de white folks allowed dey was abolitioners, come down for ter raise a ruction 'mong de colored people."

And on inquiring if any of the colored people had joined them, "No-sah-ree!" was his prompt and emphatic answer, at the same time striking the ground with his stick, as if to give additional force to the denial.[13]

None was more painfully aware of the truth in the old slave's statement than John Brown. His well-laid plans were quickly unraveling. The hoped-for insurrection had thus far failed to materialize. What had materialized, however, was an angry and thoroughly aroused citizenry who, locating a cache of overlooked weapons near the arsenal, escalated their attack on the raiders. When a company of townsmen crossed the Potomac, then opened fire from the Maryland shore, the abolitionists found themselves assailed on two sides. Nonetheless, as the fighting continued and as his position became increasingly perilous, John Brown remained "cool" and committed, confident that thousands of slaves were on the way.[14]

Themselves nervous over this possibility, fearful lest hundreds of abolitionists and slaves should suddenly sweep into Harpers Ferry and join their comrades, citizens and some of the first militia units to reach the town agreed to storm the arsenal. The initial target was the rifle factory edging the Shenandoah, where John Kagi of Kansas and several others were holed up.

"[We] came down the hill . . . ," the Reverend Charles White later wrote, "and fired so heavily upon the insurgents at the Rif[l]e factory that they had to run. . . . We ran immediately toward the whole of them—the Bolivar men pressing on them from the mountain—we on one side."[15] Alexander Boteler continued:

Kagi and his party [fled] pell-mell out of the rear of the building into the Shenandoah River. . . . [A]s soon as the insurgents were recognized attempting to cross the river, there was a shout among the citizens, who opened a hot fire upon them from both banks. The river at that point runs rippling over a rocky bed, and . . . is easily forded. The raiders, finding their retreat to the opposite shore intercepted . . . made for a large flat rock near the middle of the stream. Before reaching it, however, Kagi fell and died in the water, apparently without a struggle. Four others reached the rock, where, for a while, they made an ineffectual stand, returning the fire of the citizens. But it was not long before two of them were killed outright and another prostrated by a mortal wound, leaving [John] Copeland, a mulatto, standing alone and unharmed upon their rock of refuge.

Thereupon . . . James H. Holt, dashed into the river, gun in hand, to capture Copeland, who, as he approached him, made a show of fight by pointing his gun at Holt, who halted and leveled his; but, to the surprise of the lookers-on, neither of their weapons were discharged . . . from being wet. Holt, however, as he again advanced, continued to snap his gun, while Copeland did the same. Reaching the rock, Holt clubbed his gun and we

*Charles White.* KANSAS STATE HISTORICAL SOCIETY, TOPEKA.

expected to see a hand to hand fight between them; but the mulatto, show-ing the white feather, flung down his weapon and surrendered. Copeland, when he was brought ashore, was badly frightened, and well he might be in the midst of the excited crowd who surrounded him, some of whom began to knot their handkerchiefs together, with ominous threats of "Lynch law." But better counsels prevailed, and he was taken . . . to jail to await his trial.[16]

Another black captured when the rifle works were stormed was a bondsman of John Allstadt. With a long, sharp pike in his hands, the slave walked out and quickly surrendered. According to Reverend White:

> I asked him how came he there & what he was doing with the pike—he said they had taken him and his master the night before—brot them down—& told him if he didn't keep guard at [the] Rifle factory they would kill him. . . . While talking a reckless fellow came up—levelled his musket at the negro's head within an inch or so—and was about to pull the trigger. I asked him not to fire as did others. He swore he'd kill him & that he had orders from the Captain of Charlestown Company. I told him no matter what the Capt said we had the man prisoner—perhaps he was innocent . . . and stepping between the two, I ordered him not to fire. Several then took hold of his gun & saved the negro.[17]

Across the Potomac, meanwhile, townsmen encountered several raiders guarding the bridge, and a short, sharp fight ensued. With one comrade dead, and another, William Thompson, captured, a third abolitionist ran for the river. Recorded a witness:

> [A] dozen shots were fired after him; he partially fell, but rose again, threw his gun away and drew his pistols, but both snapped; he drew his bowie knife and cut his heavy accoutrements off and plunged into the river; one of the soldiers was about ten feet behind; the man turned round, threw up his hands, and said, "Don't shoot;" the soldier fired, and the man fell into the water, with his face blown away. . . .[18]

With the bridges recaptured, several raiders now found themselves on the Maryland shore, cut off from Harpers Ferry. Frantic to help his friends, John Cook decided to act.

> After going down opposite the Ferry, I ascended the mountain in order to get a better view of the position of our opponents. I saw that our party

were completely surrounded, and as I saw a body of men on High Street firing down upon them,—they were about half a mile distant from me,— I thought I would draw their fire upon myself; I therefore raised my rifle and took the best aim I could and fired. It had the desired effect, for the very instant the party returned it. Several shots were exchanged. The last one they fired at me cut a small limb I had hold of just below my hand, and gave me a fall of about fifteen feet, by which I was severely bruised, and my flesh somewhat lacerated.[19]

Sensing that further fighting on their part would be "sheer madness," Cook and the others, including Brown's son Owen, withdrew and soon vanished among the mountains.[20]

"For nearly two hours," said a spectator on the heights above the town, "a running and random firing was kept up by the troops against the raiders. . . . During the firing the women and children ran shrieking in every direction." [21]

By 3 P.M., the number of militiamen in Harpers Ferry had grown to several hundred. To root out the raiders and free the sixty or so hostages, a final attempt was made to storm the arsenal. Wrote Captain Ephram Alburtis:

We entered the armory at the upper end of the shops, and after some consultation I directed that twenty-five men should proceed down the main avenue or centre, that a like number should take the rear of the shops, and the remainder should proceed down through the shops the best way they could. I took command of those who came down the main avenue. Upon arriving nearly opposite the first and second buildings . . . we were fired upon by the men in the [fire] engine house, and on the corner between the engine house and the pay office. The fire was returned and they retreated into the engine house, from which they kept up a continual fire through the door, which was kept four or five inches ajar. This fire was very briskly returned by our men, eight of whom were wounded, and two it is feared mortally. During the fight we found in the room adjoining the engine house some thirty or forty prisoners who had been captured and confined by the outlaws. The windows were broken open by our party, and these men escaped. The whole of the outlaws were now driven into the engine house. . . . [N]ot being supported by the other companies as we expected, we were obliged to return. . . . [22]

Realizing that too many prisoners were a liability, Brown released several more of those still with him.[23] Said one of the eleven yet remaining, a nervous John Daingerfield:

After getting into the engine-house with his men, [Brown] made this speech: "Gentlemen, perhaps you wonder why I have selected you from the others. It is because I believe you to be the most influential, and I have only to say now that you will have to share precisely the same fate that your friends extend to my men." He began at once to bar the doors and windows, and to cut port-holes through the brick wall.

Then commenced a terrible firing from without, from every point from which the windows could be seen, and in a few minutes every window was shattered, and hundreds of balls came through the doors. . . . [S]trange to say, no prisoner was hurt, though thousands of balls were imbedded in the walls, and holes shot in the doors almost large enough for a man to creep through.[24]

Despite his predicament, Old Brown remained as defiant as ever, stalking with Lewis Washington's sword in hand from one wall to the next, directing the fire of his decreasing number of men. Though Brown continued to caution his followers about firing on unarmed civilians, the hard-pressed abolitionists aimed at anything that moved.[25]

"While they were thus shooting at every one they saw, without regard to his being armed or not," a witness wrote, "Mr. Fountain Beckham, station agent, who was . . . mayor of the town, happened to walk out upon the depot platform near his office . . . [with] his hands in his pockets. . . . He was instantly shot. . . ."[26]

"[H]e bent forward, doubled down and dropped dead," gasped a stunned bystander.[27]

In Alexander Boteler's words:

When Mr. Beckham's friends upon the platform saw him fall dead in their presence,—shot through the heart without a word of warning,—killed without having taken any part in the fight . . . their rage became uncontrollable, and they impulsively rushed into the railroad hotel to take summary vengeance on the prisoner, Thompson, who was confined there.[28]

One of those in the frenzied mob was a relative of Beckham's, twenty-two-year-old Henry Hunter. "He was my grand-uncle and my special friend," Hunter cried, "a man I loved above all others."

After he was killed, Mr. Chambers and myself moved forward to the hotel for the purpose of taking the prisoner out and hanging him; we were joined by a number of other persons, who cheered us on in that work; we went up into his room, where he was bound. . . . [A]t the door we were stopped by persons guarding the door, who remonstrated with us, and the excitement was . . . great. . . . [W]e burst into the room where he was, and found several around him, but they offered only a feeble resistance; we brought our guns down . . . for the purpose of shooting him in the room. There was a young lady there, the sister of Mr. Fouke, the hotel keeper, who sat in this man's lap, covered his face with her arms, and shielded him with her person whenever we brought our guns to bear; she said to us, "For God's sake, wait and let the law take its course;" my associate shouted to kill him. . . . [A]ll round were shouting, "Mr. Beckham's life was worth ten thousand of these vile abolitionists. . . ."

[A]fter a moment's thought, it occurred to me that [this] was not the proper place to kill him; we then proposed to take him out and hang him; some portion of our band then opened a way to him, and first pushing Miss Fouke aside, we slung him out of doors; I gave him a push, and many others did the same; we then shoved him along the platform and down to the trestle work of the bridge; he begged for his life all the time, very piteously at first. . . .

[W]e bore him out on the bridge with the purpose then of hanging him; we had no rope, and none could be found; it was a moment of wild excitement; two of us raised our guns . . . and pulled the trigger; before he had reached the ground, I suppose some five or six shots had been fired into his body; he fell on the railroad track, his back down to the earth, and his face up.[29]

After flinging the corpse from the bridge, the enraged crowd peered over the edge to see the victim "lying at the bottom of the river, with his ghastly face still exhibiting his fearful death agony."[30]

Now "wild and madly excited," the mob, which had spent its only live abolitionist, turned its fury on those in the streets who were dead. "Curses were freely uttered against them, and kicks and blows inflicted upon them," reported a Maryland newsman.

The huge mulatto that shot Mr. Turner was lying in the gutter in front of the Arsenal, with a terrible wound in his neck, and though dead and gory, vengeance was unsatisfied, and many, as they ran sticks into his wound, or beat him with them, wished that he had a thousand lives, that all of them might be forfeited in . . . avengement of the foul deed he had committed.

[Another body] lay upon a rock in the river, and was made a target for the practice of those who had captured Sharpe's [*sic*] rifles in the fray. Shot after shot was fired at him, and when tired of this sport, a man waded out to where he lay, and set him up, in grotesque attitudes, and finally pushed him off, and he floated down the stream.[31]

Unaware of the savagery taking place around the town, Brown's son Watson and Aaron Stevens stepped from the engine house bearing a flag of truce. Both were instantly shot down. Stevens was quickly captured, but young Brown, mortally wounded and vomiting blood, managed to crawl back into the building.[32]

In such a murderous climate, Harpers Ferry was no place for a stranger, especially a stranger from the North. Soon after his train was mysteriously halted on the outskirts of town, one impatient attorney—who was both a stranger and a Northerner—foolishly decided to continue on foot in hopes of catching a connecting line at Harpers Ferry. When he found himself surrounded by a crowd of shouting men, the traveler suddenly realized his mistake. The man was arrested and jailed with six others who likewise blundered into town.

Now and then an ugly-looking fowling-piece or an awkwardly handled pistol was threateningly pointed at us, with a half-laughing and half-drunken threat of keeping us safe. Toward afternoon we were ordered for the night to Charlestown. . . . My special guard was a gentlemanly young lawyer . . . and to his cleverness I think I owed my safe arrival at the end of our journey. Every turn in the road brought us face to face with an angry crowd, gathering from far and near, armed and ready to do instant justice on a helpless victim. [My guard], however, gracefully waived [*sic*] them back to the wagons behind us, where other prisoners, in less skilled hands, were pretty badly used. The houses on the road were utterly deserted; on the first news of an outbreak by the slaves, the women and children were hurried off to the larger towns. . . .[33]

Though the nervous attorney and his fellow prisoners were later released, he and the others were nonetheless struck by the contrast between the frightened adults they met in Charles Town and a group of black and white children they saw, "playing soldiers, led by a chubby black boy."[34]

Meanwhile, as night approached, the fight at the engine house continued. Lewis Washington:

[O]ld Brown . . . was the busiest and most vigilant of all the rebels in watching through the loopholes and crevices for opportunities to kill those outside. Whilst he was thus watching, rifle in hand, one of his own sons was shot through the body and fell within four or five feet of him. The young man groaned and cried aloud in his agony, begging that some of his comrades would kill him at once. Thereupon old Brown, turning for a few moments an unmoved and unsympathizing glance . . . sternly bade him be silent and die like a man, and then instantly turned his attention back to his own work of killing.[35]

As darkness descended on Harpers Ferry, a cold, drizzly rain began to fall, cooling passions a degree and ending most of the gunfire. Although the engine house was surrounded by hundreds of men as well as cannon, the Virginians hesitated to attack.[36] Congressman Alexander Boteler:

> At this time a conference was held by three or four of the principal officers in command, to which two or three civilians, including myself, were invited,—the object of the consultation being to determine whether or not to take the engine-house by assault at once, or to wait until morning. It was represented to us by the prisoners whom Brown had released . . . that, if an attempt should be made to carry it by storm at night, it would be impossible to distinguish the hostages from the insurgents; and that Brown would probably place the former in front of his own party as a protection, and thereby cause them to receive the brunt of the attack. It was also urged that the raiders were then as securely imprisoned in their place of refuge as if incarcerated in the county jail, and could be taken in the morning without much risk to our friends.[37]

Curiously, while all the captives had miraculously escaped the day unscathed, most of the raiders in the engine house were either dead, dying, or wounded. Only Brown and three others remained untouched.[38] Nevertheless, when the summons for unconditional surrender was made, the old man flatly refused. With his grand dream of liberating the slaves of the South fading more and more with each passing hour, Brown held tenaciously to his hope that an army of blacks was marching to join him. But not only had the slaves of Virginia and Maryland failed to heed his call, even those in the immediate vicinity were strangely silent.

"[T]he negroes about H[arpers] F[erry] were terribly alarmed and clung as closely as they could to master & mistress," Charles White acknowledged. "One negro hid under a water wheel in the armory canal and [wouldn't] come out . . . afraid Brown might catch him." [39]

And perhaps most painful of all to the old man, even those slaves he had liberated seemed supremely indifferent to the fight for freedom going on around them. "About a dozen black men were there," noted prisoner John Daingerfield, "armed with pikes, which they carried most awkwardly and unwillingly. During the firing they were lying about asleep, some of them having crawled under the engines." [40]

Soon, a "dead stillness" settled over the arsenal. In the engine house, Brown and his handful of followers kept watch throughout the rainy night, waiting for what the morning would bring. Eighty miles down the Potomac, the nation's capital was experiencing anything but a "dead stillness." When word first arrived of a "disturbance" at Harpers Ferry, many in Washington treated the news as a hoax. As the day progressed, however, the reports became increasingly ominous until by nightfall, the streets were filled with flying rumors stating that hundreds, even thousands, of abolitionists and slaves were sweeping through northern Virginia with fire and sword. "We found all the volunteers and regular soldiers at Washington on duty patrolling the city," one visitor remarked, "as well as the police force of some one hundred men, expecting an attack upon the city. . . ." [41]

"[N]othing is talked of but the insurrection," added a newsman from Baltimore to the north. [42]

With a scratch force of ninety marines and two fieldpieces, Colonel Robert E. Lee was ordered to rush by train to Harpers Ferry and put down the insurrection. Rising in his wake were hundreds of Virginia militiamen, rallying and making ready to move in the same direction. Coincidentally, one such company was holding its regular drill and inspection in Richmond when the startling news arrived. As militiaman Parke Poindexter later wrote to his sister:

> [We] had barely assembled, when an order from Governor [Henry] Wise arrived that we should immediately repair to Harper's Ferry, and in ten minutes after the order was received we were upon the cars. . . . The people all along the road were in a great state of excitement. Men, women, and children cheered vociferously, waving their handkerchiefs, as the train bore on our splendid company at almost lightning speed. . . . [I]n this state of excitement we dashed on, meeting at every cross-road excited and alarmed crowds of country-people. . . . [43]

By 1:00 A.M. on October 18, Colonel Lee and his troops had reached Harpers Ferry and assumed positions near the engine house. Anxious to avoid a bloody assault, Lee sent under a flag of truce an impetuous young aide to demand a surrender. Hostage John Daingerfield looked on as Brown cautiously opened the door to greet Lt. J. E. B. Stuart.

When Stuart was admitted, and a light brought, he exclaimed, "Why, aren't you old Ossawatomie Brown, of Kansas, whom I once had there as my prisoner?" "Yes," was the answer, "but you did not keep me. . . ." When . . . [Stuart] advised Brown to trust to the clemency of the Government, he responded that he knew what that meant,—a rope for his men and himself,—adding, "I prefer to die just here." Stuart told him he would return at early morning for his final reply, and left him.

When he had gone, Brown at once proceeded to barricade the doors, windows, etc., endeavoring to make the place as strong as possible. During all this time no one of Brown's men showed the slightest fear, but calmly awaited the attack, selecting the best situations to fire from upon the attacking party, and arranging their guns and pistols so that a fresh one could be taken up as soon as one was discharged.[44]

Now realizing that he was dealing with a determined, desperate foe, Lee wisely decided to delay any action until morning light. While many of the weary militiamen retired for a well-deserved rest, Lee, Stuart, and their marines kept the rainy vigil near the engine house.

Finally, wrote one of the numerous newsmen covering the story,

the anxiously looked for dawn . . . broke slowly and dully. . . . [T]hrongs of citizens and soldiers crowded around the besieged in ill-defined expectation of the bloody tragedy which they were assured would ensue. . . . About seven o'clock, a detachment of Marines, two of whom concealed heavy sledge hammers behind their backs, were brought up . . . separated from the engine house but by six or eight feet, but, from their position, entirely concealed from the view of those within it.

All being now in readiness, Col. Lee, (dressed in citizen's clothes) took a position outside the armory yard, and concealed from the view of the fanatic rebels by a heavy brick column, beckoned to . . . Stuart, who, accompanied by an aged man holding an umbrella, to which was attached a white handkerchief, entered the yard and approached the engine house, the door of which was opened for a few inches, and the parley commenced. The actions of the officers were watched with breathless attention by the vast throng. . . .[45]

"When Lieutenant Stuart came . . . ," remembered John Daingerfield, "I got up and went to Brown's side to hear his answer. Stuart asked, 'Are you ready to surrender and trust to the mercy of the Government?' Brown answered promptly, 'No! I prefer to die here.' His manner did not betray the least fear."[46]

"This closed the interview," noted Alexander Boteler, who, with other nervous citizens, was watching the drama unfold.

Thereupon Stuart bowed, and as he turned to leave made a sign, previously agreed upon, to Colonel Lee, who immediately raised his hand, which was the signal of assault. Instantly the storming party under Lieutenant [Israel] Green, consisting of a dozen marines, sprang forward from behind the angle of the wall that had concealed them, and for perhaps two minutes or more the blows of the sledge-hammers on the door of the engine-house sounded with startling distinctness. . . .

As yet, to our surprise, there was no shot fired by the insurgents, nor any sound heard from within the engine-house. Unable to batter down its door, the men with the sledges threw them aside, at a sign from Stuart, and withdrew behind the adjoining building. Then there was a brief pause of oppresive silence, as some twenty-five or thirty more marines were seen coming down the yard with a long ladder that had been leaning against one of the shops. Nearing the engine-house they started into a run, and dashed their improvised battering ram against the door with a crashing sound, but not with sufficient force to effect an entrance. Falling back a short distance they made another run, delivering another blow, and as they did so a volley was fired by the conspirators, and two of the marines let go the ladder—both wounded and one of them mortally. Two others quickly took their places, and the third blow, splintering the right-hand leaf of the door, caused it to lean inward sufficiently to admit a man. Just then Lieutenant Green, who had been standing close to the wall, sword in hand, leaped upon the inclining door-leaf, which, yielding to his weight, fell inside and he himself disappeared from our view in the interior of the building.[47]

John Daingerfield:

Lieutenant Green . . . jumped on top of the engine, and stood a second in the midst of a shower of balls, looking for John Brown. When he saw Brown he sprang about twelve feet at him, and gave an under-thrust of his sword, striking him about midway the body and raising him completely from the ground. Brown fell forward with his head between his knees, and Green struck him several times over the head. . . . I was not two feet from Brown at that time . . . It seems that in making the thrust Green's sword struck Brown's belt and did not penetrate the body. The sword was bent double. The reason that Brown was not killed when struck on the head was that Green was holding his sword in the middle, striking with the hilt and making only scalp wounds.[48]

Behind Lieutenant Green, troops poured through the breach. "The moment the marines entered," said a friend of Lewis Washington, "[Lewis] sprang upon one of the engines, told his fellow-prisoners to hold up their hands . . . and then rapidly pointed out the outlaws to the vengeance of the soldiers. . . ."[49]

The fight inside was "rapid and sharp" and outside, the anxious spectators were wrought to a "pitch of frenzy."[50] In seconds, however, the firing ceased and all defenders were either dead or hiding among the captives and slaves. Wrote a spellbound reporter of the *Baltimore American:*

When the insurgents were brought out, some dead and others wounded, they were greeted with execrations, and only the precautions that had been taken saved them from immediate execution. The crowd, nearly every man of which carried a gun, swayed with tumultuous excitement, and cries of "Shoot them! shoot them!" rang from every side. The appearance of the liberated prisoners, all of whom, through the steadiness of the marines, escaped injury, changed the current of feeling, and prolonged cheers took the place of howls and execrations.[51]

With tears of relief, Lewis Washington, John Daingerfield, and the other hostages ran to meet families and friends. Continued the Baltimore journalist:

The lawn in front of the engine house, after the assault, presented a dreadful sight. Lying on it were two bodies of men killed on the previous day, and found inside the house; three wounded men, one of them just in the last gasp of life and two others groaning in pain. One of the dead was Brown's son Oliver. The wounded father and his son Watson were lying on the grass, the old man presenting a gory spectacle. He had a severe . . . wound in his side, and his face and hair were clotted with blood.[52]

"[S]o great was the curiosity to see him," added Alexander Boteler, "that the soldiers found some difficulty in keeping back the crowd. . . ."[53]

While some still cried for Brown's blood and would have gleefully murdered him on the spot, a grateful John Daingerfield was not one of them: "He had made me a prisoner, but had spared my life and that of other gentlemen in his power; and when his sons were shot down beside him, almost any other man similarly situated would at least have exacted life for life."[54]

As surgeons removed a number of wounded to a nearby hospital or simply let the hopeless cases lie "without sympathy or medical relief," Colonel Lee ordered John Brown carried to an adjoining building where a strong guard was quickly posted.[55] Eager to learn more, Congressman Boteler gained permission to talk with the old man.

> On entering the room where he was I found him alone, lying on the floor on his left side, and with his back turned toward me. The right side of his face was smeared with blood from the sword-cut on his head, causing his grim and grizzly countenance to look like that of some aboriginal savage with his war-paint on. Approaching him, I began the conversation with the inquiry:
>
> "Captain Brown, are you hurt anywhere except on your head?"
>
> "Yes, in my side,—here," said he, indicating the place with his hand.
>
> I then told him that a surgeon would be in presently to attend to his wounds, and expressed the hope that they were not very serious. There-upon he asked me who I was, and on giving him my name he muttered as if speaking to himself:
>
> "Yes, yes,—I know now,—member of Congress—this district."
>
> I then asked the question;
>
> "Captain, what brought you here?"
>
> "To free your slaves," was the reply.

*The capture of John Brown.* KANSAS STATE HISTORICAL SOCIETY, TOPEKA.

"How did you expect to accomplish it with the small force you brought with you?"

"I expected help," said he.

"Where, whence, and from whom, Captain, did you expect it?"

"Here and from elsewhere," he answered.

"Did you expect to get assistance from whites here as well as from the blacks?" was my next question.

"I did," he replied.

"Then," said I, "you have been disappointed in not getting it from either?"

"Yes," he muttered, "I have—been—disappointed." [56]

Disheartened as Brown undoubtedly was, when Governor Wise and others visited the prisoner they soon discovered that the will of the old abolitionist was as indomitable as ever. "[N]o signs of weakness were exhibited," noted a stunned reporter. "In the midst of enemies whose home he had invaded; wounded and a prisoner; surrounded by a small army of officials and a more desperate army of angry men; with the gallows staring him full in the face, Brown lay on the floor, and, in reply to every question gave answers that betokened the spirit that animated him." [57]

"He is the gamest man I ever saw," Governor Wise announced in awe. [58]

Although Brown and the surviving raiders were now safely caged, the respite in northern Virginia proved brief. That only a handful of men would dare challenge the might of state and federal governments seemed too preposterous to believe. Many felt that the failed foray was only the first step in a much wider conspiracy. On the very night following the fight at the engine house, the great terror began.

"The abolitionists are coming down the Valley, killing all the citizens!" a white-eyed farmer shouted as he galloped through a village just down from Harpers Ferry. [59] The horrifying words ignited mass panic. "Our people gathered all their families and put them in the cellars," remembered a terrified Jennie Chambers. "The church was full of them, mostly women and children. All night long the men of the town waited in terrible suspense, the women and children crying and screaming." [60]

Though this alarm like all the rest was false, tremulous citizens along the Potomac heeded every cry. By day, ominous gunfire was heard echoing in the mountains, and at night "mysterious Roman lights" were seen arcing in the sky. Hand in hand with the fear of an abolition army marching down from the north was the horror of a slave revolt rising up from the south. While the fight at Harpers Ferry was in progress, cowering blacks had quaked in their cabins. But now as the days passed, many Virginia and Maryland masters found it "almost impossible" to manage their unruly chattel. [61]

"The slaves," wrote one Washington witness, "were in many instances insolent to their masters, and even refused to work." [62]

"All Virginia was in alarm," gloated abolitionist newsman James Redpath. "Her militia forces were every where called out, and all business for the time was suspended. They, who had boasted of the stability of slave society, now acknowledged that its foundations lay in fire, whose irruption they daily feared would overwhelm them with ruin." [63]

In such a terror-filled setting, it is not surprising that many Southerners prayed nightly that the author of so much misery and woe should be speedily hung. That this would be the fate of Brown and his cohorts there was never a doubt. Indeed, several Slave States even vied with one another to provide the rope with which to strangle the abolitionists. While hemp from Missouri seemed appropriate, a Kentucky product was finally chosen. [64] Few took more satisfaction in the capture of Brown and his impending doom than Mahala Doyle, formerly of Kansas, now a "poor disconsolate widow, with helpless children," forced back on friends and family in Tennessee.

> I confess that I do feel gratified to hear that you were stopped in your fiendish career at Harper's Ferry, with the loss of your two sons. You can now appreciate my distress in Kansas, when you then and there entered my house at midnight and arrested my husband and two boys, and took them out in the yard, and in cold blood shot them dead in my hearing. ... Oh, how it pained my heart to hear the dying groans of my husband and children. ... You can't say you did it to free our slaves; we had none, and never expected to own one. ... My son, John ... is very desirous to be at Charlestown on the day of your execution ... that he might adjust the rope around your neck ... I do hope and trust you will meet with your just reward. [65]

But while many in the South screamed for his blood, a growing sympathy for Brown was developing in the North. Although abolitionists had naturally cheered his attempt to foment a slave insurrection, the vast majority of Northerners viewed the raid on Harpers Ferry as a wild and reckless act of a maniac. As the days passed and the trial at Charles Town continued, however, a transformation took place in the public mind. Beaten and stabbed, wounded and bleeding, unable even to stand, the old man, far from bowing down to the mighty, hateful host all around him, remained true as steel to himself, clinging throughout the trial to his beliefs with a tenacity that impressed even his enemies. From a crazed old fool with a bloodstained past, John Brown was increasingly viewed by those of the North as an incredibly brave, solitary soldier who saw his duty to God and, in the teeth of man and law, did not hesitate to do it.

Hundreds of letters poured into Brown's Charles Town jail cell from people thrilled by his example. "Manly," "heroic," "saintly," even "Godly"; the words of support lifted the old man's spirits. "He shall . . . make the gallows glorious like the cross," Ralph Waldo Emerson declared with a smile.[66]

Never fearful of death himself, Brown soon came to see, to his surprise, that by dying he would do more to end slavery than ever he could by living.

Nov. 30, 1859

My Dearly Beloved Wife, Sons, and Daughters, Every One. . . .

I am waiting the hour of my public murder with great composure of mind and cheerfulness; feeling the strong assurance that in no other possible way could I be used to so much advantage to the cause of God and of humanity, and that nothing that either I or all my family have sacrificed or suffered will be lost. . . . I have now no doubt but that our seeming disaster will ultimately result in the most glorious success. So, my dear shattered and broken family, be of good cheer. . . . I never felt stronger confidence in the certain and near approach of a bright morning and glorious day. . . .[67]

At 11:00 A.M. on December 2, 1859, John Brown emerged from the jail in Charles Town to travel the last road of his long life. Waiting for him at the end of his short journey was old, white-haired Edmund Ruffin and young, raven-headed John Wilkes Booth. Hundreds of other Virginia militiamen were also on hand, hoping by their presence to forestall any rescue attempt. Their concerns were needless. Brown was happiest where he was. Even as he stepped into the crude wagon and seated himself upon his own coffin, a chorus of church bells were pealing throughout the North. From New York and Boston to Chicago and St. Paul, those who only a fortnight before had pronounced him a madman and murderer now announced to the world his martyrdom.[68]

Southerners also heard the tolling bells. Indeed, it was these sounds more than anything else—more than the raid at Harpers Ferry, more even than the loss of Kansas—that finally convinced many in the South that the America of their fore-fathers, the America of their hopes and dreams, could no longer live with itself.

Even as Brown was mounting the scaffold, a thousand miles to the west a tall, ambitious lawyer from Illinois was spreading his antislavery message to the towns and hamlets of Kansas.[69] He was as yet an unannounced candidate for president, but as he moved inexorably toward his quest, the sputtering fuse, ignited in 1854 and now flashing fiercely as it swept past Harpers Ferry, hissed nearer and nearer the terrible, waiting powder keg.

# EPILOGUE—THE STRANGER

To THE SURPRISE OF NO ONE, WHEN THE PROSLAVERY CONSTITUTION WAS FINALLY placed on the block in 1858, it was soundly rejected by the voters of Kansas. And thus, as the people of the territory registered their determination to wait—forever, if necessary—until a friendly federal government admitted them into the Union as a free and equal member with no strings attached, the last hope of the South in Kansas was dashed forever. And with that grim understanding, secession voices, crying so long in the wilderness, now began to be heeded in deadly earnest.

Although the last proslavery threat to Kansas had been finally erased, James Montgomery and Charles Jennison acted as if the territory was still at war. Continuing the rampage begun in 1857, these men and their Jayhawkers scoured southern Kansas, looting homes, stealing livestock, aiding fugitive slaves, and killing any who got in their way. During one week in December 1860, three men were murdered in succession, ostensibly because they were proslavery or had helped return runaways to Missouri.[1] When the supply of southern victims ran low, the Jayhawkers turned their sights on free-state Democrats, and when this quarry, too, became scarce, moderate Republicans were next in line.

"We are neither Democrats nor Republicans," announced Montgomery, "but abolitionists. We are determined that slaves shall never be retaken in Kansas. We intend to operate against South-west Missouri as soon as we clear out all opposition in the Territory."[2]

As prophets North and South had warned, and as the words and deeds of Montgomery, and John Brown before him, revealed, radical abolitionists cared for Kansas only insofar as it provided a fortress for attacks against slavery in Missouri and Arkansas. With the black clouds of war lowering over the nation following the election of Abraham Lincoln and the consequent secession of southern states, and with the ravenous Kansas Jayhawkers poised for a swoop into the state at the first opportunity, many Missouri slaveholders now began to voluntarily dismantle the system. While some masters allowed their "runaways" to simply walk away to

Kansas and freedom, others shipped their bondsmen to southern markets by the thousands.[3]

"[A]t the rate slaves have been sold South for the past six months," a happy Kansas editor reported, "slavery in western Missouri will cease before the end of three years."[4]

For some Kansans, three years was too long to wait. Although slave raids into Missouri were still relatively rare, several had occurred. One foray stood out from the rest. On a sunny afternoon in mid-December 1860, a tall, handsome stranger approached the Blue Springs plantation of wealthy slave owner Morgan Walker. The stranger was dirty and unshaven for he had been hiding in a heavy thicket only a mile from the home.[5] The stranger was also troubled. A former free-soiler from Kansas, he had of late undergone a powerful, wrenching change. As a letter to his Ohio mother makes clear, the transformation had been well on its way to completion one year before.

> You have undoubtedly heard of the wrongs committed in this territory by the southern people, or proslavery party, but when one once knows the facts they can easily see that it has been the opposite party that have been the main movers in the troubles & by far the most lawless set of people in the country. They all sympathize for old J. Brown, who should have been hung years ago, indeed hanging was too good for him. May I never see a more contemptible people than those who sympathize for him. A murderer and a robber, made a martyr of; just think of it.[6]

Now, at Walker's, the young stranger was about to turn his back forever on the old life and cross the threshold to a new. According to Walker's grown son, Andrew:

> He told my father that he was with a party of three men who had come over from Kansas to rob us of our money, horses and mules and run off our niggers. He said he would aid us in thwarting their designs. We got several men together between that time and dark. . . . We had it all arranged that when the robbers came to the door a lighted candle was to be placed in one of the windows.[7]

That moonless night, as promised, the Kansan led his three companions to the Walker home. "We have come to take your niggers with us to Kansas," the stranger announced as he stepped into the house. "We also want your horses and mules and what money you have in the house."

Andrew Walker:

My father replied that if his niggers wanted to go to Kansas they were at liberty to do so, but he did not see any reason why those who did not want to go should be compelled to leave him and he thought he ought to have his stock and money left him. The other three were standing outside the door, which was then shut; a candle was put in the window and the other lights turned out. We then opened fire on the three. . . .[8]

In the blaze of buckshot that swept the yard, one abolitionist dropped dead while another helped his wounded comrade into the night. The respite was brief. "A negro servant of my father's saw them in the brush a few days later," concluded young Walker. "My father and I shouldered our guns . . . and went after them, and they were buried right there."[9]

For his role in the affair at Morgan Walker's, the stranger was awarded a horse, one hundred dollars, and a warm welcome to his new home and new life in Missouri.

One month later, on the evening of January 29, 1861, Benjamin Simpson and other members of the territorial legislature were sitting in session at the Eldridge House in Lawrence. "There were from three to four inches of snow on the ground," Simpson noted, signifying an end to a terrible, year-long drought, "and the night was windy and cold."

It must have been as late as nine o'clock when D[aniel] R. Anthony . . . came into the hotel with sturdy stride and flashing eyes, and told us that the President of the United States had that day signed and approved the bill admitting Kansas into the Union. He brought with him and scattered around extras issued by a newspaper published at Leavenworth . . . announcing the joyful tidings in flaring headlines.[10]

With one voice, the assembly exploded in a wild celebration of shouts, cheers, and laughter. "Men ran from place to place proclaiming the glad tidings," rang one reveler. "Cheering and music and all manner of exultation was heard everywhere through our streets."[11]

"[T]he news ran through the town like wildfire," an elated—and now inebriated—Ben Simpson added. "Houses were lighted, doors were thrown open (and some were broken open), the people gathered in public places . . . toasts were drunk; songs were sung; speeches were made, and well, the truth is, that my recollection is not good after midnight."[12]

With incredible speed, the glorious word spread until the entire new state had joined the jubilation. While a grateful Charles Robinson quietly prepared to don his well-earned and long-postponed mantle as the first governor of Kansas, and while his archenemy, James Lane, after a miraculous political comeback, schemed his way toward the U.S. Senate, those Kansans of more modest aspirations were merely thankful that the territorial days were mercifully at an end and that their new western home had finally "moved to America."

"At last," sighed a Manhattan editor, "the great victory, for which the people of Kansas have fought so many hard battles against the slave power, suffered so many acts of injustice, at the hands of a corrupt and vindictive Administration, and submitted to so many sacrifices and privations, is won! We are a FREE and Sovereign State!!" [13]

The celebration on this snowy winter's eve was not dampened in the least by the looming prospect of war nor the growing national crisis that would increasingly focus on a fort in Charleston Harbor. For seven long years the people of Kansas had fought the fight of the North, and the moment to set down a heavy load was at hand. And if the horrors of civil war did indeed engulf the nation, many in Kansas felt it was only fitting that all of America should finally join in. Some, like James Redpath, Julia Lovejoy, and James Montgomery, actually welcomed war. Even had these individuals, and many more just like them, been able to peer into the future and see what lay ahead for America, their attitude would not have changed in the least. Even could they have viewed for themselves the blood-soaked sod at Shiloh and Antietam or the hideous heaps of corpses at Fredericksburg, Franklin, and a score of other slaughter pens, they would have felt the sacrifice a necessary one to atone for the sin of all sins: slavery. However, could these same people, now so lighthearted and gay, have looked ahead into their own future, it might have given them reason to pause. Could they have but gazed at the death and destruction and desolation that was coming to Kansas, at their own towns and villages enveloped in smoke and flame, at the bodies of friends, neighbors, and loved ones strewn about the fields and streets, it is doubtful few, if any, would have been so eager for the terrible storm that was now rushing down on them with the force of a tornado.

None were aware of the fact, of course, but the lead player in the coming drama who would transform this horrifying Kansas vision into reality had already stepped upon the stage at Morgan Walker's. He was destined to be loved and revered on one side of the state line and despised and demonized on the other, but ultimately, and almost single-handedly, this man would make all that came before in "Bleeding Kansas" seem like child's play by comparison. A few along the line had known him as Charley Hart; the world would soon hear of him as William Quantrill.

But for the moment, at least, war was far from the collective heart and soul of Kansas. The well-earned victory celebration had begun—the victory of freedom over slavery. A few courageous men and women, a few who never quit believing, had finally conquered against almost overwhelming odds. And because of their heroic efforts, the face of America had been altered forever.

"Our State . . . ," saluted the *Lawrence Republican* in one final toast, "may her ways be ways of pleasantness, and all her paths be peace." [14]

# NOTES

## PROLOGUE

1. Webb Scrapbook, Kansas State Historical Society, Topeka, 17:104.
2. P. Poindexter, "The Capture and Execution of John Brown," *Lippincott's Magazine* 43 (Jan. 1889): 125.
3. James Redpath, *The Public Life of Capt. John Brown* (Boston: Thayer and Eldridge, 1860), 40l.
4. William Ansel Mitchell, *Linn County, Kansas—A History* (Kansas City, Mo.: 1928), 228.
5. Redpath, *John Brown,* 403.
6. Webb Scrapbook, 17:107.
7. *Elwood (Kans.) Free Press,* Dec. 10, 1859.
8. Mitchell, *Linn County,* 228–29.

## CHAPTER 1

1. Eli Thayer, *A History of the Kansas Crusade—Its Friends and Its Foes* (1889; reprint, New York: Books for Libraries, 1971), 13.
2. Charles Robinson, *The Kansas Conflict* (New York: Harper and Brothers, 1892), 148–49.
3. Ibid., 148.
4. Thayer, *Kansas Crusade,* 3.
5. Robert W. Richmond, *Kansas—A Land of Contrasts* (St. Charles, Mo.: Forum Press, 1974), 63.
6. Albert Castel, *William Clarke Quantrill—His Life and Times* (New York: Frederick Fell, 1962), 1.
7. Robinson, *Kansas Conflict,* 97.
8. Ibid., 73.
9. A. T. Andreas, *History of the State of Kansas* (Chicago: A. T. Andreas, 1883), 85.
10. Thayer, *Kansas Crusade,* 184.

11. Robinson, 97.

12. Ibid., 73.

13. Thayer, 69–70.

14. F. W. Blackmar, "Charles Robinson," *Kansas Historical Collections* 6 (1887–1900): 195.

15. Alice Nichols, *Bleeding Kansas* (New York: Oxford University Press, 1954), 12.

16. Patrick Brophy, *Three Hundred Years—Historical Highlights of Nevada and Vernon County Missouri* (Boulder, Colo.: Donna G. Logan, 1993), 110.

17. *Atchison (Kan.) Squatter Sovereign,* Feb. 19, 1856; Webb Scrapbook, Kansas State Historical Society, Topeka, 3: 48.

18. Nichols, *Bleeding Kansas,* 59; Jay Monaghan, *Civil War on the Western Border, 1854–1865* (Boston: Little, Brown, 1955), 30.

19. Robinson, *Kansas Conflict,* 76–77.

20. Miriam Davis Colt, *West to Kansas—Being a Thrilling Account of an Ill-fated Expedition to that Fairy Land, and Its Sad Results* (1862, reprint; Ann Arbor, Mich.: University Microfilms, 1966), 28.

21. "Some Ingalls Letters," *Kansas Historical Collections* 14 (1915–1918): 96.

22. Russell K. Hickman, "A Little Satire on Emigrant Aid—Amasa Soule and the Descandum Kansas Improvement Company," *Kansas Historical Quarterly* 8, no. 4 (Nov. 1939), 346.

23. "Thomas C. Wells: Letters of a Kansas Pioneer, 1855–1860," *Kansas Historical Quarterly* 5, no. 2 (May 1936): 146.

24. Ibid.

25. Richard Cordley, *Pioneer Days in Kansas* (Boston: Pilgrim Press, 1903), 32–33.

26. "Ingalls Letters," *Kansas Historical Collection* 14, 97.

27. Ibid., 98.

28. "Letters of John and Sarah Everett, 1854–1864—Miami County Pioneers," *Kansas Historical Quarterly* 8, no. 1 (Feb. 1939): 4.

29. "Wells: Letters," *Kansas Historical Quarterly* 5, no. 2, 146.

30. "Letters From Kanzas—Julia Louisa Lovejoy," *Kansas Historical Quarterly* 11, no. 1 (Feb. 1942): 33.

31. Edward Fitch Letters, to "Friends," July 30, 1855, Douglas County Historical Society, Lawrence, Kansas.

32. "Letters From Kanzas," 34.

33. Louise Barry, "The Emigrant Aid Company Parties of 1854," *Kansas Historical Quarterly* 12, no. 2 (May 1943): 120.

34. Hannah Anderson Ropes, *Six Months in Kansas* (Boston: John P. Jewett, 1856), 34.

35. Albert D. Richardson, *Beyond the Mississippi—From the Great River to the Great Ocean, Life and Adventure of the Prairies, Mountains, and Pacific Coast, 1857–1867* (Hartford, Conn.: American, 1867), 26.

36. Barry, "Emigrant Aid Company," 138.

37. "Letters From Kanzas," 34.

38. "Letters of Julia Louisa Lovejoy, 1856–1864, Part Three," *Kansas Historical Quarterly* 15, no. 4 (Nov. 1947): 369.

39. "The Letters of Joseph H. Trego, 1857–1864—Linn County Pioneer," *Kansas Historical Quarterly* 19, no. 2 (May 1951): 116.

40. Robinson, *Kansas Conflict,* 34.

41. Edward P. Bridgman, "Notes and Documents—Bleeding Kansas and the Pottawatomie Murders," *Mississippi Valley Historical Review* 6, no. 4 (Mar. 1920): 557.

42. Ropes, *Six Months in Kansas,* 36.

43. Glenda Riley, ed., "Kansas Frontierswomen Viewed Through Their Writings—The Diary of Chestina Bowker Allen," *Kansas History* 9, no. 2 (Summer 1986): 84–85.

44. "Letters of Julia Louisa Lovejoy, Part Three," 368.

45. Thayer, *Kansas Crusade,* 71–72.

46. Barry, "Emigrant Aid Company," 122.

47. Robinson, *Kansas Conflict,* 81.

48. Ibid.

49. Ibid., 81–82.

50. Ibid., 79.

51. Robert W. Richmond, "A Free-Stater's 'Letters to the Editor'—Samuel N. Wood's Letters to Eastern Newspapers, 1854," *Kansas Historical Quarterly* 23, no. 2 (Summer 1957): 188–89.

52. "Wells: Letters," 146

53. Don Russell, ed., "Julia Cody Goodman's Memoirs of Buffalo Bill," *Kansas Historical Quarterly* 28, no. 4 (Winter 1962): 458–59.

54. Ibid., 459.

55. William F. Cody, *An Autobiography of Buffalo Bill* (New York: Rinehart, 1920), 12.

56. Russell, "Julia Cody's Memoirs," 459–60.

57. Robinson, *Kansas Conflict,* 129; George W. Martin, "The First Two Years of Kansas," *Kansas Historical Collections* 10 (1907–1908): 129; Webb Scrapbook, 3: 1.

58. Barry, "The Emigrant Aid Company," 146–47.

59. "Letters of John and Sarah Everett," no. 1: 23.

60. Barry, 139.
61. Louise Barry, "The New England Emigrant Aid Company Parties of 1855," *Kansas Historical Quarterly* 12, no. 3 (Aug. 1943): 236.
62. Cora Dolbee, "The Second Book on Kansas—An Account of C. B. Boynton and T. B. Mason's 'A Journey Through Kansas; With Sketches of Nebraska,'" *Kansas Historical Quarterly* 4, no. 2 (May 1935): 136.

## CHAPTER 2

1. David Rice Atchison Papers, 1837–1953, to "Dear Davis," Sept. 24, 1854, folder 4, Western Historical Collections, Columbia, Missouri; W. M. Paxton, *Annals of Platte County, Missouri* (Kansas City, Mo.: Hudson-Kimberly, 1897), 833.
2. Atchison Papers, Letter from William Walker, July 6, 1854.
3. Ibid., Letter from C. F. Jackson, Jan. 18, 1854.
4. Frederick Starr Papers, to "Dear Father," Aug. 1, 1854, folder 1, Western Historical Collections, Columbia, Missouri; Robinson, *Kansas Conflict*, 133.
5. Thayer, *Kansas Crusade*, 64–65.
6. "The Letters of the Rev. Samuel Young Lum—Pioneer Kansas Missionary, 1854–1858," *Kansas Historical Quarterly* 25, no. 1 (Spring 1959): 50.
7. Andreas, *History of Kansas*, 93.
8. *Kansas City (Mo.) Enterprise*, June 28, 1856; *Liberty (Mo.) Tribune*, April 6, 1855.
9. Robinson, *Kansas Conflict*, 98–99.
10. Thayer, 168–70.
11. Richmond, "Wood's Letters," 186.
12. Robinson, 109.
13. Ibid., 98.
14. Ibid., 102.
15. *St. Joseph (Mo.) Commercial Cycle*, Feb. 9, Mar. 30, 1855.
16. Andreas, *Kansas*, 99.
17. Robinson, 93–94.
18. Martin, "The First Two Years of Kansas," 126.
19. Floyd C. Shoemaker, "Missouri's Proslavery Fight for Kansas, 1854–1855," *Missouri Historical Review* 48, no. 4 (July 1954): 328.
20. Sara T. D. Robinson, *Kansas—Its Interior and Exterior Life* (Boston: Crosby, Nichols, 1856), 20.
21. "Wells: Letters," 149.
22. *Lawrence (Kan.) Herald of Freedom*, June 2, 1855.
23. G. Douglas Brewerton, *The War in Kansas* (1856, reprint; Freeport, N.Y.: Books For Libraries, 1971), 287.

24. Sara Robinson, *Kansas,* 16.

25. Brewerton, *War in Kansas,* 287.

26. Sara Robinson, 17.

27. *Lawrence (Kans.) Herald of Freedom,* Mar. 31. 1855.

28. Ibid.

29. Shalor Winchell Eldridge, *Recollections of Early Days in Kansas* (Topeka: Kansas State Historical Society, 1920), II:19.

30. Sara Robinson, 18.

31. Ibid., 19.

32. *Lawrence (Kans.) Herald of Freedom,* June 2, 1855.

33. Sara Robinson, 20.

34. Lela Barnes, "Letters of Cyrus Kurtz Holliday, 1854–1859," *Kansas Historical Quarterly* 6, no. 3 (Aug. 1937): 257.

35. Robinson, *Kansas Conflict,* 112.

36. Webb Scrapbook, 3: 93.

37. Robinson, *Kansas Conflict,* 113.

38. Ibid., 113.

39. Ibid., 112–13.

40. Ibid., 115.

41. Ibid., 116–17.

42. Ibid., 114.

43. Ibid., 133.

44. Kenneth M. Stampp, *America in 1857—A Nation on the Brink* (New York: Oxford University Press, 1990), 145.

## CHAPTER 3

1. *Lawrence (Kans.) Herald of Freedom,* Aug. 18, 1855.

2. Robinson, *Kansas Conflict,* 142.

3. Ibid., 140.

4. Ibid., 115.

5. Brewerton, *The War in Kansas,* 87–88; *Parkville (Mo.) Industrial Luminary,* Feb. 9, 1855; Nichols, *Bleeding Kansas,* 29; *Liberty (Mo.) Tribune,* Mar. 2, 1855.

6. Robinson, 111.

7. *Atchison (Kans.) Squatter Sovereign,* Mar. 13, 1855; Shoemaker, "Missouri's Proslavery Fight," 326.

8. Robinson, *Kansas Conflict,* 121.

9. *Lawrence (Kans.) Herald of Freedom,* May 19, 1855.

10. *Weston (Mo.) Weekly Platte Argus,* May 5, 1855.

11. *Atchison (Kans.) Squatter Sovereign,* Apr. 24, 1855.

12. Roy V. Magers, "The Raid on the Parkville Industrial Luminary," *Missouri Historical Review* 30, no. 1 (Oct. 1935): 46.

13. Ibid.

14. Martin, "The First Two Years of Kansas," 130.

15. Robinson, *Kansas Conflict,* 131; *Weston (Mo.) Weekly Platte Argus,* May 3, 1855.

16. *Lawrence (Kans.) Herald of Freedom,* Sept. 8, 1855.

17. Ibid., June 9, 1855.

18. Ibid.

19. *Weston (Mo.) Weekly Platte Argus,* May 5, 1855.

20. Andreas, *Kansas,* 99.

21. *Weston (Mo.) Weekly Platte Argus,* May 5, 1855.

22. Andreas, 99.

23. Ibid., 425.

24. *Leavenworth Kansas Weekly Herald,* May 25, 1855.

25. Monaghan, *Civil War on the Western Border,* 20.

26. Andreas, *Kansas,* 425.

27. *Leavenworth Kansas Weekly Herald,* May 25, 1855.

28. Martin, "The First Two Years," 131.

29. Ibid.

30. John H. Gihon, *Geary and Kansas—Governor Geary's Administration in Kansas With Complete History of the Territory Until June 1857* (1857, reprint; Freeport, N.Y.: Books For Libraries, 1971), 34.

31. *Lawrence (Kans.) Herald of Freedom,* June 30, 1855.

32. Webb Scrapbook, 3: 116.

33. *Leavenworth Kansas Weekly Herald,* June 15, 1855.

34. Robinson, *Kansas Conflict,* 130.

35. James A. Rawley, *Race and Politics—"Bleeding Kansas" and the Coming of the Civil War* (Philadelphia: J. B. Lippincott, 1969), 88.

36. James C. Malin, *John Brown and the Legend of Fifty-Six* (Philadelphia: American Philosophical Society, 1942), 520.

37. Ibid.

38. Robinson, *Kansas Conflict,* 135.

39. *Atchison Squatter Sovereign,* Apr. 10, 1855; *Leavenworth Kansas Weekly Herald,* Sept. 29, 1855.

40. Robinson, *Conflict,* 134.

41. Ibid., 151.

42. Andreas, *Kansas,* 105.

43. Robinson, *Conflict,* 162.

44. Nichols, *Bleeding Kansas,* 39.

45. *Parkville (Mo.) Weekly Southern Democrat,* July 21, 1855.

46. Robinson, *Conflict,* 164.

47. Ibid., 165.

48. Ibid., 160–61.

49. Ibid., 147, 152.

50. Gunja SenGupta, *For God and Mammon—Evangelicals and Entrepreneurs, Masters and Slaves in Territorial Kansas, 1854–1860* (Athens: University of Georgia, 1996), 64.

51. Wendell Holmes Stephenson, *The Political Career of General James H. Lane* (Topeka: Kansas State Historical Society, 1930), 42, 45.

52. Ibid., 47.

53. *Parkville (Mo.) Weekly Southern Democrat,* Apr. 24, 1855.

54. Andreas, *Kansas,* 115, 371.

55. *Lawrence (Kans.) Herald of Freedom,* Mar. 22, 1856.

56. Ibid., Aug. 18, 1855.

57. Andreas, 115.

58. *Lawrence (Kans.) Herald of Freedom,* Mar. 22, 1856.

59. Gihon, *Geary and Kansas,* 49.

60. Pardee Butler, *Personal Recollections of Pardee Butler, With Reminiscences of His Daughter, Mrs. Rosetta B. Hastings, etc.* (Cincinnati: Standard, 1889), 66.

61. Gihon, *Geary,* 49.

62. Butler, *Personal Recollections,* 67–68; David Edwin Harrell, Jr., "Pardee Butler: Kansas Crusader," *Kansas Historical Quarterly* 34, no. 4 (Winter 1968): 390; *Lawrence (Kans.) Herald of Freedom,* Sept. 8, 1855.

63. Butler, 70–71.

64. Ibid., 71–72; Harrell, *Pardee Butler,* 391.

65. Gihon, *Geary.* 48–49.

66. Charles S. Gleed, "Samuel Walker," *Kansas Historical Collections* 6 (1897–1900): 254.

67. Ibid., 252.

68. Ibid., 253.

69. Ibid., 254.

70. Robinson, *Kansas Conflict,* 159.

71. Ibid., 171–72.

72. *Lexington (Mo.) American Citizen,* Oct. 10, 1855.

## CHAPTER 4

1. Eldridge, *Early Days in Kansas,* n.17; Andreas, *Kansas,* 316.

2. Andreas, 316.

3. Sara Robinson, *Kansas,* 543.

4. Colt, *West to Kansas,* 72.

5. Richmond, *Kansas—A Land of Contrasts,* 65–66.

6. Richardson, *Beyond the Mississippi,* 53; Sara Robinson, 165.

7. Andreas, *Kansas,* 317.

8. *Lawrence (Kans.) Herald of Freedom,* Mar. 10, 1855.

9. Louise Barry, "The New England Emigrant Aid Company Parties of 1855," *Kansas Historical Quarterly* 12, no. 3 (Aug. 1943): 246.

10. M. A. DeWolfe Howe, ed., *Home Letters of General Sherman* (New York: Charles Scribner's Sons, 1909), 159.

11. Sara Robinson, 50–51.

12. Colt, *Went to Kansas,* 69.

13. Isaac Moffatt, "The Kansas Prairie or, Eight Days on the Plains," *Kansas Historical Quarterly* 6, no. 2 (May 1937): 170; "Letters From Kanzas," 39.

14. Barnes, "Letters from Cyrus Kurtz Holliday," 280.

15. "Letters of John and Sarah Everett," no. 1: 20, 22.

16. "Letters of Julia Louisa Lovejoy, Part Four," 69.

17. *Lawrence (Kans.) Herald of Freedom,* Aug. 15, Dec. 22, 1855; *Lexington (Mo.) American Citizen,* Sept. 4, 1855.

18. Ropes, *Six Months in Kansas,* 61, 64.

19. William Stanley Hoole, "A Southerner's Viewpoint of the Kansas Situation, 1856–1857—The Letters of Lieut. Col. A. J. Hoole, C. S. A.," *Kansas Historical Quarterly* 3, no. 1 (Feb. 1934): 60.

20. Letter of Sarah Everett to "Sister Cynthia," Sept. 1, 1855. Kansas State Historical Society, Topeka.

21. *Fort Scott (Kans.) Democrat,* Sept. 8, 1859.

22. Colt, *Went to Kansas,* 81–82.

23. "The Diary of James R. Stewart, Pioneer of Osage County," *Kansas Historical Quarterly* 17, no. 1 (Feb. 1949): 16.

24. "Letters of Julia Louisa Lovejoy, 1856–1864, part four," *Kansas Historical Quarterly* 16, no. 1 (Feb. 1948): 67.

25. Colt, 104.

26. Richardson, *Beyond the Mississippi,* 137.

27. "Lovejoy Letters, part two," 307–08.

28. Ibid., 285, 308.

29. Donald M. Murray and Robert M. Rodney, eds., "The Letters of Peter Bryant, Jackson County Pioneer," *Kansas Historical Quarterly* 27, no. 3 (Autumn 1961): 337.

30. "The Diary of James R. Stewart," no. 1:14.

31. Gleed, "Samuel Walker," 255.

32. Colt, *Went to Kansas,* 49, 70–71.

33. William H. Mackey, "Looking Backwards," *Kansas Historical Collections* 10 (1907–1908): 644–45.

34. "Letters of John and Sarah Everett," no. 1: 20–21.

35. "Letters from Kanzas," 35.

36. Colt, 70–71.

37. Ibid., 77.

38. Ibid., 78.

39. Ibid., 80.

40. Barnes, "Letters of Cyrus Kurtz Holliday," 246.

41. James C. Malin, "Housing Experiments in the Lawrence Community, 1855," *Kansas Historical Quarterly* 21, no. 2 (Summer 1954): 97–98.

42. Ropes, *Six Months in Kansas,* 217.

43. "Letters of John and Sarah Everett," no. 2: 145.

44. Richmond, *Kansas,* 67.

45. Sara Robinson, *Kansas,* 63.

46. T. H. Gladstone, *The Englishman in Kansas—or Squatter Life and Border Warfare* (1857, reprint; Lincoln: University of Nebraska Press, 1971), 112.

47. Webb Scrapbook, 3: 79.

48. Andreas, *Kansas,* 135.

## CHAPTER 5

1. Charles Howard Dickson, "A True History of the Branson Rescue," *Kansas Historical Collections* 13 (1913–1914): 286, 288.

2. Ibid., 288–89.

3. F. B. Sanborn, ed., *The Life and Letters of John Brown, Liberator of Kansas, and Martyr of Virginia* (Boston: Roberts Brothers, 1891), 208.

4. Robinson, *Kansas Conflict,* 186.

5. Brewerton, *The War in Kansas,* 151.

6. Sanborn, *John Brown,* 208–09.

7. Dickson, "Branson Rescue," 289–90.

8. Brewerton, 159–60.

9. Sara Robinson, *Kansas,* 116.

10. Brewerton, 163.

11. Robinson, *The Kansas Conflict,* 213.

12. Ibid., 190.

13. *Lawrence (Kans.) Herald of Freedom,* Jan. 19, 1856.

14. Robinson, *Kansas Conflict,* 196.

15. Ibid., 191.

16. "The Letters of the Rev. Samuel Young Lum," 66; Stephenson, *Lane,* 56.

17. Cordley, *Pioneer Days,* 72.

18. Sara Robinson, *Kansas,* 142–43.

19. Brewerton, *The War in Kansas,* 126.

20. *Kansas City (Mo.) Enterprise,* Feb. 16, 1856; Sara Robinson, 143.

21. *Kansas City (Mo.) Enterprise,* Feb. 16, 1856.
22. Stephenson, *Lane,* 56.
23. Sara Robinson, 123.
24. Brewerton, 166.
25. Ibid., 168.
26. *Leavenworth (Kans.) Weekly Kansas Herald,* Dec. 15, 1855.
27. *Atchison Squatter Sovereign,* Jan 1, 1856.
28. Brewerton, 140.
29. Gladstone, *The Englishman in Kansas,* 292–93.
30. Ibid., 293.
31. Brewerton, 326.
32. Ibid., 320.
33. Ibid., 327.
34. Ibid., 321.
35. Sara Robinson, 135.
36. Ropes, *Six Months in Kansas,* 136.
37. Sara Robinson, *Kansas,* 145–46.
38. Elvid Hunt, *History of Fort Leavenworth, 1827–1927* (Fort Leavenworth, Kans.: General Service Schools, 1926), 112–113.
39. Robinson, *The Kansas Conflict,* 215.
40. Sara Robinson, 146–47.
41. Joseph Savage, ed., "Captain Bickerton's Recollections of 1856," no. 3, Douglas County Historical Society, Lawrence, Kansas: 1; Brewerton, 186.
42. Sara Robinson, 155.
43. Nichols, *Bleeding Kansas,* 61.
44. Sara Robinson, 120.
45. Malin, *John Brown,* 17.
46. Stephen Oates, *To Purge This Land With Blood—A Biography of John Brown* (Amherst: University of Massachusetts Press, 1984): 107.
47. Ibid.; Nichols, 70.
48. Robinson, *Kansas Conflict,* 264.
49. Sara Robinson, 133.
50. Brewerton, 191.
51. Sara Robinson, 152.
52. Nichols, *Bleeding Kansas,* 75; Kendall E. Bailes, *Rider on the Wind—Jim Lane and Kansas* (Shawnee Mission, Kans.: Wagon Wheel, 1962), 32.
53. Nichols, 75.
54. Ibid.; *Atchison Squatter Sovereign,* Jan. 1, 1856.
55. Brewerton, *The War in Kansas,* 198–99.
56. Ibid., 199.
57. Robinson, *Kansas Conflict,* 206.

58. Ropes, *Six Months,* 144–45.
59. Ibid., 145.
60. Floyd C. Shoemaker, "Missouri's Proslavery Fight for Kansas, 1854–1855," *Missouri Historical Review* 49, no. 1 (Oct. 1954): 53.
61. Sara Robinson, 158.
62. Ibid., 182.
63. Ibid., 166.
64. Brewerton, 366.
65. "Letters of John and Sarah Everett," no. 1: 24.
66. "Letters of Julia Louisa Lovejoy, Part One," 127; Nichols, 87.
67. Brewerton, 78–79.
68. *Doniphan Kansas Constitutionalist* article in the *Atchison Squatter Sovereign,* May 20, 1856.
69. Ibid.
70. Brewerton, 226; *Leavenworth Kansas Weekly Herald,* Jan. 12, 1856.
71. Brewerton, 202.
72. *Leavenworth Kansas Weekly Herald,* Jan. 12, 1856.
73. Ibid., Jan. 19, 1856.
74. Ibid., Jan. 5, 1856.
75. Ibid., Jan. 12, 1856; Malin, *John Brown,* 36.
76. Brewerton, *The War in Kansas,* 395–96, 400.
77. *Lexington (Mo.) American Citizen,* Feb. 6, 1856.
78. *Parkville (Mo.) Weekly Southern Democrat,* Jan. 24, 1856; Gihon, *Geary and Kansas,* 71; *Leavenworth Kansas Weekly Herald,* Jan. 26, 1856.
79. *Lawrence (Kans.) Herald of Freedom,* May 3, 1856.
80. Redpath, *Capt. John Brown,* 95–96.
81. *Lawrence (Kans.) Herald of Freedom,* May 3, 1856.
82. Ibid., Mar. 29, 1856.
83. *Atchison Squatter Sovereign,* Jan. 22, 1856.
84. Nichols, *Bleeding Kansas,* 84.
85. Sara Robinson, 180.
86. *Topeka Kansas Freeman,* Feb. 9, 1856.
87. Malin, *John Brown,* 66–67.
88. Ibid., 526.
89. Robinson, *Kansas Conflict,* 223.
90. Martin, "The First Two Years of Kansas," 136; Rawley, *Race and Politics,* 113.
91. *Lawrence (Kans.) Herald of Freedom,* Feb. 23, 1856.
92. Robinson, *Kansas Conflict,* 226.
93. Andreas, *Kansas,* 125.
94. James C. Malin, "Judge Lecompte and the 'Sack of Lawrence,'" *Kansas Historical Quarterly* 20, no. 7 (Aug. 1953): 478.

95. Brewerton, 367.

96. *Atchison Squatter Sovereign,* Dec. 4, 1855.

97. Sara Robinson, 181.

98. Robinson, *Kansas Conflict,* 224.

99. Brewerton, 366.

100. Oates, *To Purge This Land With Blood,* 258.

**CHAPTER 6**

1. Martin, "The First Two Years of Kansas," 136.

2. Hoole, "A Southerner's Viewpoint of the Kansas Situation," 44–45; *Leavenworth Kansas Weekly Herald,* Mar. 15, 22, 1856; *Lexington (Mo.) American Citizen,* Mar. 12, 1856.

3. *Lawrence (Kans.) Herald of Freedom,* Feb. 9, 1856.

4. Ibid., Oct. 13, 1855, Feb. 9, 1856.

5. Ibid., Feb. 9, 1856.

6. Gihon, *Geary and Kansas,* 107.

7. Gladstone, *The Englishman in Kansas,* 128.

8. Brewerton, *The War in Kansas,* 248–49.

9. Ibid., 74.

10. *Topeka Kansas Freeman,* Nov. 28, 1855; Gihon, 106; Sara Robinson, 294; Gladstone, 129.

11. *Lawrence (Kans.) Herald of Freedom,* Mar. 24, 1855.

12. Richardson, *Beyond the Mississippi,* 144.

13. "The Letters of the Rev. Samuel Young Lum," 49; *Lawrence (Kans.) Herald of Freedom,* July 14, 1855.

14. Brewerton, 75.

15. Colt, *Went to Kansas,* 188; *Parkville (Mo.) Weekly Southern Democrat,* Nov. l, 1855; "Letters of Julia Louisa Lovejoy, Part Four," 50.

16. Brewerton, 65–66, 68–69.

17. *Leavenworth Kansas Weekly Herald,* June 29, 1855.

18. Brewerton, 65.

19. Nichols, *Bleeding Kansas,* 5–6.

20. *Leavenworth Kansas Weekly Herald,* Dec. 1, 1855.

21. Ibid., Sept. 20, 1856.

22. Brewerton, 209.

23. Ibid., 75.

24. Barry, "The Emigrant Aid Company," 120.

25. *Leavenworth Kansas Weekly Herald,* Dec. 15, 1855.

26. *Kansas City (Mo.) Enterprise,* May 31, 1856.

27. *Atchison (Kans.) Squatter Sovereign,* Jan. 22, 1856.

28. Robinson, *Kansas Conflict,* 227.

29. *Leavenworth Kansas Weekly Herald,* July 26, 1856.

30. Monaghan, *Civil War on the Western Border,* 49–50; *Atchison (Kans.) Squatter Sovereign,* May 27, 1856.

31. Robert H. Williams, *With the Border Ruffians—Memories of the Far West, 1852–1868* (1907, reprint; Lincoln: University of Nebraska Press, 1982), 59–60.

32. *Atchison (Kans.) Squatter Sovereign,* May 27, 1856.

33. Ibid.; Pardee Butler, *Personal Recollections,* 106–07.

34. *Lawrence (Kans.) Herald of Freedom,* May 17, 1856; Gihon, 76.

35. *Atchison (Kans.) Squatter Sovereign,* May 6, 1856.

36. Nichols, 86.

37. *Lawrence (Kans.) Herald of Freedom,* Oct. 13, 1855.

38. Malin, *John Brown,* 79; James C. Malin, "The Hoogland Examination—The United States v. John Brown, Jr., et al," *Kansas Historical Quarterly* 7, no. 2 (May 1938): 146.

39. Savage, "Captain Bickerton's Recollections, no. 3,": 1.

40. Ibid., 1–2.

41. Malin, *John Brown,* 65.

42. *Atchison (Kans.) Squatter Sovereign,* Feb. 19, 1856.

43. Malin, *John Brown,* 67–68; Gihon, 51; Robinson, *Kansas Conflict,* 241; Brewerton, 136.

44. Malin, *John Brown,* 45.

45. Sara Robinson, 197; *Kansas City (Mo.) Enterprise,* May 10, 1856.

46. Sara Robinson, 197.

47. *Kansas City (Mo.) Enterprise,* May 10, 1856.

48. "Sixth Biennial Report," *Kansas Historical Collections* 4 (1886–1888): 418.

49. *Kansas City (Mo.) Enterprise,* May 10, 1856.

50. Malin, *John Brown,* 47.

51. *Lecompton (Kans.) Union,* Apr. 28, 1856.

52. *Kansas City (Mo.) Enterprise,* May 10, 1856.

53. Ibid., May 3, 1856.

54. Malin, *John Brown,* 47.

55. *Atchison (Kans.) Squatter Sovereign,* June 10, 1856.

56. Robinson, *Kansas Conflict,* 282.

57. *Doniphan Kansas Constitutionalist* article in *Lexington (Mo.) American Citizen,* May 28, 1856.

58. Hoole, "A Southerner's Viewpoint," 48.

59. Robinson, *Kansas Conflict,* 244.

60. Sara Robinson, 221–23.

61. Gihon, *Geary and Kansas,* 82–83.

62. Hoole, 52.

63. Robinson, *Kansas Conflict,* 246–47.

64. Ibid., 247–48.

65. "May 21st, Let the Day be Remembered . . . ," Douglas County (Kans.) Historical Society *Newsletter* 10, no. 1 (May 1981): 1.

66. Stephenson, *James H. Lane,* 70.

67. Malin, "Judge Lecompte," 476; Eldridge, "Recollections," 49; "May 21st," Douglas County (Kans.) Historical Society *Newsletter,* 1.

68. *Parkville (Mo.) Weekly Southern Democrat,* May 29, 1856.

69. Eldridge, 50.

70. Ibid., 52.

71. Sara Robinson, 243.

72. Malin, "Judge Lecompte," 581.

73. Nichols, *Bleeding Kansas,* 107.

74. Eldridge, 53.

75. Gihon, *Geary,* 84.

76. Ibid.

77. Eldridge, "Recollections," 90.

78. Ibid., 53–54.

79. Ibid., 54.

80. "Sixth Biennial Report," *Kansas Historical Collections* 401.

81. Bridgman, "Bleeding Kansas," 559.

82. Gihon, 85; Malin, "Judge Lecompte," 477; *Leavenworth Kansas Weekly Herald,* May 31, 1856.

83. Gladstone, *The Englishman in Kansas,* 40–41.

84. Gihon, 85.

85. Sara Robinson, 249.

86. Andreas, *Kansas,* 136.

87. Stephenson, *Lane,* 70.

88. Andreas, 136.

89. Monaghan, *Civil War,* 54.

90. Ibid., 55.

91. David Donald, *Charles Sumner and the Coming of the Civil War* (New York: Alfred A. Knopf, 1967), 290–91.

92. D. A. Harsha, *The Life of Charles Sumner—With Choice Speeches of His Eloquence, etc.,* (New York: Dayton and Burdick, 1856), 146–47.

93. Donald, *Charles Sumner,* 294–95.

94. Ibid., 296.

95. Ibid., 296–97.

96. Ibid., 297.

97. *Kansas City (Mo.) Enterprise,* June 7, 1856.

98. Donald, *Charles Sumner,* 299.

99. Sanborn, *The Life and Letters of John Brown,* 249.

100. Donald, 299.

101. Ibid., 298.

102. "The Letters of the Rev. Samuel Young Lum," 176.

103. Edward Fitch Letters: 1855–56, to "Dear Father," May 26, 1856, Douglas County Historical Society, Lawrence, Kansas.

## CHAPTER 7

1. George W. Brown, *Reminiscences of Gov. R. J. Walker; With the True Story of the Rescue of Kansas From Slavery,* second part (Rockford, Ill.: G. W. Brown, 1902), 67; Louis Ruchames, ed., *A John Brown Reader—The Story of John Brown in his Words, in the Words of Those Who Knew Him and in the Poetry and Prose of the Literary Heritage* (New York: Abelard-Schuman, 1959), 192; Oates, *To Purge This Land With Blood,* 129.

2. Oates, 130.

3. Brown, *Gov. R. J. Walker,* 67–68.

4. Nichols, *Bleeding Kansas,* 113.

5. Brown, *R. J. Walker,* 73.

6. Ruchames, *John Brown Reader,* 193.

7. Ibid., 236; Richard J. Hinton Journal, Kansas State Historical Society, Topeka, 47; Sanborn, *The Life and Letters of John Brown,* 628.

8. Ruchames, 236.

9. Oates, 144.

10. Brown, *R. J. Walker,* 73.

11. Ely Moore, Jr., "The Naming of Osawatomie, and Some Experiences With John Brown," *Kansas Historical Collections* 12 (1911–1912): 345.

12. Robinson, *Kansas Conflict,* 396.

13. Brown, *R. J. Walker,* 73.

14. Robinson, 396.

15. Brown, *R. J. Walker,* 73–74.

16. Robinson, 396.

17. Ibid., 396–97.

18. Ruchames, 200; Robert W. Johannsen, ed., "A Footnote to the Pottawatomie Massacre, 1856," *Kansas Historical Quarterly* 22, no. 3 (Autumn 1956), 238–239.

19. Sanborn, 265–66.

20. Ruchames, 200.

21. Malin, *John Brown,* 99.

22. Hoole, "A Southerner's Viewpoint," 54.

23. Bridgman, "Bleeding Kansas," 559.

24. Robinson, 291.

25. Ibid., 281.

26. Ibid., 280.

27. Eldridge, *Recollections,* 58.

28. Andreas, *Kansas,* 135.

29. Ibid.

30. Robinson, 268.

31. Ibid.

32. Redpath, *The Public Life of Capt. John Brown,* 111–12.

33. Gihon, *Geary,* 100.

34. Oates, *To Purge This Land With Blood,* 138.

35. Malin, *John Brown,* 260; Robinson, *Kansas Conflict,* 278.

36. Redpath, 112–13.

37. Robinson, 287–88; Ruchames, 95.

38. Malin, 55, 115; Malin, "The Hoogland Examination," 136–37; Brown, *Walker,* 80.

39. Webb Scrapbook, 17:1.

40. G. W. E. Griffith, "The Battle of Black Jack," *Kansas Historical Collections* 16 (1923–1925): 524–25.

41. Malin, *John Brown,* 76; Ruchames, 95; Loren K. Litteer, *Bleeding Kansas— The Border War in Douglas and Surrounding Counties* (Baldwin City, Kans.: Champion, 1987): 48.

42. Ruchames, *John Brown Reader,* 95.

43. August Bondi Manuscript, Kansas State Historical Society, Topeka: 38–39.

44. Ibid., 39.

45. *Lexington (Mo.) American Citizen,* June 11, 1856.

46. Bondi manuscript, 39–40.

47. Oates, 153; Malin, *John Brown,* 590.

48. Luke F. Parsons Manuscript, Kansas State Historical Society, Topeka: 3.

49. Malin, *John Brown,* 62.

50. Edward Payson Bridgman and Luke Fisher Parsons, *With John Brown in Kansas— The Battle of Osawatomie* (Madison, Wis.: J. N. Davidson, 1915), 26; Robinson, *Kansas Conflict,* 295.

51. *Territorial Kansas—Studies Commemorating the Centennial* (Lawrence, Kans.: University of Kansas Press, 1954), 96.

52. Andreas, 133.

53. Riley, "Kansas Frontierswomen," no. 1:6; Malin, *John Brown,* 592.

54. Robinson, *Kansas Conflict,* 294.

55. "Bypaths of Kansas History—The Chicago Company and the Missouri River Pirates," *Kansas Historical Quarterly* 15, no. 2 (May 1947): 211.

56. Ibid.

57. Edgar Langsdorf and R. W. Richmond, "Letters of Daniel R. Anthony, 1857–1862," *Kansas Historical Quarterly* 24, no. 1 (Spring 1958): 22.

58. Andreas, 138.

59. Ibid., 135.

60. Sara Robinson, 291–92.

61. Eldridge, *Recollections,* 42–43.

62. Ibid., 43–44.

63. Richardson, *Beyond the Mississippi,* 81.

64. Brown, *R. J. Walker,* first part, 79.

65. Robinson, *Kansas Conflict,* 279.

66. Sara Robinson, 302.

67. Nathan Smith, ed., "Letters of a Free-State Man in Kansas, 1856," *Kansas Historical Quarterly* 21, no. 3 (Autumn 1954): 168–69.

68. Robinson, *Kansas Conflict,* 277; Malin, "The Hoogland Examination," 137.

69. Ruchames, 209.

70. Barnes, "Letters of Cyrus Kurtz Holliday," 285.

71. Malin, *John Brown,* 112.

72. Ruchames, 96.

73. Bondi Manuscript, 36.

74. Ruchames, 213.

75. *Territorial Kansas,* 91; Ruchames, 209.

76. Sara Robinson, 310–11.

77. Gleed, "Samuel Walker," 265.

78. Sara Robinson, 312–13.

79. Ibid., 313–14.

80. Gleed, 265.

81. "Sixth Biennial Report," *Kansas Historical Collections* 4 (1886–1888): 449.

82. V. E. Gibbens, "Letters on the War in Kansas in 1856," *Kansas Historical Quarterly* 10, no. 4 (Nov. 1941): 371.

## CHAPTER 8

1. Monaghan, *Civil War on the Western Border,* 71.

2. *Lexington (Mo.) American Citizen,* Aug. 20, 1856; Eldridge, *Recollections,* 99, 101.

3. Eldridge, 101.

4. *Lexington (Mo.) American Citizen,* Aug. 20, 1856; *Atchison (Kans.) Squatter Sovereign,* Sept. 23, 1856; *Kansas City (Mo.) Enterprise,* Aug. 23, 1856.

5. *Atchison (Kans.) Squatter Sovereign,* July 22, 1956.

6. *Leavenworth Kansas Weekly Herald,* Oct. 4, 1856.

7. Eldridge, n. 84; Gleed, "Walker," 267.

8. Gleed, 268; Eldridge, 83; Malin, *John Brown,* 173.

9. Gleed, 268.

10. Ibid.

11. Robinson, *Kansas Conflict,* 300.

12. Gleed, "Walker," 268.

13. Gihon, *Geary and Kansas,* 94.

14. "Selections from the Hyatt Manuscripts," *Kansas Historical Collections* 1–2 (1875–1878): 218–19; Gibbens, "Letters on the War in Kansas in 1856," 374; *Leavenworth Kansas Weekly Herald,* Aug. 23, 1856.

15. "Hyatt Manuscripts," 219; Savage, "Captain Bickerton's Recollections of 1856," 1–2; *Kansas City (Mo.) Enterprise,* Aug. 16, 1856; Robinson, *Kansas Conflict,* 310.

16. Andreas, *Kansas,* 142.

17. Ibid.; Savage, 2.

18. Gibbens, "Letters," 375.

19. Savage, 2.

20. Samuel Walker Papers, box "History H," folder "Territorial History, 1854–1861."

21. Andreas, 142; "Hyatt Manuscripts," 218–219; *Leavenworth Kansas Weekly Herald,* Aug. 23, 1856.

22. Sara Robinson, 326.

23. Savage, "Captain Bickerton's Recollections," no. 5: 1.

24. Sanborn, 308; *Leavenworth Kansas Weekly Herald,* Sept. 6, 1856.

25. *Leavenworth Kansas Weekly Herald,* Sept. 6, 1856; Gleed, "Walker," 269.

26. Gleed, 269.

27. *Leavenworth Kansas Weekly Herald,* Sept. 6, 1856.

28. Gibbens, 375.

29. Sanborn, 309.

30. Gibbens, 376.

31. Savage, no. 5: 2; Gleed, 269.

32. Gleed, 269–70.

33. Ibid., 270.

34. Malin, *John Brown,* 119.

35. Savage, no. 5: 2.

36. Malin, *John Brown,* 240; Andreas, *Kansas,* 320; *Leavenworth Kansas Weekly Herald,* Oct. 25, 1856; Sara Robinson, 255; Sanborn, 312.

37. "Battle of Fort Titus—An Eye Witness Account," *Bald Eagle* 9, no. 3 (Fall 1983): 3; Gibbens, 376; "Capture of Col. Tutus—The Treaty—The Exchange," *Kansas Historical Collection* 1–2 (1875–1878): 228.

38. "Battle of Fort Titus," 3; Gleed, "Walker," 270, 273; Malin, *John Brown,* 608.

39. Gleed, 270.

40. Ibid., 270–71.

41. Luke F. Parsons Manuscript, 4.

42. Gleed, 271.

43. "Battle of Fort Titus," 2; "Capture of Col. Titus," 228.

44. Gleed, "Walker," 271.

45. Parsons Manuscript, 5.

46. Gleed, 271.

47. Parsons Manuscript, 4–5.

48. Gleed, 271.

49. "Captain Bickerton's Recollections," no. 5: 2.

50. Sara Robinson, 326; O. G. Richards, "Kansas Experiences of Oscar G. Richards of Eudora, in 1856," *Kansas Historical Collections* 9 (1905–1906): 547.

51. "Battle of Fort Titus," 2.

52. Gibbens, 377; Gihon, *Geary and Kansas,* 95.

53. Sanborn, *The Life and Letters of John Brown,* 311; Sara Robinson, 325.

54. Sanborn, 311.

55. Malin, *John Brown,* 607.

56. Richards, "Kansas Experiences," 547; "Capture of Col. Titus," 228–29.

57. Eldridge, 86; "Battle of Fort Titus," 2.

58. Gleed, 271–72.

59. Gibbens, 376.

60. "Battle of Fort Titus," 2.

61. *Leavenworth Kansas Weekly Herald,* Oct. 25, 1856.

62. Andreas, 320.

63. "Capture of Col. Titus," 229.

64. Gleed, 272; Robinson, *Kansas Conflict,* 312; Andreas, 320.

65. "Sixth Biennial Report," 461–62.

66. Nichols, *Bleeding Kansas,* 139.

67. Redpath, 148.

68. *Lexington (Mo.) American Citizen,* Aug. 27, 1856.

69. *Kansas City (Mo.) Enterprise,* Sept. 13, 1856.

70. *Leavenworth Kansas Weekly Herald,* Nov. 8, 1856.

71. Andreas, 320.

72. Malin, *John Brown,* 647.

73. Ibid., 613–14.

74. "Hyatt Manuscripts," 211.

75. *St. Louis Weekly Missouri Democrat,* Sept. 9, 1856; G. Murlin Welch, *Border Warfare in Southeastern Kansas—1856–1859* (Pleasanton, Kans.: Linn County Historical Society, 1977), 4–5.

76. Sanborn, *Life and Letters of John Brown,* 314–15.

77. *St. Louis Weekly Missouri Democrat,* Sept. 9, 1856.

78. B. F. Blanton, "A True Story of the Border War," *Missouri Historical Review* 17, no. 1 (Oct. 1922): 58.

79. *St. Louis Weekly Missouri Democrat,* Sept. 9, 1856; Sanborn, n. 245–46, 322–23.

80. Sanborn, 322–23.

81. *St. Louis Weekly Missouri Democrat,* Sept. 9, 1856.

82. Malin *John Brown,* 113, 618; *St. Louis Weekly Missouri Democrat,* Sept. 9, 1856.

83. Andreas, 876; Malin, *John Brown,* 158.

84. Andreas, 876; Nichols, *Bleeding Kansas,* 142; Joanna L. Stratton, *Pioneer Women—Voices From the Kansas Frontier* (New York: Simon and Schuster, 1981), 241.

85. George Gardner Smith, ed., *Spencer Kellogg Brown, His Life in Kansas and His Death as a Spy, 1842–1863* (New York: D. Appleton, 1903), 68–69.

86. *St. Louis Weekly Missouri Democrat,* Sept. 9, 1856.

87. Sanborn, 285.

88. Ibid., 318–19.

89. Ibid., 319.

90. Bridgman, *With John Brown in Kansas,* 18–19.

91. Ibid., 19; Luke Parsons Manuscript, 7; Ruchames, *John Brown Reader,* 99.

92. Sanborn, 286.

93. Bridgman, 19.

94. Ibid.

95. Blanton, *A True Story,* 59.

96. Ibid.

97. Luke Parsons Manuscript, 7.

98. Oates, 170.

99. Parsons Manuscript, 7.

100. *Leavenworth Kansas Weekly Herald,* Sept. 6, 1856; Andreas, 145, 877; *St. Louis Weekly Missouri Democrat,* Sept. 9, 1856.

101. Gerald W. McFarland, *A Scattered People—An American Family Moves West* (New York: Pantheon, 1985), 151.

102. "Letters of John and Sarah Everett," 148.

103. Robinson, *Kansas Conflict,* 330; Oates, *To Purge This Land With Blood,* 170–71.

104. Andreas, 877; Smith, *Spencer Kellogg Brown,* 75.

105. Samuel Walker Papers.

106. Gihon, 115–16; *Leavenworth Kansas Weekly Herald,* Nov. 1, 1856.

107. *Leavenworth Kansas Weekly Herald,* Nov. 1, 1856.

108. Ibid.

109. Andreas, *Kansas,* 427.

110. Ibid.

111. *Leavenworth Kansas Weekly Herald,* Nov. 1, 1856.

112. "Letters of Julia Louisa Lovejoy, part one," 135.

113. Ibid, "part two," 283.

114. Sara Robinson, 328.

115. *Atchison (Kans.) Squatter Sovereign,* Sept. 23, 1856.

116. *Leavenworth Kansas Weekly Herald,* Oct. 4, 1856.

117. Ibid., Nov. 8, 1856.

118. Brown, *R. J. Walker,* second part, 20.

119. John C. Van Gundy, *Reminiscences of Frontier Life on the Upper Neosho in 1855 and 1856,* pamphlet, Kansas State Historical Society, Topeka: 21–22.

120. "Letter of John C. Van Gundy," *Kansas Historical Collections* 17 (1926–1928): 597; Flora Rosenquist Godsey, "The Early Settlement and Raid on the Upper Neosho," *Kansas Historical Collection* 16 (1923–1925): 461.

121. Stephenson, *James H. Lane,* 91; *Ottawa (Kans.) Herald,* Feb. 27. 1988; Charles Frederick William Leonhardt Papers, 1827–1884, box 2, Kansas State Historical Society, Topeka: Richard J. Hinton to Zu Adams, Winter, 1900.

122. James Redpath, *The Roving Editor, or, Talks with Slaves in the Southern States* (New York: Burdick, 1859), 347–48.

123. Ibid., 348.

124. Robinson, *Kansas Conflict,* 335.

125. "Sixth Biennial Report," *Kansas Historical Collections* 4 (1886–1888): 489; Andreas, 542; *Leavenworth Kansas Weekly Herald,* Sept. 13, 1856.

126. Gleed, *Walker,* 273; "Diary of James Stewart," part two, 152.

127. *Leavenworth Kansas Weekly Herald,* Aug. 23, 1856; Sara Robinson, 335; Andreas, 146; "Sixth Biennial Report," 488.

128. Gleed, 274.

129. Hoole, "A Southerner's Viewpoint," 64–65.

130. "Sixth Biennial Report," 488; Hinton Journal, 46.

131. Sara Robinson, 335.

132. Gleed, 274.

133. "James Stewart," 152.

134. Nichols, *Bleeding Kansas,* 143.

## CHAPTER 9

1. *Leavenworth Kansas Weekly Herald,* Sept. 13, 1856; Malin, *John Brown,* 218; *Atchison (Kans.) Squatter Sovereign,* Sept. 9, 1856.

2. Gihon, *Geary and Kansas,* 103–05.

3. Ibid., 106–07.

4. Ibid., 115; Williams, *With the Border Ruffians,* 88.

5. Gihon, 118.

6. Ibid., 117.

7. Ibid., 118.

8. Ibid., 119.

9. Ibid., 119–20.

10. *Atchison (Kans.) Squatter Sovereign,* Sept. 16, 1856; Andreas, 501.

11. *Atchison (Kans.) Squatter Sovereign,* Sept. 16, 1856.

12. Andreas, 501.

13. George A. Root, "The First Day's Battle at Hickory Point—From the Diary and Reminiscences of Samuel James Reader," *Kansas Historical Quarterly* 1, no. 1 (Nov. 1931): 39.

14. "Executive Minutes of Gov. Geary," *Kansas Historical Collections* 4 (1886–1888): 578.

15. *Leavenworth Kansas Weekly Herald,* Oct. 4, 1856.

16. Root, "Hickory Point," 39–40.

17. Ibid., 39.

18. Ibid., 40–41.

19. *Atchison (Kans.) Squatter Sovereign,* Sept. 30, 1856.

20. Root, 44.

21. Ibid., 42–43.

22. Ibid., 43.

23. *Atchison (Kans.) Squatter Sovereign,* Sept. 16, 1856.

24. Savage, "Bickerton's Recollections, no. 7," 1.

25. *Atchison (Kans.) Squatter Sovereign,* Sept. 16, 1856.

26. "Dr. Albert Morrall: Proslavery Soldier in Kansas in 1856—Statement and Autobiography," *Kansas Historical Collections* 14 (1915–1918): 133–34.

27. *Atchison (Kans.) Squatter Sovereign,* Sept. 16, 1856; Richardson, *Beyond the Mississippi,* 84.

28. "Dr. Albert Morrall," 134.

29. *Leavenworth Kansas Weekly Herald,* Oct. 4, 1856; "Executive Minutes of Gov. Geary," 576, 578; Savage, "Bickerton's Recollections, no. 7," 1.

30. "Letters of Julia Louisa Lovejoy, part one," 133.

31. Franklin B. Sanborn, "Some Notes on the Territorial History of Kansas," *Kansas Historical Collections* 13 (1913–1914): 250–51.

32. Ruchames, *A John Brown Reader,* 100.

33. "Letters of Julia Louisa Lovejoy, part one," 133.

34. Ibid., 133–34.

35. Robinson, *Kansas Conflict,* 326.

36. "Letters of Julia Louisa Lovejoy, part one," 134.

37. Brinton W. Woodward, "Reminiscences of September 14, 1856—Invasion of the 2700," *Kansas Historical Collections* 6 (1897–1900): 81.

38. "Edward Fitch Letters," no. 34: 2.

39. "Sixth Biennial Report," 500.

40. Gihon, 150; Otis E. Young, *The West of Philip St. George Cooke, 1809–1895* (Glendale, Calif.: Arthur H. Clark, 1955), 282; "Sixth Biennial Report," 500.
41. Nichols, *Bleeding Kansas,* 156.
42. Gihon, *Geary,* 151; Fitch Letters, no. 34: 2.
43. Gihon, 151–52.
44. Ibid., 152.
45. Ibid., 152–53.
46. Ibid., 153.
47. Ibid., 196.
48. Ibid., 166–67.
49. *Leavenworth Kansas Weekly Herald,* Sept. 27, 1856.
50. Malin, *John Brown,* 193.
51. "Richard B. Foster's Statement," *Kansas Historical Collections* 1–2 (1875–1878): 227.
52. Joseph G. Rosa, *They Called Him Wild Bill—The Life and Adventure of James Butler Hickok* (Norman: University of Oklahoma Press, 1964), 18.
53. Sanborn, *Life and Letters of John Brown,* 320.

**CHAPTER 10**
1. *Atchison (Kans.) Squatter Sovereign,* Aug. 14, 1855.
2. Robert W. Johannsen, "The Lecompton Constitutional Convention: An Analysis of Its Membership," *Kansas Historical Quarterly* 23, no. 3 (Autumn 1957): 228, 231, 232.
3. Gihon, *Geary and Kansas,* 217, 220.
4. "Letters of John and Sarah Everett," no. 3: 285; Gihon, 194.
5. Gihon, 121.
6. Gladstone, *The Englishman in Kansas,* 313–14.
7. Gihon, 183.
8. Ibid., 183–84.
9. Ibid., 219–20.
10. Hoole, "A Southerner's Viewpoint," 157.
11. Eldridge, *Recollections,* 125.
12. *Atchison (Kans.) Squatter Sovereign,* Feb. 24, 1857; Gihon, 230, 231.
13. Eldridge, 123.
14. Gihon, 234.
15. Gihon, 236; Martin, "The First Two Years of Kansas," n. 144.
16. Gihon, 237–38, 239.
17. Ibid., 241–43.
18. *Leavenworth Kansas Weekly Herald,* Mar. 28, 1857.
19. Eldridge, 126, 127; Gihon, 222, 257, 291; Andreas, 157.

20. *Leavenworth Kansas Weekly Herald,* Nov. 8, 1856, Mar. 28, 1857; Malin, *John Brown,* 198–99, 735–36.

21. Gihon, 271.

22. Hoole, "A Southerner's Viewpoint," 151; *Leavenworth Kansas Weekly Herald,* Jan. 3, 1857.

23. "Letters of John and Sarah Everett," *Kansas Historical Quarterly* 8 no. 2: 169; Eldridge, *Recollections,* 129.

24. Malin, *John Brown,* 207.

25. Ibid., 341.

26. *Leavenworth Kansas Weekly Herald,* May 23, 1857.

27. Stampp, *America in 1857,* 148.

28. Malin, 695.

29. "Letters of John and Sarah Everett," no. 3: 284; Martha B. Caldwell, "The Diary of George H. Hildt—June to December, 1857: Pioneer of Johnson County," *Kansas Historical Quarterly* 10, no. 3 (Aug. 1941): 286.

30. *Doniphan Kansas Constitutionalist,* Oct. 7, 1857; Caldwell, "Hildt," 286; Monaghan, *Civil War on the Western Border,* 98.

31. Hinton Journal, 44.

32. Brown, *R. J. Walker,* 108; Stephenson, *Lane,* 91; Malin, *John Brown,* 258, 707.

33. Brown, 109–10.

34. Brown, 111.

35, Nichols, 214; Robinson, *Kansas Conflict,* 379.

36. "Some Ingalls Letters," *Kansas Historical Collections* 14 (1915–1918): 115.

37. Caldwell, "Hildt," 290.

38. "Some Ingalls Letters," 96.

39. Brewerton, *The War in Kansas,* 259.

40. Gladstone, *The Englishman in Kansas,* 155–56.

41. Moffatt, "The Kansas Prairie," 162.

42. *Leavenworth Kansas Weekly Herald,* Apr. 4, 1857; "Letters of Julia Louisa Lovejoy," Part Three, 377; Martha Caldwell, "When Horace Greeley Visited Kansas in 1859," *Kansas Historical Quarterly* 9, no. 2 (May 1940): 125; Robert Taft, ed. "Over the Santa Fe Trail Through Kansas in 1858—H. B. Mollhausen," *Kansas Historical Quarterly* 16, no. 4 (Nov. 1948): 376.

43. Caldwell, "Hildt," 266.

44. "Ingalls Letters," 110.

45. Ibid.

46. Richardson, *Beyond the Mississippi,* 53, 58.

47. "Ingalls Letters," 100.

48. Cordley, *Pioneer Days in Kansas,* 46–47.

49. Malin, *John Brown,* 146; Richardson, 121.

50. Butler, *Personal Recollections,* 205.

51. Caldwell, "Greeley," 130, 131.

52. Howe, ed., *Home Letters of General Sherman,* 154, 158–159.

53. "Rev. Samuel Young Lum," 46.

54. Barry, "The New England Emigrant Aid Company," 260; Letter of A. J. Hoole, Nov. 2, 1856, Kansas State Historical Society, Topeka.

55. "Ingalls Letters," 103.

56. Langsdorf, "Letters of Daniel R. Anthony," part two, 211.

57. Hoole, "A Southerner's Viewpoint," 46.

58. Moffatt, "The Kansas Prairie," 172.

59. *Lawrence (Kans.) Herald of Freedom,* Feb. 24, 1855.

60. Ibid., July 14, 1855.

61. "Samuel Young Lum," 65.

62. Malin, *John Brown,* 119.

63. Murray, "The Letters of Peter Bryant," 331.

64. Gleed, "Walker," 255–56.

65. Rosa, *They Called Him Wild Bill,* 26.

66. Butler, 205.

67. Gladstone, 60.

68. Williams, *With the Border Ruffians,* 75.

69. "Letters of Julia Louisa Lovejoy, Part Two," 304.

70. Gladstone, 60.

71. Fred Starr Papers, folder 1, Starr to "Dear Father," Aug. 21, 1854.

72. "Letters of Julia Louisa Lovejoy," 388.

73. Rosa, 25–26.

74. Malin, *John Brown,* 129.

75. *Lexington (Mo.) American Citizen,* Nov. 12, 1856; *Leavenworth Kansas Weekly Herald,* Nov. 22, 1856, Mar. 14, 1857; Martin, "The First Two Years of Kansas," 145.

76. Welch, *Border Warfare,* 68.

77. *Elwood (Kans.) Weekly Advertiser,* Aug. 6, 1857.

78. Ibid.

79. *Leavenworth Kansas Weekly Herald,* July 26, 1856.

80. Brewerton, 269.

81. *Seneca (Kans.) Courier–Tribune,* Sept. 20, 1995.

82. *Kansas City (Mo.) Enterprise,* Mar. 28, 1856.

83. William E. Connelley, "The Lane–Jenkins Claim Contest," *Kansas Historical Collections* 16 (1923–1925): 123.

84. Ibid., 124.

85. Robinson, *Kansas Conflict,* 422.

86. Connelley, "Lane–Jenkins," 123.

87. Ibid., 132, 138.

88. Ibid., 132.
89. Ibid., 131.
90. Ibid., 138.
91. Ibid., 138, 139.
92. Richardson, 113.
93. Stephenson, *Lane,* 98; Monaghan, 108.
94. "Letters of Julia Lovejoy, Part Three," 387.
95. "The Diary of James Stewart," n. 259.
96. Ibid., 259.
97. Caldwell, "Hildt," 298.
98. Hoole, "A Southerner's Viewpoint," 166.

**CHAPTER 11**
1. Malin, *John Brown,* 181.
2. "Governor Denver's Administration," *Kansas Historical Collections* 5 (1889–1896): 533–34; "The Letters of Joseph H. Trego, 1857–1864—Linn County Pioneer," *Kansas Historical Quarterly* 19, no. 2 (May 1951): 126; Welch, *Border Warfare,* 56–57.
3. David Glenn Cobb, "Letters of David R. Cobb, 1858–1864—Pioneer of Bourbon County," *Kansas Historical Quarterly* 11, no. 1 (Feb. 1942): 67–68; *Fort Scott (Kans.) Democrat,* May 6, 1858; Leonhardt Papers, box 2.
4. *Fort Scott (Kans.) Democrat,* May 6, 1858.
5. Welch, 75.
6. Robinson, *Kansas Conflict,* 399–401; Welch, 93.
7. Welch, 93.
8. *From Pioneering to the Present—Linn County: Its People, Events, and Ways of Life* (Pleasanton, Kans.: Linn County Historical Society 1976): 54.
9. *Fort Scott (Kans.) Democrat,* May 6, 1858.
10. Welch, 89.
11. Ibid.
12. Ibid., 86, 88; Leonhardt Papers, box 2.
13. Mitchell, *Linn County,* 82.
14. Welch, 97.
15. Ibid., 98–99.
16. Ibid., 100.
17. Ibid., 101.
18. Andreas, *Kansas,* 1105.
19. Welch, 101.
20. *Fort Scott (Kans.) Democrat,* June 2, 1858.
21. Welch, 101.
22. Richardson, *Beyond the Mississippi,* 123; Mitchell, *Linn County,* 205, 206.

23. Richmond, *Kansas—A Land of Contrasts,* 75.

24. Richardson, 124.

25. "Governor Denver's Administration," 527; Richardson, 129, 130; Welch, 115.

26. Richardson, 125.

27. Ibid., 123; Mitchell, 279.

28. Richardson, 126.

29. Ibid.

30. Ibid., 128.

31. Ibid., 129, 130.

32. Ibid., 130.

33. Letter of James W. Denver, Lecompton, K. T., to "My Dear Wife," Jan. 4, 1858. Kansas State Historical Society, Topeka.

34. *Fort Scott (Kans.) Democrat,* July 29, 1858; "Letters of John and Sarah Everett," no. 2: 144.

35. "Governor Denver's Administration," 554; *Westport (Mo.) Border Star,* Jan. 14, 1860.

36. Mitchell, 276.

37. *Fort Scott (Kans.) Democrat,* Dec. 23, 1858.

38. Mitchell, 278.

39. *Fort Scott (Kans.) Democrat,* Dec. 23, 1858.

40. Ibid.

41. Ibid.

42. Leonhardt Papers, box 2.

43. James Montgomery Papers, 1859–1860, folder 2, letter from "Sene Campbell," Jan. 4, 1859, Kansas State Historical Society, Topeka.

44. *Fort Scott (Kans.) Democrat,* Dec. 23, 1858.

45. Ibid.

46. *History of Vernon County, Missouri* (St. Louis: Brown, 1887), 230.

47. Ibid., 226–27.

48. Ibid., 230; *Fort Scott (Kans.) Democrat,* Dec. 23, 1858.

49. Brown, *R. J. Walker,* second part, 147; Brophy, *Three Hundred Years,* 130–31.

50. *History of Vernon County,* 228–29.

51. Ibid., 229.

52. Oates, *To Purge This Land With Blood,* 262.

53. Ibid., 264.

## CHAPTER 12

1. Webb Scrapbook 17: 85.

2. Ibid.

3. "Recollections of the John Brown Raid," *The Century Illustrated Monthly Magazine* 26, no. 3 (July 1883): 404.

4. Webb Scrapbook 17: 85.

5. Ibid.

6. John E. P. Daingerfield, "John Brown at Harper's Ferry," *The Century Illustrated Monthly Magazine* 30, no. 2 (June 1885): 265–66.

7. "Recollections of the John Brown Raid," 405.

8. Ibid.

9. Ibid, 406.

10. Ibid.

11. Jennie Chambers, "What a School-Girl Saw of John Brown's Raid," *Harper's Monthly Magazine* 104 (Jan. 1902): 311.

12. Ibid.

13. "Recollections of the John Brown Raid," 400–01.

14. "John Brown at Harper's Ferry," 266; Webb Scrapbook,17: 85.

15. Rayburn S. Moore, ed., "John Brown's Raid at Harpers Ferry—An Eyewitness Account by Charles White," *The Virginia Magazine of History and Biography* 67, no. 4 (Oct. 1959): 389.

16. "Recollections of the John Brown Raid," 406–07.

17. Moore, "John Brown's Raid," 389–90.

18. Webb Scrapbook, 17: 48.

19. Redpath, *The Public Life of Capt. John Brown,* 258.

20. Ibid., 259.

21. Webb Scrapbook, 17: 48.

22. Ibid., 17: 67.

23. "Recollections of the John Brown Raid," 408.

24. "John Brown at Harper's Ferry," 266.

25. Ibid.

26. "Recollections of the John Brown Raid," 407.

27. Webb Scrapbook, 17: 67.

28. "Recollections," 407.

29. Redpath, *John Brown,* 320–21.

30. Oates, *To Purge This Land With Blood,* 297.

31. Redpath, *John Brown,* 259.

32. Poindexter, "The Capture and Execution of John Brown," 124; Redpath, *John Brown,* 326.

33. "John Brown's Raid—How I got Into It, And How I Got Out of It," *Atlantic Monthly* 15, no. 92 (June 1865): 713, 714.

34. Ibid., 714.

35. Webb Scrapbook, 17: 82.

36. Ibid., 17: 67.

37. "Recollections of the John Brown Raid," 408.

38. Redpath, *John Brown,* 260.
39. Moore, "John Brown's Raid," 390.
40. Redpath, *John Brown,* 326.
41. "The Capture and Execution of John Brown," 123–24.
42. Webb Scrapbook, 17: 46.
43. "The Capture and Execution of John Brown," 123.
44. "John Brown at Harper's Ferry," 267.
45. Webb Scrapbook, 17: 82.
46. "John Brown at Harper's Ferry," 267.
47. "Recollections of the John Brown Raid," 409.
48. "John Brown at Harper's Ferry," 267.
49. Redpath, *John Brown,* 262.
50. Ibid.
51. Ibid., 263.
52. Ibid.
53. "Recollections of the John Brown Raid," 410.
54. "John Brown's Raid," 715; "John Brown at Harper's Ferry," 267.
55. "Capture and Execution of John Brown," 124.
56. "Recollections," 410.
57. Redpath, *John Brown,* 275.
58. Ibid.
59. Chambers, "What a School-Girl Saw," 318.
60. Ibid.
61. Webb Scrapbook, 17: 48; Redpath, *John Brown,* 266.
62. Redpath, *John Brown,* 267.
63. Ibid.
64. Webb Scrapbook, 17: 107.
65. Robinson, *Kansas Conflict,* 399.
66. Malin, *John Brown,* 291.
67. Sanborn, *Life and Letters of John Brown,* 613.
68. Oates, *To Purge This Land With Blood,* 354.
69. *Elwood (Kans.) Free Press,* Dec. 3, 1859.

**EPILOGUE**
1. *Fort Scott (Kans.) Democrat,* Dec. 1, 1860, Jan. 5, 1861; *History of Vernon County, Missouri,* 244–45; Genevieve Yost, "History of Lynchings in Kansas," *Kansas Historical Quarterly* 2, no. 2 (May 1933): 186–87.
2. *Fort Scott (Kans.) Democrat,* Jan. 5, 1861.
3. Malin, *John Brown,* 252–53.
4. Ibid., 253.

5. Castel, *William Clarke Quantrill,* 36–37.

6. William Elsey Connelley, *Quantrill and the Border Wars* (1910, reprint; New York: Pageant, 1956), 90.

7. Donald R. Hale, *We Rode With Quantrill—Quantrill and the Guerrilla War as Told by the Men and Women Who Were With Him* (Lee's Summit, Mo.: Donald R. Hale, 1982), 160.

8. Ibid.

9. Ibid., 160–61.

10. Robinson, *Kansas Conflict,* 426.

11. "When Kansas Became a State," *Kansas Historical Quarterly* 27, no. 1 (Spring 1961): 7.

12. Robinson, *Kansas Conflict,* 426.

13. "When Kansas Became a State," 18.

14. Ibid., 8.

Andreas, A. T. *History of the State of Kansas.* Chicago: A. T. Andreas, 1883.

Atchison, David Rice. Papers, 1837–1953. Western Historical Collections, Columbia, MO.

Bailes, Kendell E. *Rider on the Wind—Jim Lane and Kansas.* Shawnee Mission, Kans.: Wagon Wheel Press, 1962.

Barnes, Lela. "Letters of Cyrus Kurtz Holliday, 1854–1859." *Kansas Historical Quarterly.* 6:3 (August 1937): 241–94.

Barry, Louise. "The Emigrant Aid Company Parties of 1854." *Kansas Historical Quarterly.* 12:2 (May 1943): 115–55.

——. "The Emigrant Aid Company Parties of 1855." *Kansas Historical Quarterly.* 12:3 (August 1943): 227–68.

"Battle of Fort Titus—An Eyewitness Account." *Bald Eagle.* 9:3 (Fall 1983): 1–4.

Blackmar, F. W. "Charles Robinson." *Kansas Historical Collection.* 6 (1897–1900): 187–202.

Blanton, B. F. "A True Story of the Border War." *Missouri Historical Review.* 17:1 (October 1992): 57–61.

Bondi, August. Manuscript. Kansas State Historical Society, Topeka.

Brewerton, G. Douglas. *The War in Kansas.* 1856. Reprint. Freeport, N.Y.: Books for Libraries, 1971.

Bridgman, Edward P. "Notes and Documents—Bleeding Kansas and the Pottawatomie Murders." *Mississippi Valley Historical Review* 6:4 (March 1920): 556–59.

Bridgman, Edward Payson and Luke Fisher Parsons. *With John Brown in Kansas—The Battle of Osawatomie.* Madison, Wis.: J. N. Davidson, 1915.

Brophy, Patrick. *Three Hundred Years—Historical Highlights of Nevada and Vernon County Missouri.* Boulder, Colo.: Donna G. Logan, 1993.

Brown, George W. *Reminiscences of Gov. R. J. Walker, With the True Story of the Rescue of Kansas from Slavery.* Rockford, Ill.: G. W. Brown, 1902.

Butler, Pardee. *Personal Recollections of Pardee Butler, With Reminiscences of His Daughter, Mrs. Rosetta B. Hastings, etc..* Cincinnati: Standard Publishing Company, 1889.

"Bypaths of Kansas History—The Chicago Company and the Missouri River Pirates." *Kansas Historical Quarterly.* 15:2 (May 1947): 211–13.

Caldwell, Martha B. "The Diary of George H. Hildt, June to December, 1857—Pioneer of Johnson County." *Kansas Historical Quarterly.* 10:3 (August 1941): 260–98.

———. "When Horace Greeley Visited Kansas in 1859." *Kansas Historical Quarterly.* 9:2 (May 1940): 115–40.

"Capture of Col. Titus—The Treaty—The Exchange." *Kansas Historical Collections.* 1–2 (1875–78): 228–30.

Castel, Albert. *William Clarke Quantrill—His Life and Times.* New York: Frederick Fell Inc., Publishers, 1962.

Chambers, Jennie. "What a School-Girl Saw of John Brown's Raid." *Harper's Monthly Magazine* 104 (January 1902): 311–18.

Cobb, David Glenn, ed. "Letters of David R. Cobb, 1858–1864—Pioneer of Bourbon County." *Kansas Historical Quarterly* 11:1 (February 1942): 65–71.

Cody, William F. *An Autobiography of Buffalo Bill.* New York: Rinehart, 1920.

Colt, Miriam Davis. *Went to Kansas—Being a Thrilling Account of an Ill-fated Expedition to That Fairy Land, and Its Sad Results.* 1862. Reprint. Ann Arbor, MI: University Microfilms, 1966.

Connelley, William E. "The Lane-Jenkins Claim Contest." *Kansas Historical Collections* 16 (1923–25): 21–176.

———. *Quantrill and the Border Wars.* 1910. Reprint. New York: Pageant Book Company, 1956.

Cordley, Richard. *Pioneer Days in Kansas.* Boston: Pilgrim Press, 1903.

Daingerfield, John E. P. "John Brown at Harper's Ferry—The Fight at the Engine-House, as Seen by One of his Prisoners." *The Century Illustrated Monthly Magazine* 30:2 (June 1885): 265–67.

Denver, James W. Letter to "My Dear Wife," Lecompton, K. T., January 4, 1858. Kansas State Historical Society, Topeka.

Dickson, Charles Howard. "A True History of the Branson Rescue." *Kansas Historical Collections* 13 (1913–14): 280–98.

Dolbee, Cora. "The Second Book on Kansas—An Account of C. B. Boynton and T. B. Mason's 'A Journey Through Kansas; With Sketches of Nebraska.'" *Kansas Historical Quarterly* 4:2 (May 1935): 115–48.

Donald, David. *Charles Sumner and the Coming of the Civil War.* New York: Alfred A. Knopf, 1967.

"Dr. Albert Morrall: Proslavery Soldier in Kansas in 1856—Statement and Autobiography." *Kansas Historical Collections* 14 (1915–18): 123–42.

Eldridge, Shalor Winchell. *Recollections of Early Days in Kansas.* Topeka: Kansas State Historical Society, 1920.

Everett, Sarah. Letter to "Sister Cynthia," September 1, 1855. Kansas State Historical Society, Topeka.

"Executive Minutes of Gov. Geary." *Kansas Historical Collection* 4 (1886–88): 520–742.

Fitch, Edward. Letters, 1855–56. Douglas County Historical Society, Lawrence, Kansas.

*From Pioneering to the Present—Linn County: Its People, Events and Ways of Life.* Pleasanton, Kans.: Linn County Historical Society, 1976.

Gibbens, V. E. "Letters on the War in Kansas in 1856." *Kansas Historical Quarterly* 10:4 (November 1941): 369–79.

Gihon, John H. *Geary and Kansas—Governor Geary's Administration in Kansas With Complete History of the Territory Until June 1857.* 1857. Reprint. Freeport, N.Y.: Books for Libraries, 1971.

Gladstone, T. H. *The Englishman in Kansas, or Squatter Life and Border Warfare.* 1857. Reprint. Lincoln: University of Nebraska Press, 1971.

Gleed, Charles S. "Samuel Walker." *Kansas Historical Collection* 6 (1897–1900): 249–74.

Godsey, Flora Rosenquist. "The Early Settlement and Raid on the Upper Neosho." *Kansas Historical Collections* 16 (1923–25): 451–63.

"Governor Denver's Administration." *Kansas Historical Collections* 5 (1889–96): 464–561.

Griffith, G. W. E. "The Battle of Black Jack." *Kansas Historical Collections* 16 (1923–25): 524–28.

Hale, Donald R. *We Rode With Quantrill—Quantrill and the Guerrilla War as Told by the Men and Women Who Were With Him.* Lee's Summit, Mo.: Donald R. Hale, 1982.

Harrell, David Edwin Jr. "Pardee Butler—Kansas Crusader." *Kansas Historical Quarterly* 34:4 (Winter 1968): 386-408.

Harsha, D. A. *The Life of Charles Sumner—With Choice Speeches of His Eloquence, etc.* New York: Dayton and Burdick, 1856.

Hickman, Russell K. "A Little Satire on Emigrant Aid—Amasa Soule and the Descandum Kansas Improvement Company." *Kansas Historical Quarterly* 8:4 (November 1939): 342–49.

Hinton, Richard J. Journal. Kansas State Historical Society, Topeka.

*History of Vernon County, Missouri.* St. Louis: Brown and Company, 1887.

Hoole, William Stanley, ed. "A Southerner's Viewpoint of the Kansas Sistuation, 1856–1857: The Letters of Lieut. Col. A. J. Hoole, C.S.A." *Kansas Historical Quarterly* 3:1 (February 1934): 43–68.

Howe, M. A. DeWolf, ed. *Home Letters of General Sherman.* New York: Charles Scribner's Sons, 1909.

Hunt, Elvid. *History of Fort Leavenworth, 1827–1927.* Fort Leavenworth, Kans.: General Service Schools, 1926.

Johannsen, Robert W., ed. "A Footnote to the Pottawatomie Massacre, 1856." *Kansas Historical Quarterly* 22:3 (Autumn 1956): 236–41.

———. "The Lecompton Constitutional Convention: An Analysis of Its Membership." *Kansas Historical Quarterly* 23:3 (Autumn 1957): 225–43.

"John Brown's Raid—How I Got Into It, and How I Got Out of It." *The Atlantic Monthly* 15:92 (June 1865): 711–17.

Langsdorf, Edgar, and R. W. Richmond. "Letters of Daniel R. Anthony, 1857–1862." *Kansas Historical Quarterly* 24:1–2 (Spring and Summer 1958) 6–30, 198–226.

Leonhardt, Charles Frederick William. Papers. Kansas State Historical Society, Topeka.

"Letters From Kanzas—Julia Louisa Lovejoy." *Kansas Historical Quarterly* 11:1 (February 1942): 29–44.

"Letters of John and Sara Everett, 1854–1864—Miami County Pioneers." *Kansas Historical Quarterly* 8:1–4 (February, May, August, November 1939): 3–34, 143–74, 279–310, 350–83.

"Letters of Julia Louisa Lovejoy, 1856–1864—Parts 1–3." *Kansas Historical Quarterly* 15:2–4 (May, August, November 1947): 127–42, 277–319, 368–403, and "Part 4." *Kansas Historical Quarterly* 16:1 (February 1948): 40–75.

Litteer, Loren K. *Bleeding Kansas—The Border War in Douglas and Surrounding Counties.* Baldwin City, Kans.: Champion Publishing, 1987.

Mackey, William H. "Looking Backward." *Kansas Historical Collections* 10 (1907–1908): 642–51.

Magers, Roy V. "The Raid on the Parkville *Industrial Luminary.*" *Missouri Historical Review* 30:1 (October 1935): 39–46.

Malin, James C. "Housing Experiments in the Lawrence Community, 1855." *Kansas Historical Quarterly* 21:2 (Summer 1954): 95–121.

———. *John Brown and the Legend of Fifty-Six.* Philadelphia: American Philosophical Society, 1942.

———. "Judge Lecompte and the Sack of Lawrence, May 21, 1865—Part One." *Kansas Historical Quarterly* 20:7 (August 1953): 465–94.

———. "The Hoogland Examination—The United States v. John Brown, Jr., et al." *Kansas Historical Quarterly* 7:2 (May 1938): 133–53.

Martin, George W. "The First Two Years of Kansas." *Kansas Historical Collections* 10 (1907–1908): 120–48.

"May 21st—Let the Day Be Remembered." Douglas County Historical Society *Newsletter* 10:1 (May 1981): 1.

McFarland, Gerald W. *A Scattered People—An American Family Moves West.* New York: Pantheon Books, 1985.

Mitchell, William Ansel. *Linn County, Kansas—A History.* Kansas City, MO: [?], 1928.

Moffatt, Isaac. "The Kansas Prairie or, Eight Days on the Plains." *Kansas Historical Quarterly* 6:2 (May 1937): 147–74.

Monaghan, Jay. *Civil War on the Western Border.* Boston: Little, Brown, 1955.

Montgomery, James. Papers. 1859–60. Kansas State Historical Society, Topeka.

Moore, Ely, Jr. "The Naming of Osawatomie, and Some Experiences with John Brown." *Kansas Historical Collections* 12 (1911–12): 338–46.

Moore, Rayburn S., ed. "John Brown's Raid at Harpers Ferry—An Eyewitness Account by Charles White." *The Virginia Magazine of History and Biography* 67:4 (October 1959): 387–95.

Murray, Donald M., and Robert M. Rodney, eds. "The Letters of Peter Bryant—Jackson County Pioneer." *Kansas Historical Quarterly* 27:3 (Autumn 1961): 320–52.

Nichols, Alice. *Bleeding Kansas.* New York: Oxford University Press, 1954.

Oates, Stephen. *To Purge This Land With Blood—A Biography of John Brown.* Amherst, University of Massachusetts Press, 1984.

Parsons, Luke F. Manuscript. Kansas State Historical Society, Topeka.

Paxson, W. M. *Annals of Platte County, Missouri.* Kansas City, MO: Hudson-Kimberly Company, 1897.

Poindexter, Parke. "The Capture and Execution of John Brown." *Lippincott's Magazine* 43 (January 1889): 123–25.

Rawley, James A. *Race and Politics "Bleeding Kansas" and the Coming of the Civil War.* Philadelphia: J. B. Lippincott Company, 1969.

"Recollections of the John Brown Raid, By a Virginian Who Witnessed the Fight." *Century Illustrated Monthly Magazine* 26:3 (July 1883): 399–415.

Redpath, James. *The Public Life of Capt. John Brown.* Boston: Thayer and Eldridge, 1860.

———. *The Roving Editor, or, Talks with Slaves in the Southern States.* New York: Burdick, 1859.

Richards, O. G. "Kansas Experiences of Oscar G. Richards, of Eudora, in 1856." *Kansas Historical Collections* 9 (1905–1906): 545–48.

Richardson, Albert D. *Beyond the Mississippi—From the Great River to the Great Ocean, Life and Adventure of the Prairies, Mountains, and Pacific Coast, 1857–1867.* Hartford, Conn.: American Publishing Company, 1867.

Richmond, Robert W. "A Free-Stater's 'Letters to the Editor'—Samuel N. Wood's Letters to Eastern Newspapers, 1854." *Kansas Historical Quarterly* 23:2 (Summer 1957): 181–90.

——. *Kansas—A Land of Contrasts*. St. Charles, Mo.: Forum Press, 1974.

Riley, Glenda, ed. "Kansas Frontierswomen Viewed Through Their Writings— The Diary of Chestina Bowker Allen." *Kansas History* 9:2 (Summer 1986): 83–95.

Robinson, Charles, *The Kansas Conflict*. New York: Harper and Brothers, 1892.

Robinson, Sara T. D. *Kansas—Its Interior and Exterior Life*. Boston: Crosby, Nichols and Company, 1856.

Root, George A., ed. "The First Day's Battle at Hickory Point—From the Diary and Reminiscences of Samuel James Reader." *Kansas Historical Quarterly* 1:1 (November 1931): 28–49.

Ropes, Hannah Anderson. *Six Months in Kansas, by a Lady*. Boston: John P. Jewett and Company, 1856.

Rosa, Joseph G. *They Called Him Wild Bill—The Life and Adventure of James Butler Hickock*. Norman: University of Oklahoma Press, 1964.

Ruchames, Louis, ed. *A John Brown Reader—The Story of John Brown in His Words, in the Words of Those Who Knew Him and in the Poetry and Prose of the Literary Heritage*. New York: Abelard-Schuman, 1959.

Russell, Don, ed. "Julia Cody Goodman's Memoirs of Buffalo Bill." *Kansas Historical Quarterly* 28:4 (Winter 1962): 442–96.

Sanborn, F. B., ed. *The Life and Letters of John Brown, Liberator of Kansas, and Martyr of Virginia*. Boston: Roberts Brothers, 1891.

——. "Some Notes on the Territorial History of Kansas." *Kansas Historical Collection* 13 (1913–14): 249–65.

Savage, Joseph, ed. "Captain Bickerton's Recollections of 1856." Douglas County Historical Society, Lawrence, Kansas.

"Selections from the Hyatt Manuscripts." *Kansas Historical Collections* 1 and 2 (1875–78): 203–33.

SenGupta, Gunja. *For God and Mammon—Evangelicals and Entrepreneurs, Masters and Slaves in Territorial Kansas, 1854–1860*. Athens: University of Georgia Press, 1996.

Shoemaker, Floyd C. "Missouri's Proslavery Fight for Kansas, 1854–1855." *Missouri Historical Review* 48:4 (July 1954) 325–40 and *Missouri Historical Review* 49:1 (October 1954) 41–54.

"Sixth Biennial Report." *Kansas Historical Collections* 4 (1886–88): 418.

Smith, George Gardner, ed. *Spencer Kellogg Brown—His Life in Kansas and His Death as a Spy, 1842–1863*. New York: D. Appleton and Company, 1903.

Smith, Nathan, ed. "Letters of a Free-State Man in Kansas, 1856." *Kansas Historical Quarterly* 21:3 (Autumn 1954): 166–72.

"Some Ingalls Letters." *Kansas Historical Collections* 14 (1915–18): 94–122.

Stampp, Kenneth M. *America in 1857—A Nation on the Brink.* New York: Oxford University Press, 1990.

Starr, Fred. Papers. Western Historical Collections, Columbia, Missouri.

Stephenson, Wendell Holmes. *The Political Career of General James H. Lane.* Topeka: Kansas State Historical Society, 1930.

Stratton, Joanna L. *Pioneer Women—Voices From the Kansas Frontier.* New York: Simon and Schuster, 1981.

Taft, Robert, ed. "Over the Santa Fe Trail Through Kansas in 1858—H. B. Mollhausen." *Kansas Historical Quarterly* 16:4 (November 1948): 337–80.

*Territorial Kansas—Studies Commemorating the Centennial.* Lawrence, Kans.: University of Kansas Press, 1954.

Thayer, Eli. *A History of the Kansas Crusade—Its Friends and Its Foes.* 1889. Reprint. New York: Books for Libraries, 1971.

"The Diary of James R. Stewart, Pioneer of Osage County." *Kansas Historical Quarterly* 17:1 (February 1949): 1–36.

"The Letters of Joseph H. Trego, 1857–1864—Linn County Pioneer." *Kansas Historical Quarterly* 19:2 (May 1951): 113–32.

"The Letters of the Rev. Samuel Young Lum—Pioneer Kansas Missionary, 1854–1858." *Kansas Historical Quarterly* 25:1 (Spring 1959): 39–67 and 25:2 (Summer 1959) 172–96.

"Thomas C. Wells—Letters of a Kansas Pioneer, 1855–1860." *Kansas Historical Quarterly* 5:2 (May 1936): 143–79.

Van Gundy, John C. *Reminiscences of Frontier Life on the Upper Neosho in 1855 and 1856.* Pamphlet. Kansas State Historical Society, Topeka.

Walker, Samuel. Papers. Kansas State Historical Society, Topeka.

Webb Scrapbook. Kansas State Historical Society, Topeka.

Welch, G. Murlin. *Border Warfare in Southeastern Kansas—1856–1859.* Pleasanton, Kans.: Linn County Historical Society, 1977.

"When Kansas Became a State." *Kansas Historical Quarterly* 27:1 (Spring 1961): 1–21.

Williams, Robert H. *With the Border Ruffians—Memories of the Far West, 1852–1868.* 1907. Reprint. Lincoln: University of Nebraska Press, 1982.

Woodward, Brinton W. "Reminiscences of September 14, 1856—Invasion of the 2700." *Kansas Historical Collections* 6 (1897–1900): 77–83.

Yost, Genevieve. "History of Lynchings in Kansas." *Kansas Historical Quarterly* 2:2 (May 1933): 182–219.

Young, Otis E. *The West of Philip St. George Cooke, 1809–1895.* Glendale, Calif.: Arthur H. Clark Company, 1955.

## NEWSPAPERS

*Atchison (Kans.) Squatter Sovereign* 1855–57
*Doniphan Kansas Constitutionalist* 1857
*Elwood (Kans.) Free Press* 1857, 1859
*Kansas City (Mo.) Enterprise* 1856
*Fort Scott (Kans.) Democrat* 1858–61
*Lawrence (Kans.) Herald of Freedom* 1855–56
*Leavenworth Kansas Weekly Herald* 1855–57
*Lecompton (Kans.) Union* 1856
*Lexington (Mo.) American Citizen* 1855–56
*Liberty (Mo.) Tribune* 1855
*Ottawa (Kans.) Herald,* 1988
*Parkville (Mo.) Industrial Luminary* 1855
*Parkville (Mo.) Weekly Southern Democrat* 1855–56
*St. Joseph (Mo.) Commercial Cycle* 1855
*St. Louis Weekly Missouri Democrat* 1856
*Seneca (Kans.) Courier-Tribune* 1995
*Topeka Kansas Freeman* 1855–56
*Weston (Mo.) Weekly Platte Argus* 1855
*Westport (Mo.) Border Star* 1860

# INDEX